EGYPT AND CROMER

Egypt and Cromer

A STUDY IN ANGLO-EGYPTIAN RELATIONS

Afaf Lutfi Al-Sayyid

FREDERICK A. PRAEGER, *Publishers*
New York · Washington

BOOKS THAT MATTER

Published in the United States of America in 1969
by Frederick A. Praeger, Inc., Publishers
111 Fourth Avenue, New York, N.Y. 10003

Library of Congress Catalog Card Number: 69–11866

Printed in Great Britain

TO THE MEMORY OF
MY FATHER

Contents

Illustrations

* Photographed by John Webb FRPS

Preface

The course of British policy towards Egypt in the late nineteenth century was an erratic and paradoxical one which culminated in occupation. The paradox often exasperated the European Powers as well as the Egyptians, for nowhere else was there a better example of Paul Cambon's bewildered statement, 'il y a un abîme entre ce qu'un Anglais dit et ce qu'il fait, entre ce qu'il croit être et ce qu'il est'. Between the years 1882 and 1907 England made nearly one hundred and twenty declarations and pledges of its intention to evacuate Egypt, and at the same time initiated actions, each of which established its power in Egypt more securely. But the anomaly of British behaviour was not always the outcome of deliberate perfidy as the Egyptians and the Powers suspected; it was often due to the lack of a consistent policy towards Egypt, at least during the early days of the occupation. And how could it be otherwise when British policy towards Egypt was often contingent on factors which were extraneous to Egypt—India, the Ottoman Empire, the European Powers—and when British policy fashioned in London, differed from British policy fashioned in Egypt.

Throughout the period in question one person dominated the Anglo-Egyptian scene: that was Sir Evelyn Baring, later Lord Cromer. More than anyone else Cromer was responsible for the turn that Anglo-Egyptian relations took. In one of his perceptive moments he said that in Egypt personalities counted for more than systems. Indeed, personalities mattered more than systems because the government of Egypt was autocratic, and the essence of autocracy—whether it be of the benevolent or the despotic kind—is the imposition of one man's will on a whole country, and this will can change any established system or modify it.

This book is therefore an attempt to show to what extent the strength and weakness of men's characters dominated the course of Anglo-Egyptian relations, and how far these were modified by events which lay outside the control of the men involved. And for the same reason I have not tried to produce a full history of the British occupation in Egypt, or even a history of the reforms attempted and the policies followed, but have tried to concentrate on the human relationships involved. For it is these relationships which affect Anglo-Egyptian relations to the present day and help to explain modern Egyptian attitudes towards Britain.

Wherever possible I have tried to use Egyptian sources—both written and oral in the shape of interviews with some of the people concerned in the events described, or their descendants—for two reasons. The first is that Egyptian sources have seldom been used by European writers on the period: yet they are an indispensable source for the historian, and one of which contemporary historians are indeed making full use. The second is that this is a book written by an Egyptian who would like to present the Egyptian side of the question, as well as the European one.

The idea of this book originated from a thesis which I wrote many years ago, but which I decided to modify and present to the general reader rather than to the specialist; and I can only hope that the specialist also will find it of some interest. I should therefore like to express my deep gratitude to the many friends who have given me assistance and encouragement then and now. To Albert Hourani, who supervised my original thesis, I owe more than I can express. His knowledge, perception and kindness was not only a valuable source of succour, but of inspiration, as all those who have had the good fortune to be his students well know. To Elizabeth Monroe, who has so generously given of her time and advice in reading and criticizing the manuscript I owe a deep debt of gratitude. To Gordon Waterfield, who first suggested that I rewrite the thesis into a book, I am grateful for invaluable suggestions and his constant encouragement. I am also grateful to Mrs H. Ingrams, to Mrs D. West and to Mr John Murray for taking the time and the trouble to help me.

I would also like to express my thanks to Lord Salisbury who allowed me to use his grandfather's papers and to make extensive quotations from them; to Dr J. F. A. Mason and to the staff and library of Christ Church, Oxford, where I consulted the Salisbury Papers; to Sir Ronald Wingate and Durham University for the Wingate Papers; to the Warden and Fellows of New College, Oxford, for the Milner Papers; and to Miss Elizabeth Monroe and St Antony's College, Oxford, for the Harry Boyle Papers; to the British Museum and to the Public Records in London (transcripts of Crown-copyright records in the Public Record Office appear by permission of the Controller of Her Majesty's Stationery Office); to Macmillan & Co. for permission to quote from Lord Cromer's *Modern Egypt*; and to the Egyptian Archives for the Mustafa Kamil Papers and the Urabi Correspondence.

NOTE ON TRANSLITERATION

I have tried to simplify the transliteration of Arabic words and names as much as possible by leaving out diacritical marks, which though indispensable to the Arabic speaker leave all other readers bewildered. But where a quotation from a text has used a certain form, I have retained it while using my own preference elsewhere when referring to the same person—for example, Urabi is variously referred to as Orabi and Arabi.

ABBREVIATIONS OF SOURCES QUOTED

B.P. = The Private Papers of Harry Boyle, St Antony's College, Oxford.

M.P. = The Private Papers of Lord Milner, New College, Oxford.

S.P. = The Private Papers of Robert, Third Marquess of Salisbury, Christ Church, Oxford.

W.P. = The Private Papers of Sir Reginald Wingate, Durham University.

CHAPTER I

Prelude to the Occupation

On July 11, 1882, the British fleet bombarded the city of Alexandria. Two months later, on September 13, the battle of Tal al-Kabir took place and the nationalist army under General Urabi was defeated by General Sir Garnet Wolseley. Thus ended the nationalist rebellion in Egypt, and began the British occupation of that country—an occupation that at first took on the character of a temporary expedient undertaken with reluctance, but which later became permanent, lasting seventy-two years.

The motives that lay behind the occupation of Egypt were complex and devious, but the immediate incentive was a nationalist rebellion that threatened to make an end of European intervention in Egyptian affairs. This intervention in Egypt can be directly traced to that flamboyant ruler, the Khedive Ismail. Sometimes called the 'Profligate', and sometimes the 'Magnificent', Ismail indebted Egypt by £E90,000,000, and opened the Suez Canal. Both of these events were to prove disastrous to Egyptian independence, for the existence of the Canal embroiled a number of Powers in Egyptian affairs, and the debt brought European financiers to Egypt, with a resulting increase of foreign, especially French and English, influence in the Egyptian administration.

The tale of Egypt's indebtedness is a well-known one. It is a tale of folly on the part of a ruler who borrowed beyond his means in an attempt to make his country 'a part of Europe'; of rapacity on the part of the moneylenders and bondholders, who lent him money at usurious rates which often went as high as 20%; and of intransigence on the part of certain European Powers, notably France, who espoused the cause of their bondholders, and turned private investment into an international cause. France's policy was to give the maximum protection to the interests of the French bondholders in Egypt; and, above all, to safeguard the Canal which it regarded as a French enterprise, since not only was the promoter of the company a Frenchman, but so were also the board of directors, most of the employees, and the majority of the subscribers.

England was reluctant to act as 'sheriff's officer' for the British bondholders; but since 89% of all shipping sailing through the Canal was British, and since the Canal was the artery to India and the other colonies of the Far East, England was even more anxious than France to protect her interests in Egypt. The keynote of British policy in Egypt had always been a reluctance to take on the responsibility and the expense of ruling the country, and a determination to use friendly means in her relationship both with the Sultan and the Khedive. The British government generally maintained the integrity of the Ottoman Empire. When Muhammad Ali in 1841 shook the foundations of that Empire in his bid for independence, it had been Palmerston who foiled his plans, and saved the Empire from collapse. Under British pressure, Muhammad Ali had to be content with hereditary rule over Egypt, while still remaining the vassal of the Sultan. When Napoleon III had suggested to Palmerston that France should annex Morocco, while Britain annexed Egypt, Palmerston refused, and in a letter to Clarendon explained: 'we want to trade with Egypt, and to travel through Egypt, but we do not want the burthen of governing Egypt'.[1] During the Congress of Berlin, after the Russo-Turkish war in 1878, Bismarck repeated Napoleon's proposal: the Ottoman Empire should be dismembered, France should have Tunis, while England could annex Egypt. But once again the Conservative government under Disraeli refused the offer in pursuance of their intention to maintain the integrity of the Ottoman Empire. Salisbury, who was Foreign Minister, found no arrangement to replace the Ottoman Empire that did not carry with it the risk of war in Europe; and furthermore, the dismemberment of the Ottoman Empire might place British rivals along the trade routes of Syria and Mesopotamia, which would jeopardize British interests. England was therefore content to establish a position of predominance in Egypt through the exercise of influence, rather than through actual physical possession. Salisbury explained this policy succinctly when, on July 15, 1879, he said: 'The only form of control we have is that which is called moral influence, which in practice is a combination of menace, objurgation, and worry. In this we are still supreme and have many modes of applying it . . . We must devote ourselves to the perfecting of this weapon.'[2]

But Britain did want to co-operate with France. Fear of Russian encroachment in the Mediterranean, and suspicion of Bismarck, led to an Anglo-French entente. When France, in the interests of her bondholders, determined to interfere in Egyptian affairs, Britain was forced to associate herself with that action. Salisbury's explanation on September 16, 1881, rings true: 'When you have got a . . . faithful ally who is bent on meddling in a country in which you are deeply interested—you have three courses open to you. You may renounce—or monopolize—or share. Renouncing would have been to place the French across our road to India. Monopolizing would have been very near the risk of war. So we resolved to share.'[3]

The intervention of the European Powers in the Egyptian administration first began in 1876 when Ismail appealed to the Powers to help him disentangle his finances, and to that end an institution known as the Caisse de la Dette Publique came into being. This body was composed of four Commissioners, who were to act as representatives of the bondholders in Egypt, but were appointed by the chief bondholding countries—France, Italy, Austria and England.* Alongside the Caisse, two Controllers, one British and one French, were appointed to supervise state revenue and expenditure, hence the name of 'Dual Control' by which the system became known. The Controllers were employed by the Khedive in the service of the Egyptian government, and could be appointed and dismissed by him. Unfortunately these measures were not sufficient to deal effectively with Egypt's finances, and the Commissioners and Controllers informed their respective governments that the whole of the Egyptian administration needed to

* Britain at first refused to appoint a Commissioner since it was not government policy to give official support to financial transactions of a private nature; but the following year Evelyn Baring was appointed with government approval but not official endorsement.

be changed. Whereupon Ismail was urged by the Powers to hand over the reins of government to a ministry containing two European ministers, and under the premiership of Nubar Pasha, an Armenian. This was the first step of active intervention in Egyptian political life undertaken by the Powers, and it was to prove an unsuccessful venture. Ismail, an autocrat, could bully his administration into functioning, but the European ministry did not have the same prestige, and so collapsed. Ismail once more took charge of his government.

Egyptian finances continued to deteriorate to the point where, in 1879, the Controllers found that there was no money to pay the interest due on the debt, and suggested that it should not be paid for that year. This was paramount to a declaration of bankruptcy. Ismail refused their suggestion, and put forward an alternative plan of his own, which consisted in a suggested decrease of the interest on the debt by half per cent. The Controllers resigned in protest, warning their governments that Ismail's plan was not feasible, and that the bondholders risked not being paid. The Powers, espousing the cause of their bondholders, exerted pressure on the Sultan, Egypt's suzerain, and in 1879 Ismail was deposed. This was the second, and more important, act of intervention by the Powers; it sowed the seeds of trouble to come, for, as Salisbury prophesied, 'after having a Khedive deposed the character of non-intervention is not easy to retain'.[4]

Ismail, a strong man, shrewd, forceful and dynamic—a man with a vision—was succeeded by his son Tawfiq, a weakling. In 1880 Tawfiq negotiated with the Powers a settlement of the debt which was defined in the Law of Liquidation. According to the Law, Egypt's revenue, estimated at £E9 million, was divided into two nearly equal parts, with one part assigned to the Caisse, representing the bondholders. The other part was given over to the Egyptian government, but a limit was set to its expenditure. Out of its share of the revenues, moreover, the government was expected to pay sundry items such as the tribute to the Porte, as well as any deficits that the Caisse might have incurred, which left Egypt with £E2 million to run its administration. Once again the Dual Control was established, except that, according to the new terms, the

Controllers could only be dismissed with the consent of their Governments, thereby establishing, in Gladstone's words, 'a political control' over Egypt. Moreover, since the Controllers now attended the Council of Ministers, their former function of supervising financial affairs became transformed into an active political intervention. The Law of Liquidation brought about a stranglehold of Egypt which was 'tied hand and foot, unable to move, almost unable to breathe, without the consent of Europe',[5] and with 66% of her revenues mortgaged to pay off the debt.

England claimed to find the Dual Control a distasteful expedient. As Salisbury said: 'It may be quite tolerable and even agreeable for the French Government to go into partnership with the bondholders; or rather to act as sheriff's officer for them. But to us it is a new and very embarrassing sensation . . . We have no wish to part company with France: still less do we mean that France should acquire in Egypt any special ascendency; but subject to these two considerations I should be glad to be free of the companionship of the bondholders.'[6] The Egyptian administration fervently echoed Salisbury's wish to be rid of the bondholders, and not only because they were paying exorbitant sums; for with the Dual Control, European personnel in the administration had steadily increased, and (because of Anglo-French rivalry) duplicate posts were often instituted, which became highly paid sinecures at a time when the salaries of the Egyptian employees were in arrears. The influx of foreigners into the administration was resented by the Egyptians, for the Europeans formed 2% of the total number of employees, but represented 15% of the total cost. This became a major grievance, and was to exacerbate a movement of opposition to European influence in Egypt.

But, more than anything else, the abusive system of the Capitulations made the Europeans disliked. Originally privileges of extraterritoriality granted in the fifteenth century to foreign merchants in the fields of law, taxes and tariffs, these eventually became an instrument of exploitation in the hands of the European Powers. Because of the Capitulations the Egyptian government never enjoyed complete legal control over its territories, because no law passed in Egypt could be applied to aliens unless their governments accepted it, which meant that legislation had to clear diplomatic channels, and the consent of fourteen states had to be obtained before a law became valid. Under the protective mantle of the Capitulations, and often with the complicity of their Consuls, aliens could commit any form of crime with impunity; for they could be arrested only with the consent of their Consuls, and were tried in Consular courts where, more often than not, they were released without proper trial. Egypt thus became the target of any adventurer or crook. Smuggling flourished on a large scale, since the port authorities could search ships only if they were accompanied by the Consul of the ship's nationality and the Consuls of the seamen's nationalities. Alien residents in Egypt were not taxed, merely because they refused to pay taxes; thus the burden of taxation fell on the unhappy fallahin who had to pay the exorbitant sums that were necessary to satisfy the bondholders. Levantine moneylenders ran a thriving trade by lending the fallah money at rates that often rose as high as 20% per month, and then seizing his land for non-payment of debt. Along with state debt, the insolvency of the fallah was one of the main problems the administration had to face. It was this indebtedness that had encouraged the fallah to welcome Ahmad Urabi as a saviour, and his movement as promising to lighten the yoke of taxation, and to deal summarily with the moneylenders.

Urabi's advent as head of an Egyptian national movement had been due to the coming together of three groups of people, united in their common resentment of European intervention in Egyptian affairs, but above all united in their wish to reform the administration and put an end to arbitrary government. They were: the would-be constitutionalists, who were wealthy fallah notables, and members of the Turco-Circassian aristocracy; the reformers, who were mainly fallah intellectuals; and the fallah officers in the army. The terms 'Turco-Circassian' and 'fallah Egyptian' were not only used as ethnic labels, but also carried a connotation of class. For many centuries the ruling power in Egypt had been exercised by men of foreign origin, who formed an administrative and military elite—the Mamluks. Coming from all over the Balkans, from the Caucasus mountains and even from Central Asia, they were generically referred to as Turco-Circassian. Although Muhammad Ali had broken the power of the Mamluks, yet, since he was of Turkish origin, he continued to use an amalgam of the old Turco-Circassian element, and of new imports, in his administration. It is true that he appointed fallah Egyptians in the bureaucracy; but all the highest officials, both civil and military, came from the Turco-Circassian coterie. This continued to be the rule until the advent of Said, Ismail's predecessor, who allowed fallah Egyptians to rise in the army up to the rank of colonel. Ismail had not followed this practice; and although occasionally an outstanding Egyptian was promoted to a top administrative post, the majority of administrators in the upper echelons, both civil and military, were Turco-Circassian. These despised the fallah Egyptians, and called them *pis-fallah* (dirty peasant); and in turn were disliked and feared by the latter, who were jealous of their authority and resented it.

In 1866, when Ismail called an Assembly of Notables, he had raised hopes that a real constitutional government might be in the offing; but under his iron rule the hope lay dormant, and only came to life again with the reign of the more pliable Tawfiq. At one time Tawfiq had been a member of a Masonic Lodge that included Jamal al-Din al-Afghani, the famous Islamic reformer who was said to attempt to rouse a revolution in every Muslim country he visited. Other members of the Lodge were al-Afghani's disciple, Shaykh Muhammad Abduh; Sharif Pasha, the head of the constitutionalist movement and a former Prime Minister; and Sultan Pasha, one of the richest fallah notables in Egypt. It was rumoured that Tawfiq had promised al-Afghani that he would undertake great works of reform when he ascended the throne. On becoming Khedive, Tawfiq seemed to justify these hopes for Sharif Pasha was nominated Prime Minister and set to drafting a constitution. But hopes were dashed when Sharif was soon after dismissed, and replaced by Riaz Pasha, an autocrat of the old school, but a reformer in his own way. Al-Afghani was deported, and Shaykh Abduh banished to his village. These actions were all clear indications that Tawfiq's promises of reform were not sincere, and that he intended to rule in the same autocratic fashion

7

as his father had done, save that he had neither the strength of character nor the ability of Ismail. Thus the notables who had accepted Ismail's autocracy refused to accept Tawfiq's.

Opposition to Riaz's government soon arose amongst the notables, and centred round several Pashas, who became known as the Constitutionalists; prominent amongst them were Sharif, Sultan, Umar Lutfi and Ismail Raghib. Sharif Pasha was a wealthy, highly cultured, indolent Turk, with a French training. He adopted liberal principles in the same spirit as a Florentine gentleman during the Renaissance might have patronized a new painter. All civilized countries had constitutions, therefore Sharif firmly believed that Egypt should have one as well. It would be a means of limiting Khedivial autocracy and of giving the notables a greater share in ruling the country. But Sharif was too indolent to be a good political fighter, and this role fell to Sultan Pasha. The antithesis of Sharif, Sultan—a fallah Egyptian by origin who had amassed enormous wealth—had all the characteristics of the canny peasant. A born intriguer and opportunist, he espoused the Constitutionalist cause as the surest way to power. These Pashas were to mastermind the nationalist party.

The second group of malcontents was headed by one-time supporters of al-Afghani. They were Muslim intellectuals who were fired by al-Afghani with a spirit of reform. They sought to free Egypt from arbitrary rule by means of a constitutional government, and to reform Islam by re-formulating its principles. With the exile of their leader their influence waned, but it once again revived when they joined forces with the Urabi movement and became its propagandists.

The third group consisted of army officers. The direct cause for their discontent, as with the other groups, was an internal matter. Tawfiq's Minister for War, a Circassian named Uthman Rifqi, was in process of drafting a new law which would inhibit fallah Egyptians from rising from the ranks to become officers, thereby limiting the officer class to the wealthy Turco-Circassian element who could afford to go to the military academy. Three fallah colonels, headed by Ahmad Urabi, tendered a petition protesting against the new law in January, 1881. The Council of Ministers

8

presided over by the Khedive examined this petition and decided to court-martial the colonels. The following day the Minister for War summoned the officers to the Qasr al-Nil barracks on the pretext of discussing the wedding preparations of the Khedive's sister, and arrested them. The officers, who anticipated foul play, had given prior warning to their regiments that if they did not turn up at a certain hour then their regiments should come and free them. When they did not appear at the arranged time their regiments marched up to Qasr al-Nil barracks and forcibly freed the three colonels.

The incident brought Urabi to the forefront of Egyptian political life as a potential leader. A good-looking man in middle age, Urabi was an attractive person, and a forceful speaker, often interspersing his speeches with passages from the Quran—a trait which made him popular amongst the masses, and was the result of his early training in the Azhar. Soon discontented elements gathered round him, for his bold action had shown that the army could be used as a coercive force against the Khedive. A simple man, lacking in subtlety and political refinement, but possessing courage and boldness, Urabi had had a chequered career. He had been dismissed from the army twice for insubordination, only to be reinstated; and was said to belong to a secret society of army officers who wished to rid the army of the Turco-Circassian element. His first moves had undoubtedly been prompted by motives of self-interest and self-protection; but later on, when he found himself involved in a nationalist movement, he grew into the part of a genuine nationalist leader. The party which formed itself round him was called *al-Hizb al-Watani*, the Nationalist Party, and its members were a mixture of fallah and Turk notables, united in their discontent at the autocracy of Tawfiq's rule as conducted through Riaz Pasha. Foremost among the party was Sami al-Barudi Pasha, a Turk who presented the unique combination of a general who had fought creditably in several campaigns, and a poet who had founded a new school of poetry. Al-Barudi was a minister in Sharif's first cabinet, and was said to be Urabi's *éminence grise*. Although he spoke Turkish and Persian, al-Barudi knew no European languages, hence his knowledge of international politics was somewhat limited; but he was certainly the cleverest man in the party. The members of the party blamed the bad government on the growing influence of Europe over Egyptian affairs, which explains why the slogan of the party became 'Egypt for the Egyptians'. They believed that a constitution with an assembly could be the only path to good government.

The Khedive Tawfiq was well aware of this current of opposition against him, and he turned for advice to Edward Malet, the British Consul-General, and to Auckland Colvin, the British Controller. A colourless man who lacked both vices and virtues, Tawfiq had never felt secure in his position as Khedive. Unlike his father, who had charm and a talent for managing men, as well as a great deal of political acumen, Tawfiq was totally devoid of these talents. Despised by his father, who continually intrigued to return to Egypt, Tawfiq, timorous by nature, was always haunted by the fear that he too might be deposed, and replaced by his father or by Prince Halim. Halim was Muhammad Ali's youngest son; and had not Ismail succeeded in changing the laws of succession, Halim as the eldest living member of the family would, according to Ottoman Law, have been the rightful Khedive of Egypt instead of Tawfiq. Moreover, Halim, who lived in Constantinople, was favoured by the Sultan; had strong connections with France, where he attended the academy of Saint-Cyr; and was popular in Egypt, especially amongst the Constitutionalists (Sharif used to be his private secretary). He made a formidable enemy for Tawfiq who realized that the only people he could turn to for help were the English. At that time, the French Consul-General, Baron de Ring, had become friendly with the military leaders, but was later to be replaced, at Tawfiq's request. The military group was gathering round it more supporters every day, and Tawfiq's fears grew accordingly. His immediate Turco-Circassian entourage could offer nothing more constructive than repeated attempts to assassinate Urabi and his friends; but since these attempts constantly miscarried, they only served to frighten Urabi into taking more drastic action.

Matters between the Khedive and the army came to a head in September 1881, eight months after the attempted arrest of

Urabi and his friends, when the three colonels were given orders sending their regiments to different parts of Egypt, away from Cairo. Interpreting the order as a further attempt against them, the colonels prepared for a military demonstration with a view to forcing concessions from the Khedive. In a note to the Khedive they said that, since the order given was 'intended to disperse the military power with a view of revenge upon us, and as we cannot deliver up ourselves to death, we hereby give notice to your Excellency that all the regiments will assemble today at 9 o'clock, Arabic time, in the Abdin square for deciding this question'.[7]

Their attitude suggested that the basic motive for their refusal to leave Cairo was one of fear, and many people who disapproved of open rebellion, especially Shaykh Muhammad Abduh, believed that fear was the sole motive for Urabi's actions. Yet when the army confronted the Khedive at the appointed time, Urabi lodged demands that were couched in the tone of a nationalist reformer, a 'delegate of the people' as he called himself, rather than in the tone of an insurgent army officer who wished to save his neck. With three regiments lined up behind him in the Abdin square facing the palace, and with sword unsheathed in his hand, Urabi confronted the Khedive and demanded that he comply with three requests; that the present ministry under Riaz be replaced by one sympathetic to the nationalist cause; that a constituent assembly be called; and that the army be increased to 18,000 as was originally decreed in the firmans. The first two requests were obviously inspired by Urabi's new friends, Sultan Pasha and his group, while the third request was a gambit to gain popularity with the military group. According to the terms of the firman granted Muhammad Ali in 1841, the army was limited to 18,000 men, but the Dual Control, in trying to cut down expenses, had axed a large number of army officers, and decreased the army until it reached a total of only 12,000 men.

Tradition claims that the Khedive countered these requests with a statement that he was Khedive of Egypt and would do as he pleased, whereupon Urabi is said to have answered: 'We are not slaves and nevermore shall be possessed.'[8] Cookson, the

British Consul in Alexandria, who was the only British official available to Tawfiq that day, had advised him to cow the army by a firm stand; but Tawfiq was too frightened, and pretended to give in to Urabi's requests. He was playing for time, and secretly sent a request to the Porte for twenty battalions to help quell his insurgent army. This request the Porte did not answer.

Sharif Pasha on September 14, 1881, formed the new cabinet. He was chosen by the Urabists because he was known to be an opponent to Riaz's policy of subservience to the European employees in the government, and to have said that when he came to power he would know how to put an end to European interference in Egyptian affairs.[9] He was also a firm Constitutionalist. At first Sharif demurred at accepting the premiership because he felt that the army might try to use him solely as a front, but Sultan Pasha assured him that the notables were ready to guarantee that the army would be totally submissive to his government. For the moment, there was a honeymoon period between the various factions involved. The Nationalist Party had swelled its numbers by an influx of notables, who followed the example of the four Constitutionalist Pashas, and who all looked to Sultan Pasha for guidance as one of the richest notables of fallah origin in Egypt. The only sour note came from Shaykh Muhammad Abduh, al-Afghani's disciple, and editor of the *Official Journal*. He believed that Urabi was merely trying to ward off the Khedive's impending revenge, that he was using the army to that end, and that he would try to use the notables and the Constitutionalists as he had used the army.[10] During a chance meeting between Abduh and Urabi at Sultan Pasha's house, Abduh told Urabi that if the nation were prepared to take part in the administration of the government, then to bring this end about through a military *coup d'état* would be meaningless; that what the army leaders were trying to secure was not legitimate, for if the country obtained a parliament through force of arms, this body would be neither a reflection of the nation's maturity nor the fulfilment of her aims. Hence it would soon collapse and come to an end. 'I am afraid that this turmoil will subject the land to a foreign occupation that will bring down a curse on its authors lasting till the Day of

Judgement,' he concluded.[11] But when Abduh saw how seriously the notables, Sultan Pasha and Urabi, were working at creating a constitution, he threw in his lot with them, saying that 'then and then only, along with Sultan Pasha and all Egypt, I became a follower of Ahmad Arabi.'[12] The reformers thus joined the Constitutionalists and the army to form the *Hizb al-Watani*. The chief significance of this union is that it marked Urabi's change from a man leading a military revolt into a nationalist leader. Colvin, in describing the movement to Granville the Foreign Secretary on December 21, 1881, reported that 'in its origin the movement is, I think, unquestionably an Egyptian movement against arbitrary Turkish rule . . . the movement though in its origin anti-Turk is in itself an Egyptian national movement'.* Furthermore, Colvin explained: 'What gives a show of justification to the recent conduct of the army, and gains them support among great numbers of the more respectable Egyptians is that there is a great deal of truth in their complaints.'[13]

These complaints of the Egyptians were made public, when *al-Hizb al-Watani* with the help of Wilfred Scawen Blunt, a minor poet who was married to Byron's granddaughter, published a manifesto in the London *Times* of January 3, 1882. Its authors, Abduh and Barudi, stated that the object of the nationalists was one day to see Egypt entirely in Egyptian hands. 'The Egyptians have learned in the last few years what freedom means, and they are resolved to complete their national education. This they look to find in *Majlis al-Shura* (the Consultative Assembly) just assembling, in a fair measure of freedom for the press, and in the growth of knowledge among all classes of the people.' They had confided their interest to the army as being the only power capable of protecting them, and as soon as the people should have established their rights, the army would abandon its present political attitude. 'The general end of the National Party is the intellectual and moral regeneration of the country by a better observance of the law, increased education and by political liberty.' The hand of Shaykh Abduh is obvious in the accent on education, but it is noteworthy that the manifesto expressed the sentiment of Egypt for

* FO/78/3326. Colvin was one of the two Controllers.

13

the Egyptians, and showed its discontent at foreign intervention and the abuse of power.

Gladstone sympathized at first with the Urabi movement; he said (Jan. 4, 1882): 'I am by no means pained, but I am much surprised at the rapid development of a national sentiment and party in Egypt. The very ideas of such a sentiment and the Egyptian people seemed quite incompatible. How it has come up I do not know; most of all is the case strange if the standing army is the nest that has reared it. There however it seems to be, and to claim the respect due to it as a fact, and due also to the capabilities that may be latent in it for the future. "Egypt for the Egyptians" is the sentiment to which I should wish to give scope: and could it prevail it would I think be the best, the only good solution of the "Egyptian Question".'[14] But Anglo-French co-operation was one of the corner-stones of his policy, especially since he, unlike Disraeli and Salisbury, had no thoughts of friendship with Turkey. So when Gambetta, the French Prime Minister (who believed that Egyptian national aspirations were not compatible with the international Financial Control which the French demanded, and who was nervous at the effect such a movement might have on Tunis, which France had recently occupied) suggested action against the Egyptians that same month, Gladstone, forced by the majority of the cabinet, complied. Whereas Gambetta wanted an expedition to cow the Urabists, Gladstone and Granville believed that Anglo-French pressure would be sufficient to achieve their purpose, and Gladstone wanted a 'minimum interference' in Egypt.[15] Gambetta then suggested that a Joint Note be sent to the Urabists, and Gladstone and Granville agreed.

On January 12, 1881, a few days after the first meeting of the new Assembly, and just when the army had expressed its willingness to retire from political life, England and France sent their Joint Note which stated: 'The English and French governments consider the maintenance of His Highness on the throne . . . as alone able to guarantee, for the present and future, the good order and the development of general prosperity in Egypt . . . The two governments being closely associated in the resolve to guard by their united efforts against all cause of complications, internal or external, which might menace the order of things established in Egypt.'[16]

Granville had misunderstood the terms of the Note, and had miscalculated its effect on Egypt. He believed that the object of the Note was 'to strengthen the Government of Egypt and maintain the existing order of things'.[17] It was in fact to have the opposite effect. To France, the Note logically implied a commitment on Britain's part to undertake joint action in Egypt, if the need arose; but Granville failed to see this, and assumed that the Note was merely an expression of solidarity with France, a bluff that implied no commitment to action of any kind.

The Note, interpreted by the Egyptians as a form of outside intervention, caused a new distribution of allegiances all on the side of the army. Any notables who had not previously joined *al-Hizb al-Watani* now did so; for they detected an implied threat of intervention, and felt that the army was their sole guarantee of security. France's occupation of Tunis had not strengthened faith in French intentions, and Britain was suspect by association. The Khedive, on the other hand, interpreted the Note as an implied encouragement to himself, and a hint that he need not attempt to co-operate with the Assembly, since he was backed by the Powers. He was encouraged in this attitude by the friendliness which the British and French Consuls-General, Malet and Sienkiewics, showed him, and by their open suspicions and disapproval of the army and the national party, which the Consuls continually looked on as a mutinous group rather than as a nationalist spearhead.

The Note also brought about a change in the Prime Minister's attitude. As soon as he received the Note Sharif said: 'Quelle boulette! Ils n'auraient pas pu trouver mieux pour nous perdre.' He realized that this was a warning to tread warily in matters which might lead to conflict with the Powers. This attitude soon produced a clash between Sharif and the Assembly—a clash which threatened to drag the Powers in as well. The immediate cause of disagreement was over a discussion in the Assembly on the draft of the Organic Law, Egypt's future constitution. The members indicated that they wished for the right to vote on the unassigned revenues of the budget; but there they met with the combined opposition of Sharif, the Khedive and the Controllers. Sharif refused to grant the Assembly's request, on the ground that such a move implied a shift in power from the hands of the Khedive into those of the Assembly, which would be contrary to the terms of the firmans. Sharif, an old hand at constitutions, well knew that such a request was within the normal range of an Assembly, but he was afraid of European displeasure; for the Note, as well as the stand of the Controllers on the issue, had made it very plain that such a suggested change did not meet with their approval. Europe, which had caused Ismail to be deposed to safeguard the bondholders' interests, would not stand idly by while a prospective threat to the bondholders was being discussed in the Assembly. Sharif sided with the Controllers.

The Controllers' point of view was expressed by Colvin, who said that to give the Assembly the right to vote on the unassigned revenues would imply that changes could be made in the imposition, assessment and collection of taxes, and in the administration itself. These changes might affect the Control by jeopardizing financial security and reform in the land.[18] He added that the power of the Controllers lay in advising the Council of Ministers and the Khedive, and that this power would be greatly weakened if the Control had to advise a whole chamber: the result would be financial chaos.[19] Here we see the political attributes that the Control had arrogated to itself in its role of political as well as financial mentor. Much of what followed can only be explained by the deep distrust of self-government that was felt by Europe for any Assembly in Asia or Africa. The thought that such a body as the Assembly could act in a constructive and positive way does not seem even to have entered Colvin's mind. He believed that the Assembly's aims were to possess itself of the administration of the country, to set aside the Turkish governing element. He added: 'The Egyptians being, in my opinion, incapable of conducting the administration of affairs, I think we are rapidly approaching a state of affairs which differs little, if at all, from anarchy . . . the collective note has intensified the spirit of opposition.'[20]

This devastating indictment of the Assembly was made barely three weeks after the Assembly had come into existence, and before it had even begun to control the administration. Indeed, Malet was already talking in terms of a military intervention by the Powers as the sole means of suppressing the Assembly. The Assembly, which expected just such a reaction, was very careful to point out that it had no intention of disowning its international commitments, and had every intention of fulfilling Egypt's obligations; yet it reiterated that it also intended to control the unassigned part of the budget, since that was the basic right of every parliamentary body. Moreover, the Assembly expressed its intention of instituting the principle of ministerial responsibility. It also insisted on taking a vote on the budget: this could have been delayed for another year, since the budget for that year had already been voted; but the Urabists in the Assembly determined to make an issue of the budget in order to dispose of Sharif Pasha and to make one of their own men, Sami al-Barudi, Prime Minister, with Urabi as Under-Secretary for War. This was done.

By now it was clear to most onlookers that the military were the party in power. The fallahin, thinking the military would rid them of the moneylenders, and scrap their debts, supported them; the rest of the population, regarding the army as their sole protection against foreign aggression, also supported them. Yet while the majority of the Egyptian population stood behind the Urabists, Cookson, the British Consul in Alexandria, referred to them as a military despotism; while Malet wrote, 'the country is virtually under a Military dictatorship, . . . the government is its mouthpiece, the Chamber its servant and the Khedive powerless'.[21] Three weeks later he reported that the Egyptian government was 'distinctly bent on diminishing 'Anglo-French protection', and that 'our influence is steadily decreasing. We can only regain our ascendancy by the destruction of the military supremacy'.[22] This was the real fear of Malet and Colvin. If the Control were to lose its influence in Egypt, not only would the bondholders risk not being paid, but the *status quo* might be changed, and thereby constitute a danger to the vital interests of the British Empire in the shape of a potential threat to the Suez Canal. A government subservient to the interests of the Powers was a safe one; but a government with pretensions of independence was a danger, no matter whether it were a good or a bad government. Every subsequent action that the Egyptian government took was therefore interpreted in the light of a break from Anglo-French influence. Both Consuls-General dangled the threat of anarchy in Egypt under the eyes of the Powers, for though the threat was perhaps an imaginary one, it was also the *sine qua non* of intervention. Colvin, in a memorandum to the Foreign Office, overstated the case and reported: 'It is for Her Majesty's Government to decide when, and at what point, anarchy is established . . . in my judgment, the country is at this moment without an effective government, and in imminent danger of disorder. The War Minister controls the Khedive and the Council, the army controls the War Minister.'[23] By then Urabi had become Minister for War.

Gambetta fell from power in January, 1882, and was replaced by Freycinet, who, though as reluctant to undertake a joint occupation of Egypt as Gladstone was, thought a naval demonstration by both Powers necessary to quell the nationalists. England, bound by the Joint Note, agreed, especially since Malet had urged such a step as a means of protecting the European colony in Egypt; but Malet warned the British government that 'if it is thought that the Porte and the Two Powers are not in accord, the consequences may be most serious'.[24] If the Porte were left out of a naval demonstration, the Egyptians would interpret that demonstration as an act of aggression on the part of the Powers. Since France would not accept Turkish aid, and since Turkey would not co-operate with the Powers, Malet's predictions came true, and the naval demonstration, which arrived in Alexandria on May 17, merely roused antagonism among the nationalists. As someone remarked, 'quand on veut faire quelque chose en Egypte il faut arriver par la Porte et non pas par la fenêtre'.

Urabi was emboldened in his resistance to the Powers by the Porte's refusal to co-operate with them. He interpreted its abstention as approval of his actions, the more so because the Sultan had just made him a Pasha. But relations between the Khedive and

The bombardment of Alexandria and its results, 1882

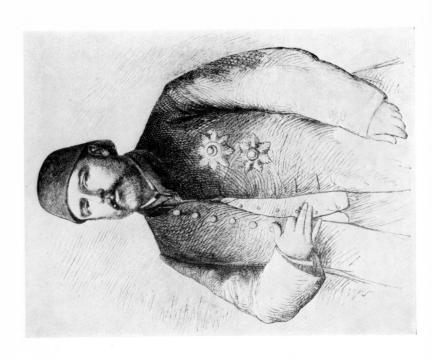

his government had deteriorated to the point where neither party trusted, or would co-operate with, the other.

Matters soon came to a head over the Khedive's handling of an alleged Circassian plot to assassinate Urabi. Several Circassian officers, including Uthman Rifqi the former Minister of War, were inculpated, and after a court martial were sentenced to death. The Khedive, on the advice of Malet, who told him that the sentence was unjust and inhuman, refused to confirm the death sentence, and issued a decree of exile instead. He then sent a report of the whole affair to the Porte. The Khedive's actions thoroughly incensed the cabinet, who detected Malet's hand behind it. They saw the Khedive's appeal to the Porte as a sign that he was attempting to diminish Egypt's autonomy by referring local matters to the Porte. The Khedive refused to retract his decision. The cabinet refused to resign, and convoked the Assembly. According to Article 9 of the new Constitution, only the Khedive had the right to convoke the Assembly, and he had refused to do so, therefore the cabinet's step in convoking the Assembly was illegal. Such a revolutionary action on their part could only bode ill for the Khedive, and it was rumoured that the cabinet intended to ask the Assembly for power to depose the Khedive. Malet, whose sources of information regarding the nationalists were the Khedive and his Greek dragoman, gave credence to the rumour and reported to the Foreign Office: 'The Chamber will meet on Saturday and will immediately pronounce the deposition of the Khedive, and sentence the whole family of Mohamed Ali to exile, appointing the President of the Council as Governor General of Egypt by the National Will.' Malet added that the Assembly went in mortal fear of the military. But the Assembly, under the Presidency of Sultan Pasha (who feared to go too far and so antagonize the Porte) belied Malet's analysis of the situation by refusing to meet unless it were convoked by the Khedive. The Prime Minister, al-Barudi, resigned on May 26.

On Barudi's resignation no one could be found to form a new ministry. Malet strongly advised the Khedive to patch up matters with his government and so end the crisis. The Khedive did so, but without any serious intention of a permanent reconciliation;

he and his government were still playing for time. Malet's next move was to send the British government a naive suggestion that it should ask Urabi and the leaders of the revolution to go into voluntary exile, after which, he assumed, matters would return to normal. Surprisingly enough, Granville agreed to Malet's suggestion, and sent a Note on May 27 asking Urabi to go into exile. The Egyptian cabinet categorically refused the terms of the Note, and one officer even threatened to kill Urabi if he accepted exile; but great was their surprise to learn that the Khedive Tawfiq had accepted it, and without consulting the cabinet. Thereupon the ministry resigned and, when no other ministry could be formed, the Khedive took the administration into his own hands.

The Khedive was not an efficient autocrat, and he was hampered by lack of co-operation from the administration. As the situation deteriorated, Tawfiq—overwhelmed by the turn of events—expected his own deposition, and the appointment of Halim Pasha, his great-uncle, as Khedive in his place.* Rumours circulated that Halim was helping the nationalists with donations of vast sums of money that were said to have reached Egypt through the intermediary of Hasan Musa al-Aqqad, a merchant. Yet the Khedive's gloomy prognostications were never fulfilled. Through the good offices of Sultan Pasha, the President of the Assembly, he finally reinstated Urabi as Minister of War, and made him responsible for maintaining order.

In Constantinople, meanwhile, the Sultan was growing perturbed about the situation in Egypt. He therefore sent an envoy, Dervish Pasha, to Egypt on June 7. Dervish Pasha was instructed to negotiate with Tawfiq, but one of Dervish's suite had secret orders to negotiate with Urabi. This standard Turkish game of diplomacy did nothing to settle the differences between the nationalists and the Khedive, and merely served to strengthen both sides in their belief that they were supported by the Porte. On June 11, the riots at Alexandria took place.

Various attempts have been made to blame the riots on the

---

* The Sultan was actually contemplating such a move. Yildiz archival collection no. 1401, group 31 in *Başbakanlik Arşivi*, also Yildiz no. 1208, Documents concerning Urabi

Khedive or on Urabi, but such evidence as is available tends to show that the riots are more likely to have arisen spontaneously than as the result of planning by either one side or the other. The British officials in Cairo and Alexandria sent back reports alleging Urabi's responsibility, and the British cabinet was led to believe these reports. According to Sir Charles Dilke, who was a cabinet minister at the time: 'I believed on the information furnished me from Alexandria and Cairo that they were the work of the revolutionary leaders in the Capital. A long time afterwards I gradually came to think that this had not been so, and that they had been purely local and spontaneous.'[25] Later, others came round to the same view. Malet (who had been away on leave at the time) in a letter to Cromer in 1907 said of the riots that they 'were the natural result of the political effervescence which was going on, and that neither the Khedive, nor Orabi "got them up" '.[26]

At the time, however, the British government certainly suspected Urabi of having caused the riots, while the nationalists suspected the Khedive—whereas their real cause lay rather in the growing tension that had been building up through the weeks. Malet had reported to the British government on May 31, 1882 that 'the whole country is labouring under a panic, and a collision might occur at any moment between the Moslems and the Christians'.[27] Anglo-French warships lay in the harbour, menacing the city, while European residents (especially Greeks and Maltese) armed themselves in expectation of a massacre, and the nationalists harangued crowds and excited them with threats of a foreign invasion. Disaster was inevitable. This was triggered off by a brawl between a drunken Maltese and an Egyptian donkey-boy, in which the Egyptian was killed. All the pent-up frustration of weeks of tension exploded in a display of mob hysteria. Several people were killed or wounded, and Cookson, the British Consul, was badly mauled by the crowd. The number of casualties were variously estimated: while a Syrian eye-witness, Salim Naqqash, puts the figure at 300 killed,[28] John Ninet, a Swiss eye-witness, and Shaykh Muhammad Abduh, estimate that the figure was some 163 Egyptians and 75 Europeans.[29] Rafii, a modern Egyptian historian, takes on the other hand, the estimate of a group of European doctors who put the number of casualties at 49, of whom 38 were European.[30] The riots were checked only in the afternoon, when word reached Urabi in Cairo, and he ordered the troops out to stop them.

The British cabinet was sorely divided over the attitude to be taken towards Egypt, and the division was an echo of the cabinet's disagreement over the Irish policy. While Gladstone and the Radicals—Chamberlain and Dilke—pressed for conciliation of the nationalists, whether in Ireland or in Egypt, the Whigs—Northbrook and Kimberley, under Hartington, Secretary for India —pressed for coercion and strong measures. The Whig attitude towards nationalists had been influenced by the Phoenix Park murders in Dublin, an act of nationalist terrorism in which Hartington's brother and Gladstone's nephew-in-law, Lord Frederick Cavendish, had been assassinated on May 5, 1882. This gratuitous murder of an innocent by-stander by Irish nationalists embittered the Whigs, who came to regard all nationalists as tarred with the same brush, and deserving of severe repression.

When the cabinet saw the failure of their Joint Note and naval demonstration with France, and when the riots at Alexandria took place, the Radicals swung over to the side of the Whigs, for they assumed that the riots were the work of the nationalists. Some blame for the Cabinet's misunderstanding of the situation in Egypt lay with Malet, who was misinformed, and Colvin, who was biased by virtue of his position as Controller. Dilke, in his memoirs, said as much: 'I cannot but think that Malet was largely responsible for the state of things in Egypt.'[31] The faith of the Radicals in Urabi as a nationalist leader waned after the Alexandria riots, and they accepted Malet's estimate of him as a military dictator who used terrorist methods.

Granville and other members of the cabinet were also worried over the safety of the Suez Canal, for rumours had spread that Urabi had sent ships filled with explosives up the Canal. On June 22 Granville said: 'I am ready to go any lengths for reparation, and I set great store about making the Canal safe. But I own to dreadful alarm at occupying Egypt militarily and politically with the French. I think the majority [in the cabinet] would rather like to do this . . . It is a nasty business, and we have been much out of luck.'[32] The Whigs were equally worried, and Hartington threatened to resign unless some action were taken. Anxiety in the cabinet increased with reports that France was negotiating on her own with Urabi.

Britain and France were by now growing suspicious of each other, and neither could decide on what action to take. Britain wished to coerce Turkey into sending an expedition under Anglo-French auspices, but France would not hear of including the Turk in an Egyptian project. Finally, to end the stalemate, Britain suggested that an International Conference be called in Constantinople, and that the problem of Egypt be discussed by all the Powers. The only hitch in this plan was that the Turks refused to have anything to do with the Conference, and warned the Powers that Egypt was a Turkish, and not a European, responsibility. Nevertheless the Conference opened on June 23, 1882, in Constantinople, but without a Turkish envoy. To allay all fears, the Powers signed a Self-Denying Protocol on June 25, which said that they undertook not to annex or occupy Egypt, and not to seek any territorial advantage. The following day Lord Dufferin, British Ambassador in Constantinople, gave the British government's reasons for calling the Conference: 'It is no exaggeration to say that during the last few months absolute anarchy has reigned in Egypt. We have seen a military faction, without even alleging those pretences to legality with which such persons are wont to cloak their designs, proceed from violence to violence, until insubordination had given place to mutiny, mutiny to revolt and revolt to a usurpation of the supreme power . . . the revenues of Egypt are failing. This state of things has placed in extreme jeopardy those commercial interests in which the subjects of all the Powers are so deeply concerned. Not only so, but those special engagements into which the governments of France and England had entered with Egypt have been repudiated.'[33] Dufferin was guilty of gross exaggeration, for there was no anarchy in Egypt. In fact, the peasants and the notables were solidly behind Urabi, who had been praised and promoted by the Sultan. The Khedive, after dismissing Urabi, had recalled him to office, as alone capable of keeping order. There was opposition to the Khedive; but if usurpation of power had taken place, it had been indirectly sanctioned by the Turkish government which had a regular correspondence with Urabi.[34] The real reason given by Dufferin is to be found in his reference to commercial interests, and to special engagements between Egypt and the Powers; for although these engagements had not been repudiated by Egypt, the Powers feared that in the future they might be repudiated. Needless to say the Conference failed to achieve anything.

The Khedive, seeing the waning of his authority, thought that the only way by which he could regain it was to appeal to the Powers. On July 7 he wrote to Cartwright, the Acting-Consul, in terms suggesting that the Anglo-French fleet should bombard Alexandria; and that British troops should disembark immediately after the bombardment to deal with the Egyptian army which— though likely to disperse after the bombardment—would, given time, be emboldened to come together again. Two days later Cartwright reported that the Khedive had asked him to 'urge on Her Majesty's Government the necessity, from his point of view, of the earliest possible action, or at least of an intimation as to what may be expected'.[35]

The British cabinet, which was threatening to collapse and thus ruin hopes for Home Rule for Ireland, had been exerting much pressure on Gladstone to take action. When fears that Urabi might block the Suez Canal worried Gladstone still further, he allowed Beauchamp Seymour, Admiral of the Fleet at Alexandria, to send an ultimatum, as a compromise with his cabinet. Granville was hopeful that the bombardment of Alexandria would bring about Urabi's collapse without necessitating an actual disembarkation of troops, and the ships sent to Alexandria carried no troops on board. But the French were unwilling to associate themselves with a bombardment, and the French fleet was given orders to withdraw in the case of such an eventuality. Freycinet, at the head of a tottering cabinet, claimed that he would have to ask the sanction of the French Parliament before taking such a step, and Parliament was not likely to give it him.

On his arrival in Alexandria in May, Seymour had informed the

British Government that the forts overlooking the harbour at
Alexandria were being manned, and guns put up. The Admiralty
sent him orders to 'destroy the earthworks and silence the bat-
teries' if he could not otherwise prevent work on the fortifications.[36] Seymour remonstrated with the Egyptian authorities, and
work ceased. The Sultan, upon learning of the fortifications,
ordered the works to stop, and warned the Khedive that 'one shot
might lose Egypt'.[37] The Khedive wired back that all work on
the forts had been stopped. Northbrook, the First Lord of the
Admiralty, reporting on the forts to Gladstone, said: 'If we want
to bring on a fight we can instruct B. Seymour to require the guns
to be dismantled. My advisers do not think they will do much
harm where they are.'[38] What both Seymour and Northbrook had
failed to tell Gladstone was that the repairs in question were being
carried out on forts that overlooked the eastern harbour, while the
British fleet lay in the western harbour, out of sight of the forts.
On July 7, Seymour once more claimed that work on the forts
had been restarted, and, although the Khedive sent a denial to the
Sultan, Seymour was allowed to send an ultimatum on July 10,
1882, demanding that work on the forts be stopped. But Seymour,
apparently over-stepping his orders, sent an ultimatum demanding
that the forts be surrendered to him for dismantling. Was it that,
in Northbrook's words, 'they wanted to bring on a fight'? The
best explanation of what happened is that there seems to have
been a lack of co-ordination between the orders of the Admiralty
to Seymour, and those of the cabinet; for when Gladstone heard
of Seymour's ultimatum he said to Granville, 'the Admiral's telegram is bad but I am at a loss to understand the meaning of the
word "surrendered". What title can he have to demand the surrender of any forts? And this without instructions?'[39] The Egyptian government was well entitled to ask by what authority
Seymour had asked them to surrender their forts to him. And at
a cabinet meeting over which Tawfiq presided, the ultimatum was
refused. The cabinet issued a decree the following day denying the
charge of installing new guns in any fort, but stated that it was
willing to allow the Admiral to dismantle three guns from any
fort he chose. If, however, Admiral Seymour still insisted on

bombarding the forts, then they would reply to British fire only after the fifth volley had been fired from the ships.[40]

Seymour refused these terms, and on July 11 the British fleet bombarded Alexandria. Two days later the Khedive sought contact with Admiral Seymour and put himself under his protection. The Urabists, convinced by this action that the Khedive had sold out to the British, declared him a traitor. In retaliation, Tawfiq dismissed Urabi from his position, and declared him a mutineer and an outlaw. General Wolseley, who had arrived in Alexandria on August 15, was empowered, in the Khedive's name, to quell the Egyptian rebellion. The nationalists, once Britain and France had set their faces against them, were doomed to failure.

After the bombardment of Alexandria, and the retreat of Urabi's forces to Tal al-Kabir, England was encouraged to take more active steps: firstly because it was understood that Urabi had threatened to block the Suez Canal, and secondly because he had declared a Holy War against England. Dufferin in Constantinople tried to get the Sultan to pronounce Urabi a rebel, to counteract the declaration of the Holy War; but the Sultan procrastinated. Urabi never attempted to block the Canal because he depended on a promise de Lesseps had made him that no British soldier would set foot on Canal territory. How Urabi could have been naive enough to believe that de Lesseps could keep his promise without the support of an army or navy, is a mystery. The British army therefore landed to Urabi's rear in the Canal Zone un-opposed, and the Egyptian army was soon defeated by a surprise attack. But even before the battle of Tal al-Kabir the insurgents realized they were fighting a losing battle. Many of their civilian colleagues defected to the side of the Khedive, and the first to do so was Sultan Pasha. Some officers also followed suit, and Urabi, whose gifts as a general were not many, soon surrendered to the British general.

When Britain first planned to send an expedition to the Canal Zone, it had invited France to join in the action. The motion had, however, been defeated in the French Parliament by Clemenceau, who saw the whole operation as part of a Bismarckian plot to lay France open to a surprise attack by Germany while France's troops were occupied in Egypt.[41] Thus it came about that France, which had inaugurated the proceedings against Egypt, defaulted because of a shaky cabinet, and out of fear of Germany; while Britain, which had not wanted to intervene in Egypt, occupied that country alone. In Freycinet's words: 'M. Gladstone a subi l'aventure égyptienne, bien plus qu'il ne l 'a recherchée.'[42] The final British plunge into Egypt is a good example of the extent to which differences of opinion within a cabinet can shape, or even twist, a policy. The cabinet's misgivings over nationalist movements, whether in Ireland or in Egypt; their despair of Turkish and international, notably French, action; and their concern for the Canal—all forced them to the point of intervention. By then Gladstone had convinced himself of the righteousness of British action in Egypt, and in the House made a statement in which he declared that 'the insecurity of the Canal, it is plain, does not exhibit to us the seat of the disease. The insecurity of the Canal is a symptom only, and the seat of the disease is in the interior of Egypt, in its disturbed and its anarchical position.'[43] The British expedition was therefore given the mission of creating law and order out of the alleged Egyptian chaos, and of restoring the rightful authority of the Khedive.

Had the two Powers not shown how easy it was to depose a ruler, even an absolute one like Ismail, and to replace him by another, perhaps Urabi would not have tried to emulate them. The extent to which the Powers had meddled in Egyptian affairs, both politically and financially, was bound to create a reaction in Egypt. They had undermined the prestige of the Khedivate, first by imposing a Dual Control on Ismail, and then by deposing him. They had paralysed the administration by the terms of the Law of Liquidation; they had prevented Urabi from disposing of the Khedive, and were soon to prevent the Khedive from disposing of Urabi. Unless they gave up their intervention in Egyptian affairs, and left the Egyptians to put their own house in order, the sequel of their constant intervention was almost bound to be a foreign assumption of the reins of authority in the country. This is what eventually happened, but the British government took some time to come to that conclusion.

When the British cabinet first decided to occupy Egypt, it did so with no thought beyond rescuing the Egyptian monarch from the nationalists, restoring his authority, effecting rapid reforms in the administration, and then retiring from Egyptian political life. The British government's aim was to be counted in terms of establishing a paramount influence in Egypt, and safeguarding British interest in the Suez Canal. Occupation of Egypt, in the sense of annexation, was out of the question. Gladstone claimed that it would be 'at variance with all the principles and views of the British Government, and the pledges they have given to Europe, and with the views, I may say of Europe itself'.[44] Although the Sultan had offered to hand over to England 'the exclusive control and administration of Egypt, reserving to himself only those rights of suzerainty which he now possessed',[45] both Gladstone and Granville had refused the offer when it was made, much to the Queen's disappointment.

After the occupation, there was soon to be strong disagreement within the British cabinet as to the future government of Egypt. The Queen, Hartington and the Whigs, feared that a liberal experiment in Egypt might bring about a repudiation of the debt, and favoured control by the British government over Egypt for a prolonged period. Gladstone felt that the best system for Egypt was to be 'found in freedom and self development as far as may be for Egypt'.[46] According to Dilke, Gladstone seems to have had in mind a plan to neutralize Egypt while reserving for England a predominance of influence. Chamberlain refused to believe that an Egyptian Assembly would repudiate the debt, since that would make it liable to further interference by the Powers, so he sent a memorandum to the rest of the cabinet, in which he wrote: 'There is great anxiety lest after all the bondholders should be the only persons who have profited by the war, and lest the phrases which have been used concerning the extension of Egyptian liberties should prove to have no practical meaning.' If the other Powers insisted on continuing the financial control in Egypt, then, Chamberlain went on, 'we should at least put forward as our own the legitimate aspirations of Egyptian national sentiment'.[47] If there were to be no guaranteed neutrality for Egypt, then England should simply evacuate at once. This suggestion did not meet with the approval of the rest of the cabinet. Dilke noted in his diary a cabinet discussion over liberal institutions and the formation of an Egyptian Chamber of Notables, and wrote: 'Chamber of Notables: decided to do nothing, at which I am furious. What do four peers know about popular feeling?'[48] The four peers were Hartington, Kimberley, Northbrook and Granville. To solve the cabinet's dilemma, Lord Dufferin was instructed to go to Egypt on October 29, 1882, and investigate the state of the administration.

Lest the existence of a British force on Egyptian soil should excite suspicion among the Powers, Granville sent a circular to the major European capitals, which said '. . . although for the present a British force remains in Egypt for the preservation of public tranquillity, Her Majesty's Government is desirous of withdrawing it as soon as the state of the country, and the organization of proper means for the maintenance of the Khedive's authority, will admit of it'. The other Powers, especially Germany, were more than content to let England handle the Egyptian question, because they thought that it would inevitably lead to the embroilment of Britain and France—a design that fitted in with Bismarck's policy of a rapprochement with France through the alienation of Britain.

In spite of its avowed intentions, every step that the British government was to take in the direction of reaffirming the Khedive's power was to have the opposite effect—to weaken it, thereby giving England a firmer hold over Egypt. For example, in its handling of the court martial of the insurgents, the British government made the Khedive look like a man of straw to the Egyptians. Since the British government did not trust the Khedive and his government to mete out justice—a feeling that was justified—it stipulated the conditions in which Urabi and his men were to be tried. 'Her Majesty's Government considered that he should not be delivered up to the vengeance of the Egyptian authorities without a guarantee that he would not be executed except after conviction of a fair trial of crimes which, according to the practice of civilized nations, call for the extreme penalty of law.'[49] Later Granville added that Urabi should only be executed if he were inculpated in the burning of Alexandria. Alexandria had caught fire during Seymour's bombardment, and opinions were divided as to whether the fire was a result of the bombardment, or whether it was a deliberate act of arson undertaken by the nationalists. The British government, needled by W. S. Blunt, let Urabi and his men have British legal counsel in a trial conducted by Egyptians, on Egyptians, using the Ottoman legal code, and the Arabic language. It also insisted that an English reporter, in the person of Sir Charles Wilson, should attend the trial and give his opinion as to the legality of the proceedings. This attitude was meant to show the Egyptians that the British government intended to exact clemency from the Egyptian government, and that people could expect justice, now that England was there to supervise things. But inevitably and perhaps even unconsciously, the British government was setting itself up as an authority, over and above the Egyptian one; an authority that was gradually to displace the Egyptian.

All these elaborate preparations for a trial were pointless, and verged on the farcical, since the verdict was agreed upon before the trial started. Riaz Pasha who, as Minister of the Interior, was President of the Tribunal, resigned in protest at this manner of conducting a trial. Dilke in his memoirs recounts the arrangement previously reached between the British and the Egyptian governments: 'With regard to Arabi's trial, it was decided that Dufferin should be told to consider the case against him, and to decide that there was no proof of common crime, after which, by arrangement between us and the Khedive, we were to put him safely in Ascencion, Barbadoes . . .'[50] Urabi had intimated that such an arrangement met with his approval, since it was the only means of saving his life; and later on he said: 'We indeed, had understood from Lord Dufferin that by so (Pleading) [sic] we should render a service to the British government in view of the reforms which it intends to carry out in our country. And solely on that account we consented to plead guilty to rebellion, contrary to the fact.'[51] Dufferin insisted on pretending that no deal had been made with the Urabists.

According to the Wilson memorandum of the trial, the case

seemed to be one of a successful military mutiny, in which the whole army took part, and towards which the native population was either sympathetic or remained apathetic. 'One remarkable feature of the examination has been the manner in which the native Egyptians have held together. Nearly all the evidence in support of the prosecution has been derived from men of Turkish or Syrian origin in government employ—no "fellah" officer has disclosed any important secret connected with the movement. The broad line which separates the Turkish governing class from the men of "fellah" origin has also been very marked . . . In conclusion, I must express my belief that on the existing evidence no English court martial would convict the prisoners . . . of any greater crime than of taking part in a successful military revolt against the Khedive.'[52] Wilson found that there was 'no evidence to connect Urabi with the riots at Alexandria on June 11, and that it is doubtful whether a deliberate massacre of Europeans was ever intended . . . [That] the evidence which connects Arabi Pasha with the burning of Alexandria is conflicting and that there is not sufficient proof that he ordered the town to be destroyed.'[53] Suspicion of the burning of Alexandria had later fallen on Hasan Musa al-Aqqad (a merchant and former slave-trader in the Sudan), and on an officer, Sulayman Sami. Sami was found guilty and hanged.*

According to most legal codes, mutiny is punishable by death. That sentence was duly passed on Urabi on December 3, 1882, and commuted to exile. And yet had Urabi actually mutinied? As Minister for War, and one who had recently been decorated by the Sultan as a sign of favour, Urabi could do no less than defend his country against foreign aggression, especially when resistance to the British had been agreed upon during a cabinet meeting presided over by the Khedive, who concurred in the decision taken. Technically the real traitor was the Khedive who, fearful for his throne, had invited the British to bombard Alexandria and to occupy Egypt, and then encouraged his own cabinet in its

---

* Al-Aqqad's grandson told the author that both al-Aqqad and Sami had organized the burning of Alexandria in an attempt to stop the advance of the British troops, but without Urabi's knowledge.

decision to resist a British attack. One cannot help but wonder how things would have turned out, if the Whigs had not been so anti-nationalist, if France had not been so intransigent in protecting her bondholders' interests, and if the Khedive had co-operated with the Urabists instead of sheltering behind the Powers. Cromer subsequently said: 'Had he [Urabi] been left alone, there cannot be a doubt that he would have been successful. His want of success was due to British interference.'[54]

At best Urabi might perhaps have been successful in controlling the country and in establishing law and order. Whether he could have introduced constitutional principles to put an end to arbitrary rule is most doubtful, for Urabi had neither the necessary stature nor the political acumen to carry out such major reforms in the teeth of opposition. Only in ideal conditions, that is, with the co-operation of the Khedive and liberal Egyptian statesmen, could the movement have succeeded. Even then, crippled as Egypt was by the Law of Liquidation and the Capitulations, his government could never have flourished. So long as the Powers put the interests of their bondholders above those of the Egyptians, no government in Egypt could have been successful.

When Dufferin arrived in Egypt in November 1882, he had found a frightened and vindictive ruler. The Khedive had been so afraid of the army that in September he had refused to return to Cairo from Alexandria so long as the rebel officers were allowed to walk around Cairo wearing their swords. He therefore asked General Wolseley to divest all Egyptian officers, from the rank of First Lieutenant to General, of their arms.[55] Such a timid Khedive was not likely to stand in the way of Dufferin's suave diplomacy. Neither was the Prime Minister, Sharif Pasha, a one-time Constitutionalist who had suffered dismissal at the hand of the Urabist nationalist Assembly. He was content to agree with Dufferin that the Egyptians were not yet ready for self-government, and to defer to his judgment on many points.

Within this context Dufferin prepared his report, which covered every facet of administrative life, and suggested its total overhaul under the supervision of British officials. But to make sure that no suspicions should be cast on the British government's motives,

Dufferin said: 'We have not the least intention of preserving the authority which had thus reverted to us, almost in spite of ourselves, by main force or any other illegitimate means. It was our intention so to conduct our relations with the Egyptian people that they should naturally regard us as their friends and counsellors but we did not propose upon that account arbitrarily to impose our views upon them, or to hold them in an irritating tutelage.'[56] And yet, after such high-sounding sentiments, Dufferin proceeded to lay down a plan whereby England could hold the Egyptians in tutelage, all the while protesting the noblest intentions. Dufferin's report was a perfect example of double-talk. He suggested that liberal institutions be introduced in Egypt, and then set out a plan for two absolutely useless bodies. These were a Legislative Council having a consultative function, and the right to 'express wishes', but not to initiate legislation; and an Assembly, with an advisory function, which was to meet 'at least once every two years'. The cabinet was not responsible to either body; and yet these chambers were to represent 'a strong and almost irresistible force of public opinion, as represented by the most intelligent men in the country', which was—by some strange process unexplained by Dufferin—to be 'focussed in such a manner as to exercise an effectual control upon the arbitrary or capricious impulses of the Khedive's ministers'. Why could not the 'most intelligent men in the country' be given a more concrete method of restraining the 'arbitrary or capricious impulses' of the cabinet? The answer was to be found in Dufferin's belief that constitutional life was premature in Egypt, since the Egyptians were characterized by 'childishness'. A strange epithet to apply to a people who had just gone through a revolution in order to acquire a constitutional life.

He said that the chief root of bitterness in the country could be traced to the indebtedness of the fallahin, then insisted that indemnities to the sum of £E4 million be paid for the loss of property incurred by the foreign community in the fire of Alexandria—even when France contended that these indemnities were not a legal obligation on the part of the Egyptian government, but were a matter of grace, since the losses arose as the result of a rebellion.[57] He could not have failed to know that the already overburdened fallahin would be the ones to pay these indemnities.

Dufferin warned the British government that Egypt could not be administered with any prospect of success from London, but he went on to add: 'Though it be our fixed determination that the new regime shall not surcharge us with the responsibility of permanently administering the country whether directly or indirectly, it is absolutely necessary to prevent the fabric we have raised from tumbling to the ground the moment our sustaining hand is withdrawn.' For this, he said, would be the signal for a return of confusion to the country with resultant discord in Europe. But if the reforms that Britain is to contrive are to have any chance of success, they cannot be allowed to operate *in vacuo*. Those who are to share in carrying out the reforms must have some guarantee. For, 'unless they are convinced that we intend to shield and foster the system we have established, it will be vain to expect the timid politicians of the East to identify themselves with its existence'.

Dufferin's report was viewed with mixed feelings by the few who read it both in England and Egypt. Some of the Egyptians failed to read between the lines, and interpreted it as a hopeful portent of a full parliamentary life in the near future. The Council and the Assembly which had come into existence with the passing of the Organic Law of May 1, 1883, were perhaps, they hoped, a prelude to full constitutional powers; and since Dufferin had correctly analysed all of Egypt's administrative diseases and suggested remedies for them, they had hopes that large-scale reforms would be instituted. This was Urabi's belief; that England would successfully put into effect all the reforms that he had hoped to carry out himself. Others, more sceptical, read into the report hints of a long occupation, camouflaged by Dufferin's diplomatic language; for what precautions to protect the 'timid politicians of the East' could he have meant, other than the continued existence of an army of occupation? Furthermore, they did not relish his adjectives, such as 'childish', nor the limited institutions that he had devised for them. The Urabi revolt had arisen to give Egypt a popular government; but, with a stroke of the pen, Dufferin wiped out that movement and all it stood for, and replaced it by

Tawfiq, Khedive

Colonel Ahmad Urabi Pasha, during the campaign against the English

the pre-revolutionary autocratic rule of Khedive and ministers, without giving the people any effective safeguards against an abuse of power, save that of public opinion. Yet the majority greeted the report passively.

In England, the more sophisticated politicians accused Dufferin of setting forth a programme in which he did not believe. This charge aroused Dufferin's indignation. He wrote to Granville: 'I have seen it constantly repeated in the newspapers and elsewhere, that I myself did not seem to believe in my own proposals . . . but I have no hesitation in declaring that if only it is given fair play, the re-organization of Egypt upon the lines now approved by the British government has every chance of success.'[58] Dufferin also wrote to Sir William Gregory who, along with Blunt, was a friend to the Urabists: 'All my instincts are with the national party in Egypt . . . They ought to be the most easily governed community in the world, as well as the best off and most contented; and if once we could get anything like self-government started upon anything like a secure basis in Egypt it might prove a beginning for the establishment of a better system of administration in other parts of the Mussulman world.'[59]

It would be unfair to accuse Dufferin and the British cabinet of deliberate hypocrisy in their attitude towards Egypt; but they had to take several factors, other than Egyptian desires, into consideration, and some of these factors ranked higher in the British list of priorities. The British government was anxious to do nothing in Egypt which might shake the foundations of the Ottoman Empire, or be used as an excuse for protest, or even intervention, by the Powers; and since the Egyptian government readily fell in with Dufferin's suggestions, the British cabinet and Dufferin, both hoping for the best, were content with a report that was nothing more than an echo of the dilemma in which the British cabinet found itself. For the report proposed a programme of reforms, to be followed by evacuation, and at the same time hinted that the reforms could only take root if the occupation were prolonged. Since reforms do not take root overnight, and Dufferin insisted that they must not be allowed to tumble down once England evacuated Egypt, then a certain period of occupation was, by implication, necessary. Although Dufferin had stressed that Egypt was not to become a 'concealed protectorate', he had not explained how this was to be avoided, especially as British officials were to be installed as Advisers, holding key positions in the government, in order to supervise the reforms. In modern parlance, an Adviser who is a technical assistant is not, strictly speaking, a political instrument; but the position of an Adviser who is supported by his government and by an army of occupation, is an entirely different matter, for even if he starts out by being non-political, he inevitably takes on political overtones. Dufferin's programme was therefore couched in terms that seemed to communicate all things to all men. It could be interpreted either as a prelude to complete self-government (and his letter to Gregory would imply as much), or it could be interpreted as an apologia for a prolonged occupation. This last was the interpretation that Evelyn Baring, who was sent to Egypt in September 1883, as Consul-General, chose.

As for the Egyptians and their nationalist aspirations, they soon crumpled in the face of the might of the British Empire. All the leaders of the Urabi revolution were sent into exile, while the minor characters were mostly in prison, awaiting judgment, or in fear and trembling awaiting a summons to trial. Their spirit was so completely broken that they had no thought beyond saving themselves from the debacle. The notables, who had been involved with the nationalists, either retired to their estates and hoped that the Khedive would forget their existence, or else threw themselves on his clemency, and begged his forgiveness—hoping that Dufferin would save them from the Khedive's vengeance as he had saved Urabi. More than one factor had broken their spirit. Apart from the actual presence of the alien army on Egyptian territory, one of the major reasons for the break-up of the movement was that the former leaders of the country, respectable notables like Sultan Pasha, hastened to play the part of Quislings. In the eyes of the nationalists, Sultan was the villain of the piece[60]—a one time Urabist, President of the Assembly of Notables, one of the founders of *Hizb al-Watani*, he had not scrupled to defect to the Khedive's side after the bombardment of Alexandria. The Khedive had then made him his liaison officer with General Wolseley, and his special task had been to woo, or bribe, Arab Shaykhs away from Urabi's army.[61] Sultan Pasha was later rewarded by both the Khedive and the British government for his share in overthrowing Urabi.* Secondly, the political leaders of the old regime, men, that is, like Sharif and Riaz—both former Prime Ministers—hastened to collaborate with England in its reforming task. As would-be reformers, whose chief object was to curb the Khedive's power, they hoped that Dufferin's proposals would promote that end, and were quick to point out this road to the disillusioned and frightened nationalists. Lastly, the Egyptian nationalist front had disintegrated. Since non-success leads to the collapse of shaky alliances, by the time the end came, the rebels were totally demoralized and in no condition to oppose any measures. It would not then be wrong to say that the impulse that had generated the revolution was virtually extinguished in Egypt, in the face of such odds, and that the Dufferin report was therefore met with a passive, if not acquiescent, attitude.

* Rida, *op. cit.*, I, p. 223. Sultan got a K.C.M.G. from Britain, and, it is alleged, £E.10,000 from the Khedive.

CHAPTER II

International Entanglements: 1882–1896

The aftermath of the occupation of Egypt promised to be an unending source of trouble to England on three levels—within the cabinet, on the international scene, and within Egypt herself. The problem of the Sudan threatened to bring down the cabinet; while international pressures exerted by France and Germany, which were a reflection of French animosity towards Britain, were to frustrate British efforts to settle the problem of Egyptian finances. These, together with the internal situation of Egypt (which will be discussed in a subsequent chapter), served to show that a policy of 'rescue and retire' was not feasible, and to prolong the occupation.

In 1881 a man calling himself al-Mahdi had roused a revolution in the Sudan. Originally a holy man who had gained great repute for piety, al-Mahdi started a movement of religious reform, somewhat akin to the Wahhabi movement in Arabia, which stressed a return to the original purity of Islam. From a religious reformist, al-Mahdi soon developed into a political and revolutionary leader.[1] The Sudan, which had been conquered piecemeal from the time of Muhammad Ali until Ismail, was an enormous tract of land divided into provinces each having a Governor nominated by Cairo and responsible to Cairo. Because of the size of the provinces and the lack of adequate means of communication, little contact between one Governor and another took place. So by the time word spread of a revolutionary movement, al-Mahdi had already gained a large following. The government in Cairo, which was in the throes of a political revolution, paid too little attention to Sudanese affairs, and the Governors had to make do with their own resources, which were at best slim. By 1882 when the Egyptian administration was in a position to devote part of its attention to the Sudan, al-Mahdi had gained a series of crushing victories over the separate Egyptian Governors of the Sudan, and had established a reputation for invincibility among his people.

The Egyptian government, which was misinformed as to the extent of al-Mahdi's influence, assumed that a simple military expedition would be sufficient to break his forces, known as the dervishes; and sent an army of sorts under Hicks Pasha, a retired Indian army officer. The regular Egyptian army had been disbanded by the Khedive after the Urabi revolution, so the Hicks force was a motley crew made up of prisoners, pensioned officers, and mercenaries. It lacked the basic elements of a military expedition, namely discipline, money and a unified command. Hicks was given half the number of men and funds that he had asked for, and was saddled with an aged Egyptian general as co-commander. As the two commanders could never agree, the result was chaos.

Evelyn Baring, the Consul-General, whose main problem was restoring Egyptian finances to solvency, was sceptical as to the efficacy of the expedition, and begrudged it any funds, which he believed were merely an added drain on the Egyptian treasury. On October 26, 1883, he warned the British government that the Sudan presented a barrier to the settlement of Egypt's finances, for it was a 'bottomless hole' as far as money was concerned. Moreover, incoming reports from the Sudan were far from reassuring. In a pessimistic letter to Granville written on November 19, Baring voiced the view that if General Hicks' army were destroyed, then the Egyptian government would lose the whole of the Sudan, unless some assistance from outside was given to them. It would therefore be wiser for them to accept the fact, and 'to withdraw to whatever point on the Nile they can be sure of defending'.[2] On November 25, the Hicks army was massacred by the dervish forces.

News of the disaster came as a tremendous shock to the Egyptian authorities, the more so when Baring and Wood, the Commander in Chief of the forces of occupation, reported that Mahdist forces were likely to invade Egypt proper. They both pointed out that Egypt, without an army, was in no position to defend herself, and that the British army of occupation would have to take over that duty. Evacuation would have to be postponed until the danger of an invasion was over. This announcement came just when Sharif Pasha's negotiations with the British government over the withdrawal of British forces from Cairo to Alexandria had met with success, so that the blow of delayed evacuation was doubly bitter to the Egyptians.

Although the British government had announced its willingness to protect Egypt from invasion, it pointed out that it was not willing to help Egypt reconquer the Sudan. Baring was firm on the point. In the first place reconquest would cost too much; and in the second place, it would make the policy of withdrawing the British garrison from Egypt difficult, since it involved the risk that British authority would be established in a permanent manner over the Nile Valley.[3] There was in all British eyes a tremendous difference between remaining in Egypt as reformers, and carving out an African empire—such as the conquest of the Sudan implied. This latter alternative neither Baring nor the British government could in 1884 morally justify. Here was the dilemma of Britain-in-Egypt. Haunted by its promises of quick evacuation, by its fear of being accused by Europe of harbouring covetous thoughts towards Egypt, and even more by the spectre of managing a large area of unwanted and doubtless expensive territory, the British government could only agree with Baring's analysis of the situation. Baring put the matter even more strongly by writing to Granville, 'if we are to become responsible for the government of the Sudan, I think, we may at once, for all practical purposes, abandon any hope of getting away from Egypt at all'.[4] That was precisely what the British government did not wish to do. The only policy then was to force Egypt to abandon the Sudan, and to prolong the occupation until such time as Egypt was able to rely on her own army.

The next step was to evacuate the Egyptian garrisons in the Sudan, and General Gordon was chosen to carry out that task. Gordon, who had won fame in China and had served under Ismail as Governor-General in the Sudan, was an eccentric and forceful person, accustomed to acting on his own, even in defiance of orders. He was given a sufficiently vague mandate to go to the

Sudan and see what he could do, although the authorities were under the impression that they had asked him to evacuate the Sudan. Once Gordon arrived at Khartum he made the mistake of underestimating the Mahdi's power and overestimating his own influence there, and decided to reconquer the Sudan. Soon the remaining Egyptian garrisons, which had not previously been over-run by dervish forces, fell; and Gordon's position became so critical that he asked for reinforcements. Gladstone's cabinet then divided itself into two camps, those who threatened to resign if reinforcements were sent, and those who threatened to resign if reinforcements were *not* sent. Gladstone himself would not present to the House a request which implied further financial commitment in Egypt. While indecision tore the cabinet apart, news of Gordon's death reached England on February 5, 1885. As Gordon, who was a public hero, could not be massacred with impunity like the unknown Hicks, a public outcry was made, and directed against Gladstone. The Queen rebuked him in an open telegram, the populace hissed him in the streets, the music-hall acts dubbed him M.O.G.—for the Grand Old Man had now become the Murderer of Gordon. The cabinet seriously considered resignation.[5] Fortunately for the Liberals, Russian advances into Pendjeh in Afghanistan saved the cabinet, but only for a few months, and it eventually fell in June 1885. The Sudan was shelved for the time being, and left to the Mahdi's followers.

While the Sudan problem was occupying the British and Egyptian governments, trouble was simultaneously brewing with France. France was coming to realize that her failure to co-operate with England in the occupation of Egypt was easing her out of the picture. Quite unwittingly the Egyptian government had made it easier to establish British domination over Egypt's finances, when, on October 22, 1882, Sharif had sent a Note to Malet asking for the abolition of the Dual Control, and the substitution of a single Adviser (British for choice). This step, though sensible enough, roused France's wrath, and helped England to acquire a free hand in directing Egyptian affairs, untrammelled by any necessity for joint action with France. Sharif's reasons for suggesting such a step were that the Dual Control, 'in consequence of its dual nature and semi-political character, has produced undeniable abuses of administration, has excited the legitimate susceptibilities of the Egyptians, and has in consequence dangerously impaired the authority of the government in the eyes of the country'.[6] The Note met with the British Government's approval, and was eventually circulated to the other Powers. As soon as France received the Note she assumed that it was written at the instigation of the British government, and let fly a barrage of invective against Britain. In a communication handed to the British Ambassador in France, Lord Lyons, France asked: 'In intervening to suppress a military revolt, was it the intention of England to free herself from her previous agreements . . . to repudiate . . . the work hitherto pursued in concert? . . . The cancelling of the Agreements of 1879, without any really serious compensation, amounts to the loss, pure and simple, of the position which our past, our traditions, and our legitimate interests ought to secure for us in Egypt.'[7] The government of the day tried to mollify France by offering her the Presidency of the Caisse de la Dette; but France refused, on the grounds that it was inconsistent with her dignity to accept—as an equivalent for the abolition of the Control—a position which would be simply that of a cashier, after having held the keys to the safe.[8] Since England was in possession, there was very little that France could actually do, apart from remonstrating. But from then on she pursued a retaliatory 'pinprick' policy of pique against England—a policy which was to last until 1904 and the signing of the Entente Cordiale.

By the end of 1883 Egypt's financial deficit, aside from the debt, amounted to over £E8 million. Nearly £E4 million had been adjudged as indemnities to be paid for the property lost during the burning of Alexandria; £E1·5 million was the estimated cost of evacuating the Sudan; deficits on the budgets of the years 1881–4 amounted to nearly £E3 million. A loan was the only means of saving Egypt from bankruptcy. According to the terms of the Law of Liquidation, a loan could be negotiated only with the concurrence of Turkey and the Powers. Therefore, on June 28, 1884, the British government called an International Conference in London to settle Egyptian finances. Unfortunately the

Powers differed on many items, and when they failed to come to an agreement, the Conference adjourned *sine die*.

The failure of the Conference was due to France's lack of co-operation. The French cabinet assumed that if **it** succeeded in sabotaging the efforts of 'perfidious Albion' in Egypt, then England would be constrained to seek French assistance. Germany, which could have brought about a compromise in the course of the conference, chose to remain neutral. Bismarck had already begun his campaign of rapprochement with France, and this was a way of demonstrating his goodwill towards her, as well as embarrassing Britain.

Since the British government was unable to solve Egypt's financial tangle with the co-operation of the Powers, it was obliged to do so on its own. Northbrook, First Lord of the Admiralty, was sent to Egypt in November 1884 to report on the situation and to see if England could solve the impasse. He arrived in Egypt to find that the government lacked the wherewithal to pay the administrative expenses of the following month. Northbrook recommended that Britain should guarantee a loan of £E9 million to help Egypt pay off her immediate debts and finance her irrigation projects. Like his cousin Baring, he did not believe that it was safe to fix a time limit for the evacuation of Egypt; and the outcome of his proposals would have been that English financial control would have replaced international control, so that England would, of necessity, have had to prolong the occupation for an even longer period.

The thought of assuming the onus of Egyptian finances alarmed Gladstone, and awed even Granville, who wrote to Baring in a plaintive vein: 'There is an immense and powerful combination to force us into a more exclusive administration of Egypt: the bondholders, Bismarck, the English and foreign press, the Tories and the Jingoes. But many of these disclaim annexation, and short of that I myself (apart from our pledges) do not see how we could strengthen affairs . . . the misfortune during the last two years has been that we hardly ever had anything but bad alternatives to choose from.'[9] Gladstone therefore refused to accept Northbrook's suggestions, and once more an attempt was made to negotiate with France. This time the attempt met with success, and the Powers came to an agreement in 1885, by which Egypt was granted a loan of £E9 million, guaranteed by all the Powers involved in Egyptian finances.

The financial agreement introduced a new principle in the previous distribution of the revenues between the Caisse and the government. The government was now entitled to a larger share of the revenues than the £E4 million allotted to it under the Law of Liquidation of 1880; but it was also entitled to call upon the Caisse for funds to finance any kind of expenditure which fell into a newly-defined category. This new category, however, had to be authorized by the Caisse. Moreover, when the Caisse paid off the interest to the bondholders in the yearly coupon, and found that there still remained a surplus, this was to be equally divided between the Caisse and the government. Subsequent agreements with the Powers increased the items of expenditure susceptible of falling under the new authorized category. But since the Commissioners of the Debt were the judges of whether an item of expenditure was authorized or not, the Caisse became a barometer of the international situation; and the degree of co-operation between the various Powers and England was measured by whether they helped or killed a reform that called for money. Often the Commissioners prevented the passage of important Egyptian reforms, when the French member refused to cast his vote favourably, because France was feeling antagonistic towards England on the international level. For example, three years of negotiations with France elapsed before the Egyptian government was able partially to abolish the corvée by paying for it out of the 'authorized' funds. Another example of obstructionism on the part of the Powers happened in connection with a projected increase in the Egyptian army. France refused to allow the funds for the proposed increase; and Germany was told to withhold consent because Britain had supported France, against the interests of Germany, in Constantinople, in connection with the railway in Asia Minor. The German Consul-General informed Baring that he must no longer look to German assistance on the Caisse for English projects in Egypt, until the misunderstanding had been cleared away. The projected increase of the army had to be shelved until both France and Germany had been placated.

The Caisse de la Dette Publique was thus a reflection of the power-combinations in Europe—that is, a microcosm of the European alliance and alignments; so that England's freedom of action in Egypt was limited by the political situation in Europe. Concomitantly, actions in Egypt had to be carried out with a wary eye kept open for possible international repercussions; all of which served to complicate the financial situation in Egypt even more.

Baring, the Consul-General, who had anticipated a freer hand with Egyptian finances, was disappointed with the agreement, for it did not remove Egypt from the realm of international politics, as he had hoped it would: instead, he had to carry on with a 'hybrid form of government', as he described it to Northbrook in 1884. 'It involves almost all the disadvantages of governing the country directly, without any of the advantages.'[10] To make matters worse, two more Commissioners were added to the Caisse de la Dette —one Russian and the other German—at an added yearly expense of £E4,000 to the already sorely overladen Egyptian budget.* Turkey had also asked for a representative on the Caisse, but was severely snubbed and told that such a request was hardly commensurate with her position as suzerain of Egypt.

After the agreement of 1885, the question of Egyptian finances was not examined internationally until the Entente Cordiale in 1904; but from 1885 on it was an uphill struggle for Baring and for the financial wizard, Edgar Vincent, the Adviser. They achieved solvency in 1888 by means of various domestic devices such as the *rachat militaire*,† and raising the duty on imported tobacco to over 40%, while prohibiting the culture of tobacco in Egypt on pain of a heavy fine.

In 1885 Gladstone's cabinet was replaced by a Conservative cabinet under Salisbury. Whereas Gladstone's cabinet had been

---

* The reasons given for adding them was that in view of the recent violations of the agreements about payments into the Caisse, Russia and Germany did not trust the rest of the Powers to look after their respective interests, and therefore they demanded representatives of their own.

† Purchase of immunity from military service.

paralysed by a radical faction that clamoured for evacuation, and a Whig faction that clamoured for the occupation of Egypt, as matters of principle, Salisbury's cabinet judged the situation from the angle of necessity. They wanted an occupation, but were willing to trade it in return for concessions. Evacuation was no longer a principle; to dangle it became a gambit in the game of power politics.

On first assuming power, Salisbury was worried by the 'abyss of isolation' in which Britain found herself, and he planned to end it first of all by befriending Germany; but since Germany could use her rapprochement with France as a weapon against England, Salisbury planned to settle matters with France as well. As he explained to Sir William White, his Ambassador in Constantinople: 'I do not wish to depend upon his [Bismarck's] good will, and therefore shall keep friends with France as far as we can do it without paying too dear for it. The threat of making us uneasy in Egypt through the action of France is the only weapon he has against us and we are free of him in proportion as we can blunt it.'[11] Therefore, to satisfy France, Salisbury sent Sir Henry Drummond Wolff on a mission to Turkey, with a mandate to 'secure for this country the amount of influence which is necessary for its own Imperial interest, and, subject to that condition, to provide a strong and efficient Egyptian Government, as free as possible from foreign interference'.[12] Salisbury warned him: 'Our diplomatic task is twofold: to obtain the arrangements necessary for our work in Egypt now: secondly, in leaving it to secure the privileged position which will pay us for blood and treasure spent . . . we must avoid any definite or contingent promise of evacuation: for early evacuation will be the only price we shall have to offer for this second object. If we can say to Europe "we are in possession: practically. You cannot turn us out: what will you give us to go soon?" and if the state of European politics happens to be favourable, we may gain a great deal for England.'[13]

In fact, the state of European politics was not unfavourable. Germany seemed willing to help; Herbert Bismarck assured Salisbury of his father's support of the Drummond Wolff plan for 'the co-operation of the Sultan in settling the affairs of Egypt, and in making arrangements for the military occupation by Turkey, of that country'.[14] But Prince Bismarck, who was playing his own game, said to Hohenlohe, his Ambassador in France: 'We cannot afford to embroil ourselves with England more than is necessary, owing to the danger that France may betray us with England . . . we must never lose sight of the fact that our interest in Egypt is insignificant, but that our relations towards France and England in Europe are of great importance to us.'[15] Germany suspected that England did not contemplate evacuating for a long time to come.

On October 24, 1885, a Convention was signed between England and Turkey. By its terms a Turkish Commissioner, Mukhtar Pasha Ghazi, was to go, together with Drummond Wolff, to study the Egyptian question (especially as it pertained to the Sudan frontiers) with a view to its final settlement. Drummond Wolff reported to Salisbury that the Turks themselves anticipated a long British occupation of Egypt, and that in the Convention they recognized the occupation, while leaving the date of withdrawal indefinite. A treaty with Turkey over Egypt would give England a legitimate sanction for remaining in Egypt, and if the Sultan did not co-operate with Britain, then he merely prolonged Britain's occupation. 'All the Powers at present sanction the Convention,' ended Drummond Wolff more in hopeful than in truthful vein.[16] France did not do so, nor did she approve of Turkish intervention in Egyptian affairs; and as time passed, Salisbury found that placating France was not going to be a simple matter.

Two years later the situation in Europe had changed, and Salisbury was less optimistic about it. He wrote to Baring: 'Abroad we seem to be shut up to the alternative of two wars either of which is likely to modify profoundly the face of Europe. At home we have a House of Commons paralysed by the Irish Party . . . in these circumstances you must not be surprised if we find our hands a good deal tied in many respects.'[17] Between France, Germany and England, Salisbury was having a hard time. 'English opinion is not prepared for an evacuation of Egypt—still less for the abandonment of it,'[18] he complained to Drummond Wolff. France made generous promises, but offered terms which Salisbury thought impossible. Herbette (the French Ambassador in Germany) told Malet (the British Ambassador in Germany) that if only Britain would name a date for evacuation, then the corvée would be abolished, the Capitulations reformed, and powers of re-entry to Egypt for Britain in certain contingencies would be secured—'only let us have the credit for having induced you to fix a date'.[19] That was the one thing that Salisbury would not do.

Throughout this period, France had been unco-operative. She had raised objections to the presence of Turkish troops in Egypt (save under Anglo-French auspices), on the ground that such a move would imply handing Egypt over to the uncontrolled management of the Sultan.[20] Germany also was behaving unco-operatively, so that Salisbury told Drummond Wolff: 'We must keep it diplomatically in our power to satisfy France on account of Bismarck's attitude. His policy, in a humbler walk of life, would be called *chantage* . . . I heartily wish we had never gone into Egypt. Had we not done so, we could snap our fingers at all the world. But the national, or acquisitive feeling has been roused; it has tasted the fleshpots and cannot let them go.'[21]

Baring strongly disapproved of the arrangement with Turkey. He feared the effect of a Turkish Commissioner in Egypt on a weak and unpopular ruler like the Khedive, and gloomily forecast that such an arrangement could only end in disaster. Evacuation would mean retrogression, said Baring, and he begged Salisbury 'on no account to agree to fixing *unconditionally* [*sic*] a date for our departure. I think we must leave a door open in case we should not think it wise to go . . . I am not in the least prepared to say with any degree of certainty that at the end of say five years, we shall be able to go.'[22] To support his argument, Baring insisted that both the Khedive, and the Prime Minister, Nubar Pasha, were frightened at the prospect of an early departure of British troops;[23] and Drummond Wolff, who was then in Egypt, echoed that sentiment by saying: 'Nubar feels his position and that of the Khedive untenable without the British occupation.'[24] But Salisbury had no intention of effecting an early departure from Egypt, and he had previously reassured Baring: 'I do not see any probability of our leaving Egypt under six years from this date; and

48

our stay may be much longer.'[25] However, as Salisbury reminded Baring: 'We are bound hand and foot by the pledges of retirement which our predecessors have given, and which we impliedly confirmed.'[26]

Herein lay the dilemma. Egypt was rapidly becoming a European nuisance to England, yet for Asian reasons was too valuable an asset to let go. The only possible way out was to attempt to secure an international sanction for an irregular situation. Drummond Wolff therefore returned to Turkey to negotiate another Convention. This was concluded on May 22, 1887. It stipulated that the British troops would withdraw from Egypt within three years, with the proviso that the withdrawal could be postponed 'if order and security in the interior were disturbed'. This proviso savoured of Baring's thinking, for he never tired of telling Salisbury that evacuation would not settle the Egyptian question, it would merely reopen it under a different form, for the Egyptian government would collapse immediately and the British army would be forced to return once more. However, the Convention was a mandate to Britain from Turkey to conduct Egyptian affairs, and was therefore a means of liquidating some of the influence that France and Germany had over Egyptian matters.

Turkey accepted the terms of the Convention; but France and Russia both applied strong pressure on Turkey by threatening to occupy Syria and Armenia if it gave way to Britain. France realized that the terms of the Convention gave Britain paramount influence over Egypt; Charles de Freycinet, the Prime Minister, voiced this fear in the *Chambre des Députés*, when he said, 'si une grande puissance s'installait définitivement en Egypte, ce serait un coup très grave porté à l'influence de la France dans la Méditerranée'.[27] Therefore the Convention had to be scuttled. Baron de Staal, who later became Russian Ambassador in England, humorously described the situation to de Giers, the Russian Foreign Minister: 'Assailli de terreurs dans son kiosque isolé, le malheureux Sultan fait pitié. Trois ambassadeurs, le poing levé, l'accablent de sinistres présages. Tantôt c'est la flotte Britannique qui se dirige vers la baie de Besika; tantôt les armées Russes envahissent l'Arménie, ou encore c'est la France qui prend possession de la Syrie. Le Padischah ne sait plus où chercher refuge. Il implore les uns, il conjure les autres, il change d'avis tous les jours et de guerre lasse ne fait rien.'[28] When the Sultan could not be brought to ratify the Convention, Drummond Wolff was obliged to sail away, and the Convention fell through.

Oddly enough, although the French government had been instrumental in wrecking the Convention, it really wanted to come to some sort of arrangement with England. But since France was in the throes of domestic trouble (the Boulangist movement), and the French government feared a national uproar if it compromised with England, it felt bound to behave intransigently. This attitude made Salisbury pronounce the French to be 'the most unreasonable people I have ever heard or dreamt of'.[29] He was determined not to put up with further bullying by France, and for the time being 'to sit still and drift awhile', and continue to occupy Egypt.

Two men were especially delighted over the failure of the Convention. The first was Sir William White, the British Ambassador in Constantinople; the second was Baring. Drummond Wolff had stepped on White's toes so often that the latter jovially informed the French and Russian Ambassadors that they should be given the Order of the Bath for the immense service they had done him in expediting the departure of 'ce cher Drummond Wolff'; while Baring commented that the failure of the negotiations had one great advantage in that they gave England 'a fair case for declining to negotiate again; for the time being'.[30] Like Salisbury, Baring was upset by France's intransigence, and had said earlier: 'They are themselves greatly to blame if our stay in Egypt is prolonged. They have left no stone unturned to make our task impossible. We had better make up our minds to the fact that we are not likely to solve the Egyptian Question without passing through a state of serious tension with France, which, however, will probably not lead to war if we are firm and our fleet is as strong as it ought to be.'[31] Baring's analysis proved shrewd and correct.

The failure of the Convention with Turkey made Salisbury realize that he could not trust France, nor rely on Turkey—facts which rendered Britain's position in the Mediterranean precarious. There was further cause for alarm in 1886 when France concentrated her fleet in the Mediterranean whereas previously it had been distributed between Brest, Cherbourg and Toulon. France, with an empire in Indo-China, and possessions in North Africa, and in a mood of rising hostility to England and Italy, determined to focus her interest on the Mediterranean. In doing so, France upset the naval balance there, and England—hastening to reappraise her naval strength—found this insufficient for her wants, and out of date. The Naval Defence Act, passed in 1889, decreed that the British fleet should be equal to a combination of the two next strongest fleets in Europe as an absolute minimum of security —but several years were required to bring the British navy up to the necessary standard. France countered this move by passing the Gervais Programme which, by 1893, would render the combined strength of the French and Russian navies greater than that of the British navy. Fear of German aggression, allied to anti-British feelings, had caused the French government to seek an alliance with Russia. Preliminary to the signing of an entente, the French fleet in July 1891 visited Kronstadt. In August, an exchange of notes between both countries set out the terms of the entente, and the following year a military convention was agreed upon. Rumours spread that France was turning Bizerta into a fortified naval port, and that Russia was preparing a *coup de main* in Constantinople; for while the Russian fleet grew in size, the Turkish one dwindled until it had only two vessels of fighting value.

In these conditions, Salisbury realized that the defence of Constantinople, for England alone, was out of the question, and that England's hope now lay in using Egypt as the core of Mediterranean defence plans, and as the key to India. The scramble for Africa was a direct consequence of this decision to stay in Egypt: for now none of East Africa which bordered the route to India, and none of the areas surrounding the Nile Valley, could be allowed to fall into other hands. And when, in 1888, the dervishes renewed hostilities in Suakin and Kassala, these attacks (so Gwendolen Cecil claimed) 'brought the reconquest of the Nile provinces into the foreground of Lord Salisbury's thought . . . it now became a central episode in his calculated prevision of events . . . Thus we find that, from this date the necessity of safeguarding the

Nile Valley from the intrusion of other white powers begins to appear in his correspondence as a separate and dominating factor in his policy.'[32]

During negotiations over the conversion of the Egyptian debt in 1890, Salisbury intimated as much to Hatzfeldt, the German Minister of Foreign Affairs, who reported the conversation to Chancellor Caprivi by saying that Salisbury's aim was 'to recover the lost Egyptian provinces, that the British Parliament would never vote money for it, and that the improvement of the Egyptian finances is therefore an indispensable consideration'.[33] Later that same year, Salisbury made his intentions quite clear by telling Baring that the dervishes 'were created for the purpose of keeping the bed warm for you until you can occupy it'.[34]

Although Salisbury had realized early the necessity for shifting the axis of British strategic interests from Constantinople to Cairo, it was not long before other members of the British government were impelled to the same conclusion. In March 1892, a report by the Directors of Military and Naval Intelligence stated that 'we are of the opinion that . . . unless we are acting in concert with France, the road to Constantinople for a British fleet bent on a belligerent operation, lies across the ruins of the French fleet'.[35] And in 1895 Salisbury said that the defence of Constantinople had become an 'antiquated viewpoint',[36] telling Hatzfeldt that Russia was welcome to it 'avec tout ce qui s'ensuit'.[37]

The year 1896 was one of crisis in Armenia, Venezuela and South Africa, all of which events prompted a second look at Britain's naval policy; and on October 28, 1896, the Director of Naval Intelligence drew up a memorandum of naval policy which pointed out the changes that had occurred in the Mediterranean situation, and the paramount need for holding on to Egypt. The memorandum said that, since the Sultan was now anti-British and pro-Russian, therefore: '. . . Count that as long as France and Russia act together, England must prepare to meet the Black Sea Fleet in the Mediterranean. Decide, that when a Russian Naval base is commenced in Asia Minor, an English Naval base must be created in the Eastern basin of the Mediterranean, preferably in Alexandria.'[38]

The navy was not the only department to stress the importance of continuing the occupation of Egypt. On October 13 the Director of Military Intelligence submitted a memorandum which said that Egypt was valuable as a half-way house to India; as giving control over the Suez Canal and the overland passage to India in case the Canal was blocked; and that the wisest policy was to continue the occupation.[39] By then the pattern was set for a permanent occupation of Egypt.

CHAPTER III

The Man on the Spot

Evelyn Baring, the man who was to help mould Egypt's destiny, seemed to be the inevitable choice for the post of Consul-General. On two previous occasions he had served in Egypt: from 1877–1879 he was Commissioner on the Caisse de la Dette Publique; and, after a brief and unsuccessful attempt as a candidate for Parliament in England, he returned to Egypt a few months later in 1879 as Controller. Hence his knowledge of Egypt's financial situation was intimate and thorough, and no more logical choice could be found to help unravel the financial tangle.

Though descended from a famous banking family, Baring had early in life been destined for the army. But it was an occupation that offered him little satisfaction; so when, in 1872, his cousin, Lord Northbrook, was appointed Viceroy of India, Baring was more than delighted to accept a post as his private secretary. He was then thirty-one years old, and for the next four years, until the end of Northbrook's period, he acted as his right-hand man, thereby earning the nickname of Vice-Viceroy, along with another less complimentary epithet of Over-Baring. Both these nicknames were clear indications of his character, wherein efficiency and ability to command predominated. They were invaluable traits in a man destined to become a leader, but they were not qualities conducive to popularity amongst his fellow men; so that, throughout his life, Baring was either respected and feared by his colleagues, or disliked and feared. He always held aloof from people, and had few intimates. Though civil, he was peremptory, and quite convinced that his way of doing things was the right one. Few people liked him, but no one was indifferent to him. Lytton Strachey described him as having a character that was monochromatic—cold blues and indecisive greys; and yet, though the description fits the Pro-Consul of later days, it does not fit the young

Baring, who was then the friend of Edward Lear and could appreciate the humour of notes addressed 'Thrippy Pilliwinx' and signed 'Slushypipp'. More than that, he could fall in love at the age of twenty-one and remain faithful for fourteen years until he was able to support the woman he loved and marry her. Among the blues and greys there were flashes of a different colour, but with age and responsibility and the inevitable attrition of office, they became rarer.

It was in India that Baring acquired his ideas on how to rule subject races. There he finally buried his early radical notions concerning self-determination, and decided to shoulder the White Man's Burden, and help the downtrodden peasant. His later experiences of the injustice of Ismail's rule in Egypt merely strengthened his views on the tyranny of native rulers and their incapacity to rule.

When Baring arrived in Egypt in September 1883 to take up his post as British Agent and Consul-General, he was expected to follow the policy laid down in the Dufferin Report and carry out the reforms that it had indicated. He was also expected to effect a speedy evacuation of British troops in Egypt. But whereas responsible people in England pretended to believe that both these tasks could be achieved simultaneously, Baring regarded them as incompatible. Reforms could not be carried out if evacuation was to be immediate. Therefore he believed that 'there was only one practicable method by which the Egyptian administration could be reformed. That was to place the government more or less under British guidance.'[1] He believed that this was what Dufferin was trying to say in discreet terms in his report, but that he had proposed free institutions out of deference to British public opinion. The only way to successful reforms lay in a prolongation of the British occupation. Baring was certain that he had read Dufferin rightly, because 'no one but a dreamy theorist could imagine that the natural order of things could be reversed, and that liberty could first be accorded to the poor ignorant representatives of the Egyptian people, and that the latter would then be able to evolve order out of chaos'.[2]

The alternatives as he saw them were, then, either to forget about the reforms, hand authority back to the Khedive, and effect a speedy evacuation; or else remain in occupation for an indefinite period until the reforms had taken root. But the former choice meant the return to a retrograde and autocratic form of government, and the Liberal cabinet could not agree to that: so the second choice was tacitly accepted by Baring as the only one to follow.

Though the two policies of evacuation and reform seemed to Baring incompatible for internal reasons in Egypt, they were also incompatible for international reasons, because of the Capitulations and the terms of the Law of Liquidation—both of which meant that legislation was carried out through diplomatic channels, and that no vital step towards reform could be taken without consulting fourteen European states. 'If we are to wait until all the essential reforms have been carried out by the slow process of consulting each Power separately on every question of detail, we shall wait a very long time, and there will be danger of drifting into a policy of annexation, or something tantamount to it.'[3] Therefore Baring suggested that the British government should inform the Powers of its intention to assume the government of Egypt, though only as a temporary measure. 'Give me 2,000 men and power to settle matters between the English and Egyptian governments, and I will guarantee that in twelve months there shall not be a British soldier in Egypt, and that the country is put in such a position as to render it very improbable that any Egyption question will be raised again for many years to come at all events.'[4] Granville declined to follow Baring's suggestion, and qualified it as 'too drastic';[5] Baring therefore had to try to carry out the reforms while labouring under the handicap of the Capitulations and the Law of Liquidation.

By November the problem of the Sudan had appeared in all its immensity, and thoughts of evacuation were abandoned for the next two years. The revolt in the Sudan was of paramount importance to the history of Anglo-Egyptian relations for two reasons: it formed the background to the Granville Doctrine—the principle which determined the position of the Egyptian ministers vis-à-vis the British Consul-General in the scheme of things; and it delayed the evacuation of the British forces from Egypt.

From September 1882 until November 1883 when the Hicks expedition had been massacred, the Egyptian government had been desperately trying to raise the necessary means for the re-conquest of the Sudan. Sharif Pasha tried to get help from Turkey, or even to hire Turkish mercenaries, but without avail. He could not understand why England, which had undertaken to put Egypt on its feet, not only would not help Egypt regain such an important part of her territory, but even obstructed Egypt's attempt to do so on her own. Baring realized that the loss of the Sudan would inflict a terrible blow to the prestige of the Egyptian government, which was already shaky; but he calculated the matter in terms of hard cash, especially when weighed against the risk that the attempt at reconquest might fail, and decided against taking the risk. He had to bring the Egyptian government round to his point of view. But he well knew that 'under no amount of persuasion or argument will the present Ministers consent to the adoption of the policy of abandonment'. The only way in which it can be carried out, he suggested to Granville, 'will be for me to inform the Khedive that Her Majesty's Government insist on the adoption of this course, and that if his present Ministers will not carry out the policy, others must be named who will consent to do so'.[6]

Granville agreed and sent a message saying: 'It should be made clear to the Egyptian Ministers and Governors of Provinces that the responsibility which for the time rests on England obliges Her Majesty's Government to insist on the adoption of the policy which they recommend, and that it will be necessary that those Ministers and Governors who do not follow this course should cease to hold their offices.'[7]

Sharif Pasha, who categorically refused to sanction abandoning the Sudan, had no option but to resign on receiving Granville's message. In his letter of resignation he said that evacuating the Sudan was a violation of the firmans, for these forbade the Khedive to renounce any part of his territory, forming as it did a part of the Ottoman Empire; he then added that the Granville message had made it impossible for him to continue to administer the country.[8] This then was the starting-point of Baring's policy in Egypt, and the death blow to Dufferin's pious wish that the

'Khedive and his Ministers remain the real rulers of Egypt'. The real ruler of Egypt was from now on to be the British Consul-General.

For a while after Sharif's resignation, no politician would accept the premiership, and it looked as though England would be faced with a serious crisis in Egypt. Had the Khedive refused to accept Granville's terms, and had he stood firmly behind Sharif, Baring's position in Egypt might have developed along different lines. But the Khedive as usual was afraid, and vacillated. Baring, thereupon, hinted to a few gossips that unless a premier could be found, he would be obliged to go down to the office of the President of the Council, and carry out the work himself, until he telegraphed Granville for further instructions. This so alarmed the Khedive, as it was meant to do, that he immediately forced a man into office. His choice was Nubar Pasha, an Armenian, who realized that 'ils m'ont nommé pour se sauver de vous autres Anglais'.[9] The day after Nubar had been appointed, the Khedive announced that he 'cordially accepted the policy of abandoning the Sudan'. This was a severe blow to the prestige both of the Khedive and of the government, and it served to confirm what cynics, and the French press, had said all along—that England was in Egypt to rule Egypt. When news of Gordon's death reached Egypt a year later, very little outcry was raised by the Egyptians. It was only when a nationalist movement appeared ten years later, and the reconquest of the Sudan under Kitchener was under way, that once again the Egyptians were to take an active interest in the Sudan.

Thus events in the Sudan had caused the relationship between England and Egypt to undergo a subtle change. The Granville Doctrine that ministers could be changed if they did not carry out British policy shifted decision-making from the hands of the Egyptian government into those of the British Representative. The Khedive and his government were weak and incompetent, and more and more came to rely on Baring for advice. There was little opposition worth speaking of left in the country.

Baring soon consolidated his power in Egypt. Five months after his arrival we find him writing to Northbrook that 'one of the many weak parts of the system here is that the government is just as personal as ever it was, only that the person, instead of being the Khedive, is the English Representative . . . I am expected to settle everything great and small . . . as a system, nothing can be worse.'[10] But though the system was a bad one, it was the only one that Baring would consider. The ruling classes, he claimed, were utterly incompetent. 'I have not yet come across a single man amongst the Pasha class who appears to me really to understand the main elements of the local political problem with which the Egyptian government has to deal. It should never be forgotten that the ruling classes here are almost exclusively foreign.'* The Assembly and Council which had been formed on Dufferin's suggestion were soon laid aside; because, though 'it was, without doubt, desirable to make some beginning in the way of founding liberal institutions', he claimed that no one with any knowledge of the East could for one moment suppose that the Council and Assembly could become 'either important factors in the government of the country, or efficient instruments to help in administrative and fiscal reform . . . What Egypt most of all required was order and good government. Perhaps *longo intervallo*, liberty would follow afterwards.'[11] Like Dufferin, Baring believed that 'a long enslaved nation instinctively craves for the strong hand of a master rather than for a lax constitutional regime'.[12] All of which led him to conclude that since the Khedive could not supply that strong hand, he would supply it for him, and he did so at a very early date. Baring therefore modified Britain's role in Egypt from that of an adviser to that of a mentor and guardian. Britain's duty, as he saw it, was to establish long-term reforms, and only to evacuate when that task was completed. In 1886 he wrote to Iddesleigh, then Foreign Secretary: 'The idea that we can put matters right, and then leave our work to be continued by native agents, is, in my opinion, erroneous,' though, he added: 'one ought, indeed, to try and educate the natives in administrative work.'[13]

In his report of 1885, Baring had referred to a great deal of discontent in Egypt resulting from the British occupation, and had affirmed that this could be easily solved. But Baring was too

* S.P., Baring to Salisbury, June 15, 1889. By 'foreign' he meant Turco-Circassian.

sanguine, as later events were to show. Part of this discontent stemmed from his refusal to make use of any one in the administration apart from the Turco-Circassians of the old regime. Although the occupation had arrested the national movement before it had time to breed a new ruling group, nevertheless a few men of fallah origin had managed to come to the foreground as potential leaders. But like so many of his countrymen, Baring thought that the Turks (incompetent though they were) were the only race in the East capable of ruling at all; and since they had always formed the governing class in Egypt, he continued to use them as administrators. Baring justified this choice by his claim that the Khedive would not have consented to associate himself with the former nationalists; but since Baring had succeeded in making the Khedive do many things that he did not want to do, this reason was not altogether convincing. Perhaps Baring was reluctant to use the nationalists because they were a new and untried factor, tainted with an unsuccessful revolution; or, more likely, he realized that he could more easily impose his advice on the men of the old regime, whose shortcomings he already knew, than on those who were of unknown quality. Whatever the reason, he chose to govern Egypt with the help of men whose previous rule in Egypt had given rise to a revolution. This choice caused dissatisfaction among various Egyptians, who complained to W. S. Blunt, amongst others. Blunt, who had been busy among his vast acquaintances in London, claimed in his writings that he had succeeded in convincing Randolph Churchill of the error of Baring's system, and of the need for a ministry composed of fallah Egyptians. Blunt said that Churchill had suggested that 'Tawfiq should be deposed, and his son put up under English guardianship'. Urabi could then be recalled, first in his capacity as a private citizen, then perhaps later he might be made a minister. But Churchill simultaneously believed that England must declare a protectorate over Egypt.[14] Blunt presented his plan to Gladstone, and claimed that Gladstone had agreed with him as to the necessity of restoring the National Party, *al-Hizb al-Watani*. Gladstone, said Blunt, had told him to discuss the matter with Baring, and had said that 'if Baring would help I [Blunt] would try to get the National leaders elected at the elections; but all depended on the co-operation of our officials'.[15] Blunt later added that Baring said that they could not restore the National Party without going through a second revolution in Egypt, and that since the men Blunt had in mind were as bad as the men of the old regime, the whole thing was out of the question.[16] Gladstone, on the other hand, denied that he had ever contemplated restoring the National Party in Egypt.[17]

When Gladstone fell from power in 1885, Blunt once more tried to induce the successor government to make use of new, potential Egyptian leaders, that is to say, former members of the National Party. In that context, in April 1887, he wrote a letter to Salisbury in which he explained that the Egyptians were dissatisfied with the results of the occupation, for there was not a single Egyptian Arab in the ministry; and that the revolution had, after all, arisen because of this discrimination. Blunt suggested that, amongst others, the following men were worthy of cabinet posts: Hasan Pasha Shirii, Muhammad Baligh, Ibrahim al-Wakil, Saad Zaghlul, and Shaykh Muhammad Abduh.[18]

Salisbury inquired into the matter, and Baring answered him in a long, wordy letter which said that it was quite true that no minister or Head of Department was chosen from among Blunt's friends: '. . . under present conditions, however, I should regard a proposal to make one of Blunt's friends ruler or Prime Minister of Egypt as little less absurd than the nomination of some savage Red Indian Chief to be Governor General of Canada'. He went on to say that they were 'corrupt and ignorant bigots', who represented the Arab squirearchy and religious leaders. They formed the larger part of the legislative council and are 'for the most part exceedingly ignorant and are devoted exclusively to the furtherance of their own personal interest'.[19] According to Baring the only group capable of ruling in Egypt were the Turks, for in spite of their defects they still retained some traces of their traditional ruling capacity.

Blunt may have been an eccentric poet, but from his long periods of residence in Egypt he knew something of Egyptian political life. He had referred by name to a specific number of people. Baring chose to overlook this distinction and referred to

the Egyptian notables as a whole, some of whom were undoubtedly as he described them. That the men Blunt had referred
to by name, men like Saad Zaghlul (later to become Prime Minister)
and Shaykh Muhammad Abduh (Egypt's greatest religious reformer), should have been castigated as fanatic, ignorant bigots,
or savage Red Indian chiefs, showed a deliberate inclination on
Baring's part to disregard native talent, in order to sustain the
myth that there was no one capable of ruling Egypt, other than
the puppets he appointed. Later on Baring was to become a supporter of both Abduh and Zaghlul, as two prominent reformers;
as for Hasan Shirii, he was one-time Governor of the province of
Minia, Minister of Waqfs, and President of the Committee that
set up the constitution in 1882; Baligh was the Deputy *Procureur
Général*: while the other men were prominent notables, founders
of *al-Hizb al-Watani*, and members of the Constitutional Assembly
not one of whom fitted Baring's description.

Baring's reluctance to make use of new talent may partly be
explained by a passage from an article entitled *The Government of
Subject Races* which he wrote in 1908, after he had left Egypt; for
he had never changed his mind as to the methods to be used in
governing the 'subject races'. In this article he said: 'We need not
always inquire too closely what these people, who are all, nation-
ally speaking, more or less in *statu pupillari*, themselves think is
best in their own interests, although this is a point which deserves
serious consideration. But it is essential that each special issue
should be decided mainly with reference to what, by the light of
Western knowledge and experience tempered by local consideration, we conscientiously think is best for the subject race.'[20]
Baring, a fervent believer in the White Man's Burden and in
England's divine mission of saving the downtrodden, was a good
administrator, and—like most other British administrators of the
time—he was not a believer in the value of self-rule *per se*, for
Oriental nations.* With his years in India forming the background
for his judgment, he saw great similarities between the Indian and
the Egyptian scene. He was convinced that their problems were

* This was not so surprising considering that the Morley-Minto reforms of 1909
in India set up advisory legislatures rather than independent law-making bodies.

alike,[21] that the Indian ryot was cousin to the Egyptian fallah, and that the same measures of low taxation, and remunerative public works such as irrigation schemes, were the best policy to be followed: 'the financier and hydraulic engineer . . . have probably a greater potentiality of creating an artificial and self-interested loyalty than even the judge'.[22] As for self-rule, he decreed that in countries such as India and Egypt it would be unsuitable for generations to come: 'it will probably never be possible to make a Western silk purse out of an Eastern sow's ear'.[23]

Baring had no understanding, or even sympathy, for minds that operated on other than a European model. He maintained that the reasoning of the Oriental mind was slipshod,[24] that the Oriental could only show a servile submission to authority,[25] that the educated Egyptian was a demuslimized Muslim,[26] and that the result of introducing European institutions in the East would be to enable a small minority of natives to misgovern their countrymen.[27] Yet in the same breath with which he sneered at the 'demuslimized Muslim', he quite inconsistently claimed that the Egyptian was incompetent, possessing certain faults which could only be corrected if he broke away from his Muslim background, and imbibed 'character' with the concomitant qualities of integrity and efficiency—which was of necessity a slow growth. Egypt's only hope, he believed, lay in generations of stable government that would eventually develop these qualities; and therefore Britain's primary duty in Egypt was to establish a system 'which will enable the mass of the population [Muslims] to be governed according to the Code of Christian morality'.[28]

Unfortunately, Baring's dislike of the Pasha class, the Oriental mind and Islam, blinded him to the possibility of any good seed in Egypt, and he viewed any opposition to his policy as a fifth column. Some light is thrown on his attitude by one author's remark that 'a man who believes in individual liberty for himself can deny it consciously and explicitly to other people only if he can persuade himself that the other people are really quite different, another order altogether'.[29] This Baring succeeded in doing, as his five chapters on the character of the Egyptians in *Modern Egypt* testify. He had no friends amongst the Egyptians, especially since he so held himself aloof, that his knowledge of them was mostly derived from official contacts and from reports of third parties—neither of which is conducive to genuine knowledge of a people, or to sympathy with them. And yet, as the man on the spot, he acquired the reputation of knowing more about the Egyptians than any other European. His misunderstanding of the Egyptians, whether subconscious or deliberate, was graphically revealed when on one occasion he heard a famous singer, Abduh al-Hamuli, sing a song that went 'My love is lost, O! people find him for me'. Baring commented that here was a typical example of the Egyptian character, that they could not even be bothered to look for their own loves, but had to have somebody to do it for them.[30]

Anyone reading Baring's writings cannot fail to be awed by the unshakeable self-confidence that he radiated. Edgar Vincent, who worked with Baring for many years as Financial Adviser, described him as 'not subtle or mentally agile, but endowed with that curious combination of character which lends authority even to doubtful decisions, and makes those who possess it respected in counsel and obeyed as rulers'.[31] It was this very assurance that won him the confidence of each succeeding Secretary of State, every one of whom was glad to give him a virtual *carte blanche* in Egyptian affairs. Salisbury left him an 'entirely free hand as regards all purely Egyptian affairs, Sir Evelyn frequently appealing to him for advice where he is in doubt, but at other times, rather quaintly, telling him the instructions which he wishes sent out to him'.[32] Rosebery told Baring that he was a good man to go tiger-hunting with. This faith in Baring was partly due to the fact that he managed to keep things relatively quiet in Egypt, so that it became the only calm area in an era marked by turbulence and upheaval in other parts of the world. He also won confidence by being an efficient administrator and a clever financier who had succeeded, by 1888, in saving Egypt from bankruptcy and making it solvent. This was most important, since the Powers had intervened in Egypt because of its financial tangle and its chaotic administration, and, unless these were settled, they would intervene again. Like Gladstone, Baring 'placed a sound financial system before every other consideration',[33] and was convinced that administrative efficiency was the panacea for all ills within a state, and the final goal.

This efficiency he himself supplied. But the qualities that made Baring trusted by his superiors were the very qualities that made his colleagues and underlings nickname him 'the Lord'.

Baring's reports on Egypt helped the British government to prolong the occupation. His accounts of the incompetence of the Egyptian ruling class, his repeated assurances that 'I do not believe that there are a dozen people in the country who really wish us to go',[34] and the assumption that if England evacuated Egypt then a power-vacuum would be created—one that France would hasten to fill—all pointed in the direction of a semi-permanent occupation.

Baring's analysis of the Egyptian situation was correct on two counts; the Khedive and his clique *were* indeed thoroughly incompetent—a fact which the Egyptians had recognized and tried to remedy by a revolution; the French *would* attempt to step into British shoes—but only in a moral sense. Neither of these factors made evacuation so totally impossible. More promising governors could have been found, and Britain could have gone back to her early recipe of using moral influence instead of physical presence to guide the Egyptians. But it is by no means surprising that Baring gave such a report; for the spirit of the times was not one that allowed liberal regimes to emerge at the expense of absolute monarchies—even ones as decadent as that in Egypt. Nor did it conceive that Egyptians and suchlike races were capable of learning self-rule, if only someone bothered to teach them. If the liberal experiment was not to be tried, then many Egyptians preferred the British occupation with its promise of reforms, to the rule of Tawfiq and his bungling, as the lesser of two evils. A feeling of insecurity allied with despair often pervades a country after an abortive revolution, and when a strong hand appears and brings with it promise of security and stability, it is welcomed for a while until recovery operates. This was the case with Egypt, and many Egyptians welcomed Baring as a temporary expedient.

Baring, then, stayed on to govern Egypt. As Consul-General and Agent of the British government, he had theoretically the same influence on the Egyptian government as did any other member of the diplomatic corps, and with the same rank; but in actual fact his influence was unbounded. That was to be expected: the British army was in occupation of Egypt; British officials filled key positions in the Egyptian administration as employees of the government; the ruler of Egypt and his government had accepted the principle laid down in the Granville message. But because Baring had no legal authority in Egypt the relationship between him and the Egyptian administrators, which he described as a delicate and tenuous one, worked only if all the elements concerned co-operated fully. Baring expected the Egyptian government to follow the advice offered to it by the British government in 'exceptional matters of first rate importance', but that matters of internal administration should be left to the discretion of the Egyptians. The British Advisers, he believed, should rely on their own ability and force of character, and not on his diplomatic support. He regarded it as essential that there should be no division of authority in Egypt, and that the government should feel responsible for its administration. His own function was to be limited to the offer of 'friendly advice', and his actions should not be such as to undermine the authority of the Khedive or his ministers. 'I never interfere in matters of detail,' he asserted optimistically.[35] This assertion was all very well in theory, but the practice was very different. Baring soon became the uncrowned ruler of Egypt, and two sets of government existed side by side; in his own words, there appeared 'one set of persons who carried on the government and another set of persons who told them how to do it'. And since the informal advisory government had force behind it, the nominal government collapsed when opposed by it: 'Thus advice could always take the substance, if not the form, of a command.' Advice, of course, had to be tendered in a more or less unobtrusive manner so as not to shock the susceptibilities of the Powers, notably France: but the process did not substantiate Baring's claim that the Egyptian government was 'responsible for the conduct of the Egyptian administration'.

The Veiled Protectorate, as British rule in Egypt came to be known, worked successfully under Tawfiq. Baring's power grew until he was said to have a hand in every detail of Egyptian life,

Evelyn Baring, 1st Earl Cromer

Shaykh Muhammad Abduh at the House of Commons, 1884

no matter how trivial that might be. Years later, in *Modern Egypt*, he listed the number of things in which he was asked to interfere, or in which he interfered without being asked. These ranged from major political issues, to helping an elderly shaykh elope, and attempting to prevent a female member of the royal family from striking her husband on the mouth with a slipper the moment he opened it.[36]

CHAPTER IV

The Governors of Egypt

Baring once cynically said: 'We do not govern Egypt, we only govern the governors of Egypt.' There were two sets of administrators in Egypt, the official government and the British Advisers.

The official governors of Egypt were dependent on British goodwill for survival, for without it they had practically no hold on the country. At the head of the government was the Khedive Tawfiq. Whatever power he possessed, by virtue of his position, had been shaken by the Urabi revolution and the subsequent occupation. The occupation, which ostensibly was installed to seat him more firmly on his throne, merely rendered his position more precarious by undermining what little prestige he had left, for 'on s'appuie sur des baionnettes, on ne s'y assoit pas'. All his life he laboured under the handicap of an outstanding father; for whatever Ismail's faults, and they were many, he had an arresting personality, and could rouse loyalty in those who served him. Tawfiq, timorous and suspicious by nature, constantly expected treachery, and inevitably was met by it. He was ill served, but only because he chose his servitors unwisely. Even Baring, who was one of the rare few who had a good word to say for Tawfiq, accurately described him by saying that the Khedive was very unpopular, that he was neither feared nor respected by the native population, and lived amongst a small coterie of Turks. He said that the events of the last few years had greatly weakened the Khedive's prestige. 'The Khedive's unpopularity is mainly due to his character, or perhaps, I should say, want of character. I have rarely come across anyone so wholly devoid of personal characteristics.'[1]

Baring was not quite correct in his analysis of the Khedive's character, for he did possess personal characteristics, and they were pusillanimity and vindictiveness. Tawfiq's treatment of the revolutionaries when they were imprisoned after the occupation was unworthy of a monarch, and merely brought out his pettiness; for example, he allowed his servants to go to Shaykh Muhammad Abduh in his cell and spit on him. But Tawfiq depended on Baring, and followed his advice most of the time. Occasionally he tried to intrigue against his mentor, and once, egged on by Nubar, he tried to oust Baring from power. But he invariably failed in his attempts.

Although Tawfiq's nature contributed to Baring's supremacy, his ministers, on the other hand, did not immediately take on the shape that Baring wanted, and friction arose in several instances. The first ministry to rule after the Granville doctrine of 1884 was headed by Nubar Pasha. At the time, no native Egyptian would accept office under the conditions the message had imposed, so that Nubar's acceptance of office solved a crisis that could have had serious repercussions. Nubar was a Christian Armenian. He was brought to Egypt from Turkey as a youth by his uncle Artin, one of Muhammad Ali's most trusted ministers, and became Ibrahim Pasha's secretary. Like the Turkish ruling class, he spoke no Arabic; but he spoke Turkish and French, for he had been educated in France. Under Ismail Pasha whom he had served as Minister, Nubar had suggested that England declare a Protectorate over Egypt; but since he was then in exile for displeasing the Khedive, England disregarded his suggestion. In 1878, after the Dual Control was instituted and the principle of ministerial responsibility recognized, Nubar was appointed Prime Minister in the first cabinet to have foreign ministers—these were de Blignières and Rivers Wilson; this cabinet fell after Nubar and Wilson were manhandled by a group of army officers. Nubar was disliked by the Egyptians for being pro-Western. A firm supporter of British rule in Egypt, he was quoted as saying that if the British troops were withdrawn he would leave before the last battalion. Baring, who knew Nubar well, described him as a liar and a rogue, but withal a capable man who could think in a European manner. Portal, the First Secretary at the Agency, added that Nubar was hated by the natives and Muslims, was thoroughly untrustworthy and an infernal liar.[2] Differences soon broke out between him, the

British Advisers, and Baring, and the consequences of these rows consolidated the principle of the Veiled Protectorate in Egypt.

As soon as Nubar became Prime Minister, the *Pall Mall Gazette* of January 10, 1884, implied in an article that Nubar's functions were not to govern Egypt, but to act as an intermediary between the British rulers and the Egyptian administrators. Nubar, however, saw his position in a different light. The occupation was an instrument that would help him rule Egypt as he wanted to, that is, it was to act as a buffer between the Powers and the Egyptian government. He never conceived of the occupation as an instrument that would actively interfere in the administration of Egypt, direct policies, and supervise reforms: it was merely to act as Plato's Unmoved Mover. Unfortunately for Nubar, Baring and the British Advisers thought otherwise, and they had no intention of sitting back and letting Nubar run things. Soon friction arose.

The first major crisis centred round the Ministry of the Interior. It was Britain's policy to appoint Englishmen as Advisers to the various ministries: thus the Ministry of Finance had Edgar Vincent as Adviser; the Ministry of Public Works had Scott-Moncrieff; the Ministry of War had Sir Evelyn Wood: while the Ministry of Justice had Benson Maxwell. The Ministry of the Interior was eventually handed to Clifford Lloyd, who had previously had a roving commission to reform where he saw fit. Lloyd was one of those men who invariably antagonize people. In his previous post in Ireland, he had given rise to such tension that he was recalled and sent to Egypt with the title of Inspector General of Reforms. For a time he had a finger in every pie, so that his name overshadowed that of Baring, until he was appointed Under-Secretary of the Interior in 1884 when Nubar was Prime Minister. By that time Lloyd had managed to quarrel with every English and Egyptian official, and it was rumoured that he and Benson Maxwell, at the Ministry of Justice, had even come to blows. So nobody was surprised when he quarrelled with Nubar.

The issue between Nubar and Clifford Lloyd centred round the governors of provinces and their relationship with the police. In Egypt the police department had, under the occupation, become divided into three divisions, each directed by a Deputy Inspector

General, assisted by two Inspectors—one European and one Egyptian—who all reported to the British Inspector General of Police. In the provinces the local police were responsible to the commandant of the province who, during Lloyd's period of office in the Interior, was made responsible to the Inspector General of the Police. Technically the Governor of the province, who was responsible to the Minister of the Interior, was the superior of the commandant and the Inspector of Police in his province; but these officials were more likely to obey the police authorities than the Governor, since in fact they were responsible to them. Nubar objected to this duplication of authority, or rather he objected to a system which weakened the power of the Governor in his province: above all, he resented having an Englishman as Adviser in the Ministry of the Interior. He believed that the Ministry of the Interior was the private life of a country, and that a foreigner would only introduce confusion. Moreover, the British Adviser would inevitably take over the powers of the Egyptian minister, who would become his subordinate.[3] This substitution of power was likely to take place in all the ministries which had British Advisers, and was, in fact, one of the corner-stones of the Veiled Protectorate. But it had not yet become apparent to the Egyptians, and Nubar valiantly fought to arrest the trend. But he succeeded only temporarily in the Ministry of the Interior, for, as a result of his contretemps with Lloyd, Nubar tendered his resignation. Lloyd thereupon suggested to the British government that the time had come to appoint a British President of the Council, hoping he himself would be nominated. But the British government, which needed Nubar to carry out its policy of evacuating the Sudan, and which had not yet made up its mind to rule Egypt directly, dispensed with Lloyd's advice and his services. The Egyptians were so delighted to see the last of Lloyd that when his train left the station, with true native humour they let loose several mongrels behind it, to yelp Lloyd away from Cairo.

Nubar felt that he had won that round, and it led him to believe that his position was much stronger than it really was. As time passed he became increasingly restless at Baring's tutelage, and more especially when it covered things financial. Edgar Vincent, the Financial Adviser, always kept a tight hold on the purse-strings, and Nubar (who was about sixty years old and prided himself on his financial acumen) did not relish the role of fiscal mentor that a twenty-eight-year-old held towards him. By 1887 Nubar decided to edge Baring out of Egypt; and, on a visit to Britain that summer, he surprised the Foreign Office by complaining of Baring and Vincent. Had Nubar known what Portal, from the Agency in Cairo, wrote to Villiers, Acting Private Secretary to Salisbury in London, over that situation, he might not have been so confident. Portal said that Nubar's campaign against Baring was foolish, for 'after all, Nubar, though a convenience and an "expediency" is not quite a necessity'.[4] Whereas Baring and Vincent were indispensable.

Nubar did not realize how expendable he was, and he misled the Khedive into believing that if he stood firm in the matter, the British government would recall Baring. The Khedive, who was at that time under Nubar's influence, and who had had enough of Baring and the occupation, accepted Nubar's estimate of the situation. Tigrane Pasha, the Under Secretary of Foreign Affairs, and Nubar's son-in-law, was despatched to London with more complaints. Once again the issue centred round the police. Valentine Baker, the previous head of the police, having just died, Baring wanted to appoint another Englishman in his place; whereas Nubar, who thought the police department badly run, wished to appoint an Egyptian, and to change the whole system. Nubar wanted the provincial police to be directly responsible to the Ministry of the Interior, since he considered the present system made for a division of responsibility between the police and the civil authorities, and he wished to abolish the system of Inspectors. His reasons for this move were pertinent: 'Je désire éviter, autant que possible, d'avoir des employés Européens, avec *pouvoir executif et à poste fixe* dans les provinces afin d'empêcher leur contact journalier avec les indigènes, ce qui est un mal, car appelé à exercer un pouvoir exécutif, sans connaître ni les moeurs ni la langue du pays, les étrangers se rendraient, et nous rendraient antipathiques à la population.'[5]

Nubar was determined to make an issue of the whole matter.

This was to play into Baring's hand. For the incident provided Baring with the opportunity to get rid of Nubar, who was becoming unco-operative. By turning the police question into a matter of higher politics, of Anglo-Egyptian relations, Baring made it one of the crises that his target had been to avoid, therefore the measures used to solve it had to be severe ones. He warned the British government that 'European supervision is necessary or things will go from bad to worse, and then we should be obliged to interfere once more and in a more objectionable manner.'[6] More important, Baring stressed the fact that should Nubar win that round, then British influence would receive a severe blow, and Nubar would become omnipotent, and the influence of British officials in the service of the Egyptian government would decline. Therefore the police question could not be 'considered on its own merits', and Nubar 'must be made to yield'. He added: 'This is a test case—we are on the brink of a breakdown of the system. If Nubar Pasha were told in language which was very plain without being menacing, that he was to accept the proposals which I have now made, and if at the same time Tigrane were told that your Lordship expects my advice to be followed in local matters, the decision would at once be accepted.'[7] Baring went on to say that Nubar's animosity was hard to explain, but he attributed it to the fact that a change of Consul-General would be regarded by the Egyptians as a diplomatic victory for Nubar, for a new Consul-General would be able to exert only diplomatic influence, instead of Baring's brand of administrative and financial intervention. Baring supposed that while in London the previous year (1887) Nubar had been led to believe that evacuation was more imminent than was the case; and although he was in favour of British interference, it was of the kind that preserved the peace, maintained the Khedive on his throne, and kept him (Nubar) in office—but not of the kind to control civil affairs.

Salisbury asked Baring to delay the crisis with Nubar. This was the month of the 'naval scare' when France concentrated her fleet in the Mediterranean, and England seemed to be on the brink of war. Salisbury feared that if a crisis occurred in Egypt, it might excite French public opinion into declaring war. Therefore he advised against any 'very glaring exhibition of our sovereignty in Egypt at this moment ... I do not wish our administration in Egypt to be the cause to which the long European war is to be ascribed by the future historian.'[8]

The series of disagreements that culminated in this incident formalized the main lines of Baring's policy in Egypt. It showed how strong his position was, and how much the British government relied upon him in Egyptian affairs. It also showed how weak and vacillating the Khedive was, and subsequently it was to reveal how ill he supported his government. Above all it showed how little a prime minister in Egypt was worth when he chose to cross swords with Baring, for he held his position only by Baring's grace. Baring was aware that the moment the authorities in London refused to accede to Nubar's suggestion, that was the end of Nubar, and he was content to bide his time. Nubar could remain in power only so long as Baring and/or the Khedive gave him their support. When Baring withdrew this, the Khedive—realizing that Nubar had almost brought him to the edge of a crisis—also withdrew his support. It is significant that he did so soon after a conversation between him and Baring had taken place. During the conversation, Baring had suggested that Nubar should go, and hinted that Ismail was ready to return to Egypt at any time. To this piece of gentlemanly blackmail Tawfiq pertinently remarked that a minister might be changed—that did not much matter—but that any possibility of changing a Khedive was quite a different thing.[9] But the hint did not fall on deaf ears.

Nubar therefore had to go, but he refused to resign, and asked to be dismissed. This would allow him to pose as a patriot and save his face. But the Khedive refused to play that game, and left Nubar in office only to dismiss him two months later when the crisis had been forgotten.

Baring would have done well to examine the police question on its own merits, rather than use it as a test case; for seven years later, again under Nubar's premiership, the whole Ministry of the Interior had to be re-organized, and on lines more closely following Nubar's suggestions than Baring's. The provincial police were placed under the control of the local authorities, and an English Adviser, Eldon Gorst, was appointed to the Ministry of the Interior.[10]

Nubar's fears of the conflict that might arise from the daily contact between natives and foreigners ignorant of local customs was fully justified, for it became one of the sources of discontent felt by the Egyptians. A few years later, Baring came to recognize that the reforms of the police system were unsatisfactory (even though he refused to admit that the Egyptians had any ground for complaint), because 'a reform which appears irksome, even without reason, to those for whose benefit it is intended, fails of its purpose'.[11]

When Nubar fell from power, Riaz Pasha was chosen to succeed him as Prime Minister. A sempiternal triumvirate had succeeded to the premiership from the time of Ismail, and was formed of Sharif, Nubar and Riaz. The first two had been tried and found wanting: it was now Riaz's turn. Baring described Riaz as 'the most honest man . . . a stern disciplinarian . . . he does not intrigue. Though not liked he is feared and respected.' But he was also 'stupid, obstinate and violent . . . His manners are barbarous . . . He has not the most elementary ideas of government by law.'[12] This was a fair assessment of Riaz; for though he was one of Egypt's first social reformers, he had all the faults of the tyrannical Turk. There was a rumour that he was not a Turk, but a converted Jew who came from a family of goldsmiths called al-Wazzan. But, Jew or Turk, Riaz was obstinate, retrograde and bigoted—but withal the first man to issue a decree abolishing the use of the *kurbaj* (the lash) many years before the occupation, and was the first man to prohibit the use of the corvée on the lands of the notables. It was he who had turned the *Journal Officiel* into an active instrument of governmental criticism and reform by putting Shaykh Muhammad Abduh in charge of its publications, and Abduh regarded him as a great reformer. The religious hierarchy had great respect for him as a real non-European Muslim, and they frequented his house. In the past Riaz's undoing had stemmed from the fact that he was an autocrat who, like Baring, believed that good government was better than self-government, so that

75

when the notables sounded him about a constitution during the early days of Tawfiq's reign, he turned a deaf ear, and they turned to Urabi.

Riaz was led to antagonize the British officials by his belief that good government meant acting as he saw fit, which did not necessarily mean the acceptance of British suggestions on all matters. Especially did he antagonize Milner who worked under him and described him as 'the Turk *par excellence*, with all the virtues of the Turk and all his deadly hostility to progress . . . he represented the triumph—however temporary—of the Powers of Evil in the shape of an obstructiveness, which spoilt what it could not absolutely prevent, and delayed to the last what it was often of the greatest moment to do promptly'.[13] Riaz often put up a tremendous fight against Baring, but he just as often gave in when sufficient pressure was applied; for by 1889, he and the rest of the politicians had realized that they were all expendable.

The Khedive Tawfiq did not get on with Riaz, who lacked Nubar's persuasive manners; and Baring knew that Tawfiq would be only too happy to dismiss Riaz, if only Baring would let him do so. But Riaz's dismissal would create problems, for then 'the Khedive would want to govern more actively himself with the help of a retrograde and savage old Turk as Prime Minister. I like bringing the Khedive forward, but the combination would not work. It is not desirable that the Khedive should be himself too much pledged to one side in any of the numerous disputes which arise here.'[14] This last phrase was a piece of unconscious irony since the Khedive had long since pledged himself to the occupation. But inevitably a dispute arose that brought about Riaz's downfall. This time the issue was over the Ministry of Justice.

In 1890 a judge named John Scott had been imported from India to investigate the Ministry of Justice and to make suggestions for its improvement. His report recommended various changes, and, above all, a change of personnel, with the appointment of European Inspectors over the judges, and making the investigation of crimes the prerogative of the police and the Public Prosecutor, rather than of the *Juge d'Instruction*. Fakhri Pasha, who was Minister of Justice, objected to Scott's programme, and a special committee was set up to examine the project. The committee unanimously rejected the project. Baring, however, overriding the wishes of the committee, insisted that it be accepted, and, in the teeth of the whole cabinet, Scott was appointed Judicial Adviser to the Ministry of Justice.

Fakhri tried to play a trump card by giving orders that Scott was not to become involved in administrative affairs, but was merely to act in an advisory capacity. Riaz then appointed a British army officer, Herbert Kitchener, as head of the police, in the hope that he and Scott would come into conflict, and he could get rid of both of them at once. Unfortunately for Riaz, Scott and Kitchener together drew up a report and presented it to the Khedive, thereby going over Riaz's head. Riaz knew when he was beaten, and on May 12, 1891, he resigned his post on the ground of ill health.

Baring attributed Riaz's downfall to the fact that 'the Egyptian Oriental is quite one of the most stupid . . . in the world . . . Stupidity, not cunning is his chief characteristic.'[15] But *Le Bosphore Egyptien* of May 14 sadly remarked on Riaz's resignation that 'avec lui disparait le dernier ministère Egyptien. Nous n'aurons plus à l'avenir et jusqu'à l'évacuation, que des ministères Anglais dont les membres recevront leurs instructions de Sir Evelyn Baring ou même iront les lui demander à domicile avec servilité.' The last phrase was a perfect description of the next prime minister.

Mustafa Fahmi was a rich, elegant Turk with a weakness for fine shirts which he sent to England to be washed and ironed; but apart from this one eccentricity he never departed from the norm. He was honest and hardworking, but was much happier obeying orders than giving them. Milner described him as 'the best of men, a perfect gentleman and, I believe, cordially in sympathy with our aims, is terribly weak and fears offending the Khedive too much to exercise control over him'.[16] Some of the Egyptians maintained that it was Mustafa Fahmi who had assassinated Ismail's Minister of Finance, Ismail Pasha al-Mufattish, on orders from the Khedive; and to substantiate this rumour, which has persisted to the present day, they claimed that in the struggle al-Mufattish had bitten off the tip of Fahmi's little finger. During the Urabi rebellion he had posed as a supporter of Urabi, but when matters became critical he had discreetly sailed off to Europe on grounds of ill health, and had remained there until he judged it safe to return to Egypt after everything had calmed down. Baring a long time ago had realized that Fahmi would be 'a very facile instrument in the hands of the British Representative at Cairo'. His ministry was dubbed by the Egyptians the 'ministry of dummies', and Tigrane Pasha, a Christian Armenian, and Nubar's son-in-law, was included in the cabinet just to give it some backbone. Baring described the cabinet to Milner in sneering terms: 'The main thing now is to be very respectful to the Ministers—the public tell them they were puppets—we must try to make them think they are not. The result will be just the same but they will be pleased and the whole machine will work more smoothly.'[17] The machine worked so smoothly that Baring soon complained of boredom: 'Riaz's vagaries gave immense life to the proceedings. This has now ceased. We are all *so* unanimous. *I* have nothing to do.'[18] But like his two predecessors, Fahmi did not give complete satisfaction, in spite of his pliability; and two months after his appointment he came near dismissal. Salisbury advised against such a step, and warned Baring: 'Your position as "maire du palais" will be too plainly revealed if Riaz follows Nubar at the distance of two years, and Fahmi follows Riaz at the distance of two months.'[19] So Fahmi was allowed to keep his job for the time being.

As for the rest of the Egyptian government, that is, the Council of Ministers, this was dismissed in a contemptuous phrase by Portal, the First Secretary at the Agency, as 'this collection of supine nonentities and doddering old pantaloons'.[20] And although the cap fitted most of them, one cannot help assuming that this collection of nonentities was deliberately appointed because of its apathetic quality, the more so when one comes across such revealing letters as the one Scott-Moncrieff, the irrigation expert, sent Baring, in which he said: 'If the English influence is to remain paramount in the Public Works Ministry there cannot be as Minister a capable man who would like to do things his own way and hamper our action.'[21]

Britain in Egypt did not need innovators or planners—these she supplied herself; she needed yes-men to carry out her plans. As Baring said: 'The real difficulty of the situation consisted, not in indicating the nature of the reforms required, or even the methods by which effect could be given them, but in the peculiar conditions under which the reforms had to be carried out'[22]—i.e. the Law of Liquidation and the Capitulations. Therefore Baring's moans that he found the ruling class incapable of ruling were *pour la forme*, since he did not want a ruling class that *was* capable of ruling. Weak ministers who turned to him for help whenever they had to make even a minor decision, merely strengthened his hand, even though it lessened his respect for them to such an extent that he could say: 'They are all afraid of each other . . . There is, in fact, not a man among them'[23]—a feeling which was echoed by the Egyptians.

The men Baring relied on to govern the Egyptians were the staff of British officials in the employment of the Egyptian government—they were the mainstays of the Veiled Protectorate. These men had originally been recruited at the request of the Khedive, who had asked Dufferin to furnish him with a certain number of 'highly trained, experienced and able officials',[24] who were then attached to each of the departments of state. Most of these officials had served in India. In Egypt they were given the title of Adviser, or Under Secretary, and their duties consisted in giving advice and rendering assistance whenever possible.

When was the advice proffered by the European Advisers to be taken as a suggestion, and when was it meant to be taken as an order? At first the question bewildered the Egyptian official. The Granville Doctrine in 1884 settled any doubts, and the Egyptian assumed that every suggestion was an implied order. Long years of Turkish misrule had not encouraged a spirit of initiative; and the official who realized that in a show-down he would be let down by the Khedive, was more often content to follow orders without exposing himself to any risks. Nevertheless, conflict did arise between the English official and his Egyptian superior, and when that happened Baring usually acted as mediator. His view of the situation was explained much later in a report he sent home, in which he said that whereas the European was nominally in a position of inferiority, he almost of necessity guided, whilst the Egyptian followed. If this guidance was skilfully applied, then nothing but good could come of it. 'But it is the bounden duty of every British official in Egypt, without being unduly lenient, to make every reasonable allowance for the shortcomings of his Egyptian subordinates and coadjutors; to remember that these shortcomings are largely due to the misgovernment of the past, and to the rapid introduction of novel ideas and forms of government.'[25]

There was, however, a reservation to be made. The Europeans, especially the English, were apt to forget that they were the servants, and not the masters, of the Egyptian government; especially when everything in the nature of administration and finances depended wholly on the Europeans in the Egyptian service; and although Baring thought the best plan for the English to follow was to keep in the background and work through the native minister, yet 'it would be difficult for me to exaggerate the total want of capable administrators—there are none . . . Nubar says his ministers are cyphers—so they are.'[26] The British officials, who mostly came from India, were used to ruling natives, not to proffering advice. They thought that India and Egypt were similar countries with similar problems, and their whole training in a land where Britain ruled *de jure* led them to behave in the same way where the rule was merely *de facto*. Rather than keep in the background, they took over the departments, and inevitably the minister became a figurehead whose decisions could be overruled by the Adviser. An anecdote ascribed to Ibrahim Pasha Fuad, a cabinet minister, was a telling example of the power the Adviser wielded. Fuad's secretary had brought in a sheaf of documents with a request that the minister sign them. The minister asked if the Adviser had seen them, and, when the secretary answered in the affirmative, he waved a hand towards the ministerial rubber stamp on his desk, and said: 'There is your minister.'[27]

The Anglo-Egyptian officials were often a trial, both to Baring and to the Egyptian government, and it needed Baring's strong hand to keep them in line. Eldon Gorst realized the difficulty of handling this three-ring circus. 'One of the most difficult things here,' he wrote to Milner, 'and in my opinion, the thing in which Lord Cromer shines most, is keeping the English in order. They are a difficult team to drive . . . if ever Lord Cromer goes and an ordinary diplomatist comes here who does not understand the details of the situation, you will see that this element will bring him to grief and upset the whole Egyptian coach.'[28] Prophetic words, for here was one of the elements that upset Gorst's coach when he took over Cromer's position.

Although these officials felt some degree of loyalty to Egypt, it resembled the loyalty of a baron for his serf. Elwin Palmer, who later replaced Vincent as Financial Adviser, was perspicacious enough to realize that 'although we are English our first duty is to the Egyptians, the country we serve. I think this is sometimes too often forgotten.'[29] But most of the officials felt as did Milner (who was Adviser to the Ministry of the Interior) when he said: 'Egypt is an important place, and it is important from the Imperial point of view, that Englishmen holding any sort of responsible position there, should be English-minded.' He felt that, between the service of England abroad—and, to him, Egypt was that—and the civil service at home, there was a great deal to be said for the former. 'It is more exciting. You have larger scope.'[30] Parenthetically one might add that the larger the scope of the British official, the narrower that of his Egyptian opposite number, who was meant to learn the ropes from his foreign colleague. It never struck the British official that to be English-minded in Egypt was anomalous, or that the service of Egypt was quite different from the service of England; for by the time Milner was writing this passage in 1889, England had come to regard Egypt in the light of a colony. The British official's first loyalty was, therefore, to England, not to Egypt. This could have posed an especially acute problem to those officers serving in the army, who had to swear an oath of loyalty to the Khedive, after having sworn one to the Queen. Fortunately for the peace of mind of these officials, the question of divided loyalties was never put to the test. If it had been, there would have been no doubt in their minds that their first and last allegiance lay with Queen and Empire.

The manner in which Baring and the British officials in Egypt managed to present a united front seemed most formidable to the Egyptians, who were accustomed to chicanery and backbiting in government circles. It served, indeed, as an additional demonstration of Britain's power. But behind the façade some human likes and dislikes can be detected. Letters preserved in the Milner Papers are most enlightening on that matter, for they were written by young officials to each other, and they savour of an irreverence which is often illuminating. Dawkins, who later became the Financial Adviser, one of Milner's closest friends, writing about Gorst, who was then Adviser to the Ministry of Interior, said: 'My own relations with this self-centred little cynic are quite pleasant . . . the little man has an extraordinary and rather impudent programme of his own. He believes that Cromer* must go soon; that Cromer's successor must inevitably make a mess of the job, and that, if he has gone elsewhere meanwhile and distinguished himself he must be brought back to put things straight.'[31] This did not fit in with Dawkins' own plans, for in the same letter he wished that Milner would replace Cromer, and he himself could then replace Palmer, the Financial Adviser. It is interesting to note that Cromer, writing to Rosebery three years earlier, had said: 'Who is to succeed me . . . I know of only three possible men—Nicolson, Milner and Portal.'[32] Perhaps the reason for the omission of Gorst from that list can be explained by Harry Boyle's opinion of Gorst. Boyle, Cromer's Oriental Secretary, and a close friend as well, was nicknamed 'Enoch' because he 'walked daily with the Lord'. He was of opinion that Gorst was 'brilliantly clever, more especially in the all-important matter of Finance. On the other hand, he was a hardened opportunist, and a "streber" (climber) [*sic*] of the deepest dye. He was by no means a popular character, neither could he be said to enjoy the absolute confidence of even his friends.'[33]

The *bête-noire* of most of the Anglo-Egyptian officials was Kitchener. Milner said that he was '*not absolutely straight*, he might very easily cause great trouble not only with the natives, but among the English themselves'.[34] Three years after these words were written Kitchener nearly brought about the Khedive's de-

* Baring had been made a Baron in 1892, with the title of Lord Cromer, Viscount in 1898 and Earl in 1901.

THE BEAST OF BURDEN.

Mossoo. "IF YOU CANNOT LEAD HIM, MON CHER, LET *ME!*"
John Bull. "NO, THANK YE. IF I CAN'T *LEAD* HIM, I'LL *RIDE* HIM!!"

Punch, January 19, 1884

Lord Dufferin décroche Arabi, qui, en tombant, accroche Riaz, qui, en tombant, accroche Lotfi, qui, en tombant, accroche Moubarek, qui en tombant, accroche Eyoub, qui en tombant, accroche Chérif, qui en tombant, accroche Tewfik, qui, en tombant, accroche Nobar, qui, en tombant, accroche Abbas, sous le poids de son impopulaire régence.

Notre Halim, seul; reste debout!

لورد دفرين يقطع حبل شنقة عرابي فيقع على رياض · ورياض على لطفي · ولطفي يقع على مبارك · ومبارك على ايوب · وايوب على شريف · وشريف على توفيق · وتوفيق على نوبار · ونوبار على عباس ·

حليم فقط يظل واقف ·

A contemporary caricature from the album, *Abu Naddara Zarqa*, 1886 position, as we shall see later. Wingate, who became Governor of the Sudan, and who at that time was Director of Military Intelligence, agreed with Milner, while Dawkins added that Kitchener's men disliked and distrusted him, even though they were impressed by his ability and energy. One vivid description of Kitchener is that of G. W. Steevens, a newspaper correspondent, who said: 'You feel that he ought to be patented and shown with pride at an International Exhibition—British Empire exhibit, number one, *hors concours*, the Sudan Machine.'[35]

Cromer, quite naturally, held the place of honour amongst these officials. Any flaws that his image presented were overlooked by Milner, who had a veritable hero-worship for him. When Milner first came to Egypt he wrote a letter to Goschen in praise of Cromer, saying: 'He is the real ruler of Egypt, and that, considering the enormous difficulties both native and foreign, his unostentatious supremacy is a real masterpiece of political management. I sometimes wonder whether we could possibly get on without him.'[36] Later, Milner called him the 'only thoroughly competent counsellor in Egyptian affairs'.[37]

Dawkins, who came to Egypt much later, only after Milner had left, saw Cromer in a different light. Things had changed by then. The Khedive Tawfiq had been succeeded by his son Abbas. Cromer had been offered the post of Ambassador to Vienna in 1896, but had refused it—so much to Dawkins' chagrin that he wrote to Milner: 'Cromer exults in his strength and success here. Cromer would be miserable and wasted in Vienna. But his decision not to go and his previous decision about Constantinople [he had turned down the post of Ambassador there also], and his growing belief that he is "absolutely indispensable here" (which he is not) must give pause to you and me. Cromer has rendered magnificent service in Egypt and he will again if he is called upon in a crisis. But I think a man loses something of his best when he begins to consider himself quite indispensable, and he is certainly not inclined to take trouble and use his own eyes as his Memoirs show that he used to do.'* The

---

* Dawkins meant the work that was eventually to become *Modern Egypt*. M.P. Dawkins to Milner, September 18, 1896.

inner meaning of this last sentence is clarified in a previous letter that Dawkins had sent Milner: 'Big as he is it seems that he must be under the domination of someone. The tendency will increase. It is very convenient to him, and suits an odd vein of laziness which is combined with his great energy, to work through some one agent and to hear everything through him alone. It used to be Gorst. That little man has fallen into disfavour. He mounted too quickly and then showed faults of temper and manner. Now it is Palmer.'[38] A carping tone creeps into Dawkins' letters when he says that 'Palmer is enormously important these days. We are on the best of terms, and he talks over everything. But *one is not able* to talk directly to Cromer.'*

The only non-admirer of Cromer among these officials was Willcocks, who was an Irrigation Inspector in the Ministry of Public Works. But even he said of Cromer that 'though a brute he was a just brute'. He accused Cromer of attempting to impose his ideas on the British officials, to say nothing of the Egyptians. 'I used to imagine that Lord Cromer was never so happy ordering officials to march to the right or the left as he was when ordering them to think to the right or the left. He was a thorough autocrat.'[39] Willcocks said that 'all the officials who enjoyed working under him seemed to lose their backbones',[40] and that he 'sedulously depressed and kept down every independent Egyptian and had filled all the high' posts with cyphers'.[41] As an example of Cromer's highhandedness, Willcocks recounts how, when Cromer heard that he was writing humorous skits on British officialdom in Egypt, he made Willcocks sign a statement that he would never write anything while he was an official of the Egyptian government, and would accept instant dismissal if he transgressed.[42] Lastly, Willcocks alleged that all the dailies and news-agencies had their letters and telegrams back to England corrected by the Agency, 'so that Lord Cromer was not only the real actor of the Egyptian stage, but also the critic of his own actions'.[43]

As for the Egyptian officials, they were all afraid of Cromer. They realized that they could appeal to him for the redressment

---

* M.P., Dawkins to Milner, December 6, 1896. See below Ch. V *re* Cromer's relations with Britons and Egyptians.

of their wrongs, if wrongs had been perpetrated by the government; but they also knew that he represented power, and, since the only kind of power with which they were familiar was absolute, they assumed that his power was of that variety. The myth of Cromer's authority thus grew to overwhelm Egyptian officialdom, and was only to be pricked by the young nationalists after 1895.

This then was how Egypt was ruled for the ten years from 1882 to 1892. Necessity as the mother of invention was the guiding spirit of the administration. Cromer had to devise a system that solved each crisis as it arose, since during most of the period successive British governments could not be quite sure whether they meant their promises of evacuation or not. Cromer thus had to act as though evacuation might take place soon, although he himself was sure that it would not.

In his book, *Modern Egypt*, which appeared in 1908, Cromer listed the reforms which were necessary in Egypt. The first three he mentioned were: an attempt at arresting the corruption rampant in all government departments, which was a battle constantly maintained; the abolition of the *kurbaj*, the lash; and the abolition of the corvée, unpaid forced labour. It was easy enough to abolish the use of the *kurbaj* by government decree; but to abolish the corvée, funds were needed to remunerate the labourers, which meant an appeal to the Powers for money from the Caisse de la Dette. For many years France raised all kinds of obstacles in pursuance of her pinprick policy, and it was only in 1888 that a decree was finally issued which partially abolished the corvée. Reforms of Egyptian finances, and minor changes in the Capitulatory system, also had to be wrested from the Powers. This too was a long and weary process, for solvency was reached only in 1888. In 1889 the Powers agreed to confer on the Egyptian government the right to make bye-laws applicable to all the inhabitants of Egypt, provided that the General Assembly of the Mixed Courts decreed that the laws were not contrary to the texts of the treaties and conventions. This was the beginning of legislative independence for Egypt. The most enduring reforms, and the most remunerative to Egypt, were those carried out in the irrigation system. In 1885 a loan of £E1 million had been negotiated, and a further sum of

£E800,000 in 1889. These had been expended on irrigation projects which greatly increased agricultural production; and under the direction of Colin Scott-Moncrieff and William Garstin, the Department of Public Works became the most successful department and the most popular amongst the Egyptians.

Other reforms in the departments of Justice, the Interior and Education were less successful and roused discontent amongst the Egyptians. Especially was this the case with the Department of Education. Cromer pleaded a shortage of funds to justify the deficiency of reforms there, while using Egypt's lack of education as an excuse for not extending liberal institutions. To the Egyptians, education and self-rule were Cromer's greatest failures in Egypt, just as his restoration of Egyptian finances was his greatest success. The new group of nationalists soon pointed out that the former reforms would have benefited Egypt directly, while the latter reforms were of benefit to England-in-Egypt as well as to Egypt. But these criticisms were to come at a much later period; for the time being, the Egyptian administration was content to let Cromer and the British Advisers call the tune for needed reforms.

When Tawfiq died and Abbas II came to the throne, the situation changed, and Cromer wrote to Rosebery saying that he felt that his work in Egypt had ended. He had come to Egypt under certain conditions that had now greatly changed, for all the financial and administrative questions which ten years ago had been matters of importance had been more or less solved, and the system must be modified to suit the new condition of affairs.[44] Political and not financial problems were soon to occupy the foreground; and Cromer—who did not really desire to leave Egypt—continued to rule as he had done in the past, with the difference that he now had to face a young ruler with pretensions of governing, and a rising nationalist movement.

CHAPTER V

Rumblings of Opposition

Though the Egyptian government by and large had acquiesced in Cromer's rule, there still remained traces of an opposition outside government circles. In terms of outward expression, opposition was confined, in Egypt, to the foreign press, for the native press was still too frightened and unsure of itself to speak out loud. A few French-language newspapers, sheltering behind the protective barrier of the Capitulations, violently attacked Cromer and the administration: the foremost critic was *Le Bosphore Egyptien*. But since these papers catered for a small French-speaking minority, they had little effect on the mass of the Egyptians.

The only nationalist voices that were left to cry in the wilderness were those of the nationalists in exile. Jamal al-Din al-Afghani and Shaykh Muhammad Abduh began in 1883 to publish a magazine in France which was entitled *al-Urwa al-Wuthqa*, 'The Indissoluble Bond'. A pan-Islamic paper that aimed its message at all the Muslims of the world, and urged them to unite and restore the lost glories of Islam, *al-Urwa* was specifically aimed at freeing Egypt from the British occupation. This was to be effected by stirring up public opinion in Egypt and also in India.

Pictures of al-Afghani show an intense, saturnine face bespeaking the restless revolutionary who once asked the Egyptians why they did not bury their axes in the skulls of their oppressors instead of quietly tilling the earth. Al-Afghani had such magnetism as could rouse his followers to revolutionary fervour, so that even the mildest of men, Shaykh Muhammad Abduh, planned under his influence to assassinate the Khedive Ismail. Abduh was al-Afghani's most outstanding disciple; a truly gentle man he adopted violent language only when under the spell of his teacher. The moment they parted ways his own character emerged—the kindness and compassion that was to make him beloved by so many different people, the integrity and determination that were to earn him the respect of even his enemies. Together and separately these two men dedicated their lives to the task of saving Islam from its decadence, and reformulating its principles so that once again it could become a vital force.

The ideas expounded in *al-Urwa* may be summarized into two main themes. The first is that true Islam has become corrupted through ignorance, and must therefore be reformed—otherwise the Muslims all faced extinction; the second is that the Muslim countries had been betrayed by their rulers, who, swayed by personal motives of greed and aggrandizement, gave foreigners a free hand in their countries. The consequence was that the Europeans who coveted Muslim lands took advantage of the inner discords of Islam, and sought to destroy the religious unity of the Muslim nations.

The cure for this state of affairs lay in following three guide-lines, the first of which led people back to the true faith, to the early solidarity that bound Muslims together, as in the days of the early caliphs. 'For if Muslims made the principles of their true religion their one concern, then they could not fail to progress to the limits of human perfection.' The second guide-line in the ideas of *al-Urwa* led to the definition of what was meant by true Islam. Though neither Abduh nor Afghani, being propagandists for a politico-religious purpose, were then occupied with a comprehensive elaboration of Muslim theology (although at a later period Abduh was to attempt such a work), none the less they had occupied themselves with the reformation of Islam and in so doing did expound their interpretation of Islam. They believed that it was the religion that was most in harmony with the dictates of reason and with modern progress, for it sought to liberate the mind from superstition, and gave men a divine law which was also the law of nature. Islam meant activity, but ignorance had led it towards stagnation—a stagnation that could destroy the entire Muslim world. Muslims must therefore change their behaviour and throw aside their superstitions; they must learn the techniques of the West to be able to defend themselves from encroachments by Europe. The impetus necessary for this reform could only come from the Muslims themselves: it would not appear as a divine gift, for, they said, quoting the Quran, 'God does not change what is in a people, until they change what is in themselves.' The third guide-line was definitely a revolutionary one. It expounded the right of a people to rise against a tyrannical ruler whose actions were endangering the country, lest the whole Islamic community be corrupted by this example. The right of civil disobedience is a moot point in Islamic political thought; but *al-Urwa*, which regarded Tawfiq as a traitor who had sold out to the enemies of his country, encouraged his overthrow and that of other Muslim rulers who might follow his example.

Afghani and Abduh both believed that Islam was the one bond which tied the Muslims of the world together in spite of local differences of race and language. In the past, the Muslims had once been united into a glorious community; and though they had lost this community through their decadence, and through corrupt rulers, they could still unite once again, if they could but reform themselves. The community of Islam gathered its strength from the aggregate force of its various members. Therefore, if one country became weak, it affected the totality, so that it was a religious duty incumbent upon the faithful to share a community of interests. *Al-Urwa* thus preached pan-Islam as a type of nationalist manifestation against Europe; for Islam stood, amongst Muslims, in lieu of nationality, and Muslim lands were occupied by alien powers, who were also Christian. Self-determination took on a religious colouring, and pan-Islam was another way of calling for independence from foreign domination.

The concept of a pan-Islamic nationalism was hardly compatible with the type of nationalism prevalent in Europe. It was, however, a potent indication that Muslim thinkers, too, felt the need for reform, both moral and political. It remained for a younger generation to introduce a western-style nationalism in Egypt, with its concept of loyalty to a nation as a territorial unit. But *al-Urwa* served its purpose in that it stood as a source of opposition to Britain, and maintained alive the spirit of self-determination—although amongst a minute group. The British authorities feared the effect of *al-Urwa* to the extent that it was banned in

Egypt and in India, the two countries at which its message was aimed. An aggressive pan-Islamic paper that urged Muslims to rise against the foreign invader was too dangerous an instrument to let loose on an 'easily inflamed public'. In Egypt, the Council of Ministers issued a decree forbidding the circulation of *al-Urwa*, and imposed a fine of £E5 to £E15 on anyone caught with a copy of the paper in his possession. The magazine closed down after eighteen issues had been published, but these issues had a profound influence on the Egyptians who read them. For in spite of the law, they were clandestinely read by students, *ulama* (men of religion) and intellectuals.

The effect of *al-Urwa* on British policy-makers was that they soon came to see the shadow of pan-Islam lurking behind every nationalist bush. Cromer seems genuinely to have believed that the nationalist movement in Egypt was basically a pan-Islamic one, but he was also capable of using the fear of pan-Islam as a convenient device with which to hush embarrassing questions in the House of Commons: this, as we shall see later, happened in the Dinshwai affair. Since the Power that occupied Egypt was a Christian one, it was only normal for a pan-Islamic tone to creep into nationalist propaganda, especially since Egypt's nominal suzerain, Turkey, was the seat of the Caliphate. Turks, though disliked in Egypt, were fellow-Muslims, and Egyptians could feel an affinity with them, if one based only on religion. But there was no bond to tie Egyptians to England, neither racial nor religious. Thus in most cases the reactions that Britain assumed to be dictated by pan-Islamic feelings, were really Islamic responses to the domination of an alien Power who also happened to be Christian, and whose representative showed no sympathy for Islam. These were as much cultural as political reactions to the occupation.

In August 1884, Abduh went to England and, while there, was interviewed by the *Pall Mall Gazette* on August 7. During the interview Abduh said that the only thing that the British government had taught Muslims was to become united in their wish to see England evacuate Egypt. Before the war, he said (referring to 1882), and during the war, Muslims quarrelled with each other.

They had wished to break down the tyranny of their rulers; they had complained of the Turks as foreigners; they had wished to improve themselves politically, and to advance as the nations of Europe had advanced along the path of liberty. Now they knew that there were worse evils than despotism, and worse enemies than the Turks. When Abduh was asked what he thought of Tawfiq, he said that since Tawfiq had joined the enemies of his religion at the time of war, it was impossible for him to command the respect of the Egyptians. But should he repent, and get rid of the British, he might yet be forgiven; only they did not wish for 'traitors with Egyptian faces and British hearts'. Finally Abduh said: 'Egypt is not wanting in honourable men or men of capacity. But you insist on having those who will do your work; and no honest man in Egypt will work for the British government.' His last words were a plea to the British authorities to do no more 'good' in Egypt, for their good had already done too much harm.

This was a succinct exposé of the feelings of the nationalists, which were even more poignantly expressed during a conversation Abduh had with Hartington, the Secretary for India, who asked him if it were not better for Egypt to be ruled in peace and security by England, than misruled by Turks and Pashas. Abduh answered that occupation of any kind was hateful, even to the most primitive races, and that although the Egyptian may have been ignorant, he was not so ignorant as to accept the domination of an alien race—a race that differed from him in its religion—when his own religion taught him to oppose such a domination. Here we see the two lines of thought that were to oppose colonial powers and nationalists: on the one hand, the belief that good government should be sufficient for a people, and on the other hand the belief in the value of self-rule, even that of a bungling variety, as a virtue in itself.

The fact that the Egyptians and the British had different religions often blinded both peoples to the virtues of the other race. Cromer thought very poorly of Islam, and refused to believe that it could produce any constructive reforms. 'It would be too much to expect that a fervid Moslem . . . should readily accept the facts . . . that Islamism as a social and political system—though not as a religion—is moribund, that the judicial and administrative procedures common amongst Moslems are so closely interwoven with their religion as to be almost inseparable the one from the other, and that for many a long year to come the Egyptians will be incapable of governing themselves on civilized principles.'¹ This was the very theory that *al-Urwa*, and Shaykh Muhammad Abduh, set out to disprove. On his return to Egypt Abduh struggled to show Muslims and Europe that a reformed Islam was possible.

In 1884 al-Afghani and Abduh parted, never to come together again. Al-Afghani wandered in Europe for a few years and then went to Constantinople at the invitation of the Sultan Abd al-Hamid, where he was kept under strict surveillance by that suspicious ruler until he finally died. Abduh went to Tripoli and then to Beirut, where he taught, and eventually returned to Egypt in 1888. Though he had been sentenced to three years' exile, he could not return to Egypt without the Khedive's permission; and this the Khedive refused to grant, fearing Abduh's influence as a teacher on the students at al-Azhar. Abduh's friend and disciple, Saad Zaghlul, who by then had become a successful lawyer and the protégé of Princess Nazli Fazil, pleaded Abduh's case with Cromer. Princess Nazli, Tawfiq's first cousin, and a great friend of Cromer's, also urged him to use his good offices with the Khedive to have Abduh recalled from exile. This he did, although it was alleged that Cromer allowed Abduh to return to Egypt in return for his promise not to dabble in politics again.² Whether Abduh really was asked to give such a promise, or whether his followers assumed that he had promised to abstain from political life, on his return to Egypt he set aside politics and devoted himself to social reforms and education. At first the Khedive would not allow him to return to his teaching post at al-Azhar, and nominated him to the post of Judge in the Courts of First Instance of the Native Tribunals. There Abduh's judgments became an example for other judges to follow, but eventually he was allowed to teach once again in al-Azhar. In 1899 he was appointed Grand Mufti and became a member of the Legislative Council. He died in 1905 at the age of fifty-six.

Abduh, defining his reformist intentions, said: 'I spoke out on behalf of two great causes. The first of these was the liberation of thought from the chains of imitation . . . The second cause I adopted was the reform of the Arabic Language.' He had tried his hand at a third reform which 'consisted of drawing the distinction between the government's right to the obedience of the people and the people's right to justice on the part of the government. I was among those persons who called upon the Egyptian population to recognize their right over their ruler—a notion which had not occurred to them for over twenty centuries'; but he had abandoned that task, for he came to realize that 'nations reap the fruit of what has been planted and cultivated over a long period of years, and that it is this planting with which we must now concern ourselves'.[3] Abduh saw Egypt's problem as a moral one. The Islamic mould into which Egyptian society fitted had become ossified with time, and was no longer suited to the demands of the age. It had to be re-adapted to the necessities of society, and only then could it become the life-giving force that it once was. This meant a return to the pristine purity of the early days of Islam: a move that would rid Islam of much of the traditional and shackling deadweight that it had accumulated with the passage of time. To that end, Muslims must be encouraged to examine and reassess Islam, rationally and with an inquiring mind, without having to face an accusation of heresy for such practices. For freedom from the shackles of tradition could only occur through the use of reason. 'Inasmuch as belief in the existence of God is a fundamental article of faith, and this belief is founded upon reason, the priority of reason in Islam is apparent,' he said. Moreover, where there was a conflict between reason and the meaning of the Divine Law, as given by tradition, then 'the conclusions which have been arrived at by reason are to be given the preference'.[4] This was difficult for the *ulama* to accept, especially when Abduh believed that, in matters of belief and the interpretation of religion, people should be allowed to exercise a personal freedom. But, Abduh bemoaned, the hearts of the masses have become infected by the *ulama* with the disease of dependence on precedents, *taqlid*—for the *ulama* first believed that a thing was so and then sought proofs to justify their belief.

The *ulama* in general disapproved of Abduh's ideas, which encouraged inquiry into religious matters, and threatened to upset the traditional tenets of Islam. Some of them feared that to question the dogma of Islam might bring about its total disruption, especially by the introduction of foreign elements resulting from Western methods of thought. Indeed Abduh had taken on an overwhelming task, for he was attempting to provide an answer to the modern man, 'who doubted whether someone who lived in the modern world could still be a devout Muslim'.[5]

It is not our intention to go into details of Abduh's dogma or his religious ideas. Suffice it to say that his importance to his contemporaries and followers lay in his desire that people should develop reason and a spirit of inquiry as means of evolving with the times. His greatest wish, as he once confided to a friend, was to live long enough to free Islam from its superstitions, to reform the daily beliefs of people who had replaced religion by superstition. He believed that religious reform would produce social reform, and that political independence was the inevitable and logical conclusion of a reformed society.

Education was to go hand in hand with religious reforms, for, by educating people, an enlightened public opinion could be created, and this would destroy autocracy and inhibit repression. The existing type of education in Egypt was, he said, incompatible with the needs of the society. His answer, then, was that more schools should be founded: and if the government did not devote sufficient attention to the matter, then benevolent societies should found schools and even start a university. Abduh was instrumental in founding the Muslim Benevolent Society, which still exists to this day, and which opened a large number of schools. A university project did come to fruition, although the university itself was founded after his death. But Abduh's interest in education was not only to build up an enlightened society, it was also tied up with his interest in reforming the Arabic language. For in order to reinterpret the Muslim religion a knowledge of the Arabic language was needed. Aside from that, Abduh had an interest in the language *per se*, and he communicated this feeling for the language to some of his disciples who were instrumental in reforming and

94

modernizing Arabic so that it became a vehicle for the communication of modern ideas in a language comprehensible to the man in the street, and not only confined to the chosen few.

Apart from Abduh and the group of social reformers who gathered round him, there were signs of political activity in the salons of the time. The most famous of these salons were those of Princess Nazli Fazil, Riaz Pasha, and Ali Pasha Mubarak. Nazli Fazil was the daughter of Mustafa Fazil, who lost the throne to his half-brother Ismail by being born one month later. Consequently he spent the rest of his life in Istanbul, living as a grand seigneur and intriguing, to no avail, to have his brother deposed and replaced by himself. He finally devoted himself to Ottoman politics, espoused the cause of the Young Ottomans whom he financed abroad, and then neglected when the Sultan appointed him a minister. His daughter, Nazli, had been brought up in political circles, and was a protégée of Henry Layard's when he was Ambassador in Constantinople. She had developed into a forceful but charming woman with a love for politics and intrigue, and an intense dislike for her cousin Tawfiq, which feeling was reciprocated. Nazli had espoused the cause of Urabi, in part because she believed in the liberal principles he supported, but in part out of contempt for her cousin. When the revolution failed, Nazli, who hated failures, came to despise Urabi just as fiercely as she had once supported him, and became intensely pro-British. Her salon was the meeting-ground for Englishmen and Egyptians. Amongst her regular visitors were Saad Zaghlul, whom she inspired to learn French and become a modern lawyer; Shaykh Muhammad Abduh who, on his return from exile, also learned French at her insistence at the age of forty-four; Qasim Amin, a magistrate who was to advocate women's rights; as well as Cromer, Harry Boyle, the Oriental Secretary, his successor Ronald Storrs, and Kitchener.

The second salon was that of Ali Pasha Mubarak. A fallah by origin, Mubarak had been trained as an engineer under Muhammad Ali, and had risen to become one of Egypt's foremost educators and several times a minister. The author of various works, including a twenty-volume topography of Egypt, *al-Khitat al-Tawfiqiyya li Misr al-Qahira*, Mubarak had shone as the Director of the famous School of Languages, as Minister of Public Works, and of Education. During the Urabi revolution he had tried to act as an intermediary between the Khedive and the revolutionaries in order to reconcile the two. Many of the notables of Egypt visited his house, and it was at his salon that a young Egyptian patriot, Mustafa Kamil, made his political debut by meeting the famous men of the day, and began the political agitation which was to rouse a nationalist movement.

The third salon was that of Riaz Pasha. This was frequented by the religious hierarchy, and by the anti-occupation faction who, although they were not organized as a group, needed a safety-valve for venting their feelings. This they found in Riaz's house. It was through Riaz that an obscure shaykh from al-Azhar was encouraged to found a newspaper to attack the occupation, and become the voice of the would-be nationalists. This Shaykh Ali Yusif did, by becoming co-founder of *al-Muayyad* in 1889. The two most important papers at the time were *al-Muqattam*, which was the voice of the Agency, and *al-Ahram* which spread a moderate pro-French policy. *Al-Muayyad*, therefore, was to become the voice of the Egyptians. In his autobiography, Willcocks, an irrigation expert, tells how he sympathized with this proposal and even subscribed £E5 to help found the paper. When Cromer heard that an Englishman in Egypt was subscribing to an anti-British newspaper, Willcocks came very close to losing his position.

The aims of *al-Muayyad* were expounded in the editorial of the first issue which said that the goal of any truthful press was to present and interpret the views of the rulers and the ruled, one to the other. 'Egyptians, here is a paper which aims to serve you and you only by presenting you with valuable ideas and truthful news.'

The paper soon came to be recognized as the organ of the anti-British element in Egypt. At first the Khedive looked on it with favour; but when someone told him that it was the mouthpiece of a group of men who were attempting to reconstitute *al-Hizb al-Watani*, and who aimed at deposing him, his goodwill turned into antagonism. There was no foundation to the rumour, but Tawfiq (who was permanently suspicious) did not trust a paper that attacked British policy in Egypt, and neither did the British. Yusif claimed that the Agency imposed a ban on the government departments to prevent his paper from receiving news, and that he needed the good offices of a friend who was *persona grata* at the Agency before the ban was lifted.

Ali Yusif's energy was boundless. During the early days of the paper he hawked it round the streets and cafés of Cairo. Whenever he saw a group of men gathered he would read out passages from his paper and explain them. By 1896 it reached a circulation of 6,000 per day. In 1891 the two owners of the paper disagreed with each other and it was suspended for the month of October—until Saad Zaghlul, together with a few friends, solved the deadlock by lending Yusif enough money to buy out his partner. From then on *al-Muayyad* increased in circulation until it became one of the leading newspapers in Egypt.

Ali Yusif was a moderate by nature, and his policy was to use an appeal to reason rather than to emotions, whenever he could. He was not always successful, for he wrote on many subjects and his knowledge was often superficial; but he was a good journalist, and a solid writer on matters with which he was familiar. He wrote with one eye carefully cocked towards al-Azhar, and his arguments were always Muslim-oriented, and often pro-Ottoman. When Abbas came to the throne he befriended Ali Yusif, who became one of his staunchest supporters, and the most loyal of all the Khedive's men.

From 1882–92 a good deal of discontent was growing among thinking Egyptians over Egypt's political life. The eagerly awaited parliamentary institutions proved to be ineffectual and devoid of authority. England seemed little inclined to make a move towards evacuation. There was no change in the administrative machinery: the same ministers held the same jobs they had held under Ismail, except that they were now ruled by an English Adviser as well. But although opposition was restricted to talk in salons, or to talk of social reforms, and to an occasional article in *al-Muayyad* or *al-Ahram*, nationalist yearnings were lying just below the surface, waiting for someone to goad them into becoming an active force. This goad appeared when Abbas ascended the throne.

97

CHAPTER VI

The Khedive and the Lord

Abbas Hilmi ascended the throne of Egypt in 1892, when he was barely eighteen years old. The formative years of his life had been spent at school in Switzerland, and, from 1887, at the Theresianum in Vienna. At the Theresianum Abbas had a French teacher, M. Rouiller, who introduced him to French liberal thought, and instilled in him ideas of ridding his country of the incubus of foreign domination.* During his stay in Vienna, Abbas had frequently been a guest at the court, and there he saw a monarch who not only reigned, but ruled—and in an absolute fashion. The young Prince may well have been struck by the contrast between the position of the Austrian Emperor and that of his own father; for he determined that, when the time came, he would rule his country himself.

Abbas's arrival in Egypt was the occasion of much press comment. A leader in *The Times* of January 8, 1892, said that Tawfiq's death precluded all thought of evacuation, since such a young ruler as Abbas could not be left a prey to dangerous and reactionary nationalist movements. It was Britain's duty to carry on in the role of mentor. *The Egyptian Gazette* of January 20 somewhat threateningly asserted that the death of the Khedive was not expected to effect any change in Anglo-Egyptian relations, and warned France against any attempts at making mischief. On the opposite side, *Le Bosphore Egyptien*, on March 2, 1892, took up the cudgels, insisting that Abbas was not likely to remain a puppet in British hands.

Abbas had as yet given no indication of the line that he was to take, for he was busy with his firman of investiture. The Sultan, thinking that he could hoodwink the young Khedive, had omitted

* This information was obtained during an interview with H.R.H. Prince Muhammad Abd al-Munim, the Khedive's eldest son, in Lausanne, 1963.

Jamal al-Din al-Afghani

The Khedive Abbas and his council in the 1890's. *From the left*: Fakhry Pasha; the Secretary to the Council; Mazloum Pasha; Sir Elwin Palmer, K.C.M.G.; Nubar Pasha; Ibraham Faud Pasha; Abbas Pasha, the Khedive; Boutros Pasha; Mustapha Fehmy Pasha

to mention in the firman the Sinai Peninsula as forming part of the Khedive's 'privileged territories' of Egypt. Thanks to Cromer's vigilance, and to the efforts of the British Ambassador at Constantinople, this deliberate oversight was rectified, and Sinai once more included in the list of Egyptian territories. Throughout this crisis, Abbas had relied completely on Cromer, so much so that the latter complained that both Mustafa Fahmi, the Premier, and the Khedive, 'cling to my skirts with a tenacity that is greater than I could wish'.[1]

Cromer's first impression of Abbas was a favourable one: 'He resembles a very gentlemanlike and healthily-minded boy fresh from Eton or Harrow—not at all devoid of intelligence, but a good deal bored with el Azhar . . . I really wish he was not quite so civilized.'[2] He was also 'honest and truthful, probably more so than his father . . . his judgment appears to me to be singularly sound for so very young a man'.[3] Cromer was soon to discard his favourable impression, for by the time he had been away for his summer holiday and returned to Cairo three months later, he found a different state of affairs.

Throughout the summer rumours had been flying round Cairo of an impending ministerial change. On July 10, *al-Muayyad* wrote that the government of Egypt was chaotic because authority lay in the hands of people who had been foisted upon the government as advisers, who considered themselves to be above the law, and thus were not amenable to suggestions and criticism. This article was followed two days later by a suggestion that European influence in Egypt should be limited to fiscal matters, and that Egypt should have a purely national government. Above all, *al-Muayyad* suggested, any foreign advisers used should be nationals of small or neutral states, like Belgium and Switzerland.

Further rumours of a crisis spread towards the end of the year, by which time Abbas had effected a few changes of personnel in his entourage, including his appointment of his erstwhile tutor, Rouiller, as the European Secretary in his cabinet. This brought Cromer's first rebuke, but one that was couched in a paternal tone. He reported to the British government that Abbas 'has been foolish about a number of small things but he is so young and inexperienced that he ought not to be judged too harshly. I lectured him in plain but very friendly terms, and I do not anticipate that for the time being, I shall have much difficulty with him.'⁴ There Cromer proved wrong. He was soon to have a great deal of trouble with Abbas.

In his memoirs published posthumously (but unfortunately in an expurgated edition) in *al-Misri*, April 7, 1951, Abbas gave an account of the 'small things' that had irritated him. He said that on his arrival in Egypt, while the Egyptian troops played the Egyptian national anthem, the British troops played the Turkish one, and he had interpreted this as a sign that Britain was trying to put him in his place as a vassal of Turkey rather than to recognize his as sovereign of Egypt. His next grievance stemmed from his belief that the Egyptian ministers were not allowed to visit him unless they were accompanied by Elwin Palmer, the Financial Adviser; so when Abbas left on a tour of the Delta, he deliberately refused to take Palmer with him. On his return from the tour he was met by Hardinge, the Chargé d'Affaires, who was acting for Cromer during his absence on summer leave; and Hardinge (by his own account) offended him by accusing Tigrane, one of his favourites, of being a cheat. Then Abbas heard rumours that Mustafa Fahmi, the Prime Minister, wished to have a British Adviser appointed to serve in the Khedive's cabinet, the *Maiyya Saniyya*. All of these incidents, whether true or imagined, built up the Khedive's resentment against British tutelage. His Council of Ministers seemed to him to be composed of a group of nonentities and incompetent sycophants, who answered every one of his remarks with 'as Your Highness pleases'. He therefore determined to get rid of them, and of the British influence which kept them in power. But the ground had to be prepared.

Le Bosphore Egyptien paved the way with several articles. One of them, written on November 25, 1893, and entitled, 'La mission d'un Prince', said that the ruler was the sole source of authority in a state, and that on him only fell all the responsibility. For his ministers were merely cogs in the machinery, and Egypt remained solidly behind her Prince in all his efforts. *Al-Ahram* echoed these sentiments on December 1. On December 15, the Legislative

Council felt some life for the first time since its inception. The Council was presented with the project for the budget of 1893 only thirteen days before its publication-date was due; and it therefore voted unanimously, with two abstentions, that it would not discuss the budget in such conditions. It claimed that at such short notice it was impossible for it to study the proposals and offer constructive suggestions. This was a bold step for the Council, and an indicative one, since the Council well knew that it had the right only to make 'suggestions'. A few days later Milner's book, *England in Egypt*, appeared on the market. The book, an apologia for British occupation, advocated a permanent occupation, and succeeded in rousing a wave of indignation amongst the Egyptians, for this was the first time that such a policy had been openly advocated—and by someone who had served in the Egyptian government. It could thus represent only a semi-official view of the British government's intentions—or so the Egyptians supposed. Immediately following on this turmoil, Abbas tried to oust Mustafa Fahmi from power, and to name his own ministry. That Cromer had not anticipated.

What made Abbas think that he could get his own way? For ten years his father had been dominated by Cromer, who had virtually ruled Egypt. But the essence of the Veiled Protectorate, as Abbas realized, lay in the ruler's co-operation: every step planned by Cromer could be rendered legal only through the Khedive's acquiescence. Thus it seemed to the young and ideal-istic Khedive (for one must keep in mind Abbas's extreme youth) that it was possible for a progressive monarch to take over power. In theory this was feasible. Cromer had no legal authority in Egypt: theoretically Abbas could send all the British Advisers packing whenever he wished, for they were employed by him. Theoretically, too, he could make the British army evacuate Egypt, if the Powers backed him in a request of that nature. If Abbas could prove to England and Europe that he was firmly supported by his people, and was also capable of ruling them, then he could make England release her hold on Egypt. Or so he thought.

Abbas was encouraged in his supposition by several incidents.

In the first place, on October 3, 1891, Gladstone, in a speech at Newcastle, had said that the occupation of Egypt was 'burdensome and embarrassing' to England, and that he hoped Lord Salisbury would get rid of it before he went out of power. Dilke had made similar statements in the House. Salisbury's answer, given in his Guildhall speech on November 10, was that, even if Gladstone came to power, Britain would not relinquish its work in Egypt, and would stay until Egypt was strong enough to stand on its own. When a Liberal cabinet came to power in August 1892, Abbas believed in Gladstone's desire for evacuation. During an interview that he gave at that time to a newspaper correspondent named Francis Adams, Abbas told Adams that England had pledged her word to evacuate Egypt, and he trusted Britain's word, for a promise was a promise.[5]

In the second place, Abbas may have been encouraged by articles in the British press, such as one that appeared in the *Spectator* of January 16, 1892, which said that if Abbas dismissed or appointed any minister he liked, it would not be Britain's role to interfere. For though Cromer was entitled to offer the Khedive advice, and while that advice must be followed, yet the Khedive had a free hand with his ministers, Cromer's duty 'is to support the Khedive in doing any act not clearly an interference with the mission the Minister is seated in Cairo in order to fulfil'.

In the third place, Abbas was encouraged by his advisers, especially by Rouiller, to make a bid for independence. In his memoirs, Ahmad Shafiq, who served for a long time as the Khedive's Arabic Secretary, and was also his confidant, said that Rouiller had told him that he had promised Abbas that he would help him oust the British from his country.[6] When Rouiller arrived in Egypt with Abbas and saw the welcome which the Egyptians had prepared for their ruler, he assumed that it would be an easy matter to carry out plans for making the British evacuate Egypt, and he encouraged Abbas to plot along these lines.

Lastly, Abbas was encouraged from abroad by French statesmen, notably by Etienne Deloncle and the anti-British group in the *Chambre des Députés*, who led him to believe that, were he to come to grips with Britain, Egypt would be supported by France.

Although Britain had from 1892 a Liberal government and a Premier, Gladstone, who had repeatedly stressed his intention to evacuate Egypt, it also had a Foreign Secretary, Lord Rosebery, who was a confirmed imperialist. According to Sir Henry Ponsonby, the Queen's Secretary, Rosebery had accepted office on condition 'that he shall not be interfered with especially on the question of Egypt, or briefly that he will not abandon Egypt as many insist upon'.[7] Many Liberals would have preferred to evacuate Egypt in order to draw nearer to France; but Rosebery preferred to stay on, at the risk of continuing to antagonize France, and to depend on Germany instead. Had Abbas known more of the workings of English politics he might not have been so hopeful of success.

In his bid for power Abbas relied on two important pillars of support: the first was public opinion, and the second was the army. In order to impress public opinion, Abbas needed to show that he was capable of ruling; therefore he required an occasion whereby a change in the executive machinery could take place. No doubt he had a hand in the various rumours that were spread about concerning an impending change of ministry. Mustafa Fahmi had been worried over the rumours, and had even asked the Khedive about them, but the Khedive had brushed his fears aside. Then, fortuitously, Fahmi fell seriously ill towards the end of the year, and in view of the severity of his illness, Cromer went to discuss with the Khedive the possible need to appoint a new premier. Abbas chose to nominate the Christian Armenian, Tigrane Pasha, who had served as Minister of Foreign Affairs in Fahmi's ministry. Abbas had befriended Tigrane, who was a bit of a rake and had recently been involved in a duel over a lady; he knew that Tigrane, an active and enlightened man, was no puppet. Cromer, anticipating trouble in a ministry headed by such a man, disapproved of this choice, and suggested that a Muslim premier be appointed instead. When Abbas refused to give up his nominee, Cromer sent a telegram to Rosebery saying that Abbas was 'not in the slightest degree in touch with native opinion, which he does not understand . . . if you were to telegraph to me that the appointment would be unfavourably regarded by Her Majesty's Government, the probability is that it would not be made'.[8]

Rosebery in turn wired back: 'I agree that it would be advisable to have a Mohammedan, and to avoid Tigrane if possible. If the Khedive is bent on Tigrane, I would not push the opposition too far.'[9] But Cromer did not see any necessity for giving in to the Khedive; and on January 2 he wrote back to Rosebery saying that Tigrane 'was not in touch with the Egyptian people either by race, religion, language or habits of mind, and we could not but deem his appointment as prime minister most regrettable'.[10] Cromer went on to say that Tigrane was sure to pose as an 'Anglophobe' and would give England trouble, and that he was not really so capable as to warrant taking such a risk.

The basic reason for Cromer's disapproval of Tigrane was that he was an 'Anglophobe' or, rather, that he liked to pose as one, for it made him more popular with the Egyptians. It might, moreover, disrupt Cromer's administrative machine if Tigrane tried to govern Egypt according to his own lights, which were not necessarily Cromer's. In view of Cromer's second despatch, London expressed disapproval of Tigrane, but still in mild terms which did not completely veto his appointment. Abbas seemed unmoved by the British government's wishes, and Cromer was forced to conclude his next letter: 'I do not think the Khedive has acted under any outside influence. His attitude is entirely due to the desire to show his own independence and strength of character by appointing a minister who would be disapproved by almost every class in the country.'[11] This stress on Muslim disapproval of a Christian premier influenced the British cabinet, which was always susceptible to hints of an undercurrent of Muslim fanaticism; but it did not weigh with the native population. After all, Nubar (Tigrane's father-in-law, and another Christian) had twice been foisted on Egypt within the preceding ten years.

When the crisis had blown over, Cromer said that Tigrane's appointment was not objectionable on personal grounds, but because it was desirable that the premier of Egypt should be a Mohammedan;[12] yet Cromer himself had accepted Nubar as premier, and was to appoint him to that post again a year later in 1894.

Abbas was impervious to Cromer's argument that Tigrane's appointment would be disapproved by public opinion, and had merely replied: 'Quant à l'opinion indigène, je m'en charge.'[13] This answer greatly incensed Cromer, who immediately reported to Rosebery: 'It is absurd to suppose that any lad of 19 could seriously influence native public opinion. The Khedive, moreover, has none of the qualities necessary to the exercise of a predominant influence—he is not personally popular ... I can scarcely exaggerate the impression of complete ignorance of his country and of his countrymen which the Khedive's conversation leaves on my mind ... the truth is that the Khedive is absolutely callous to Egyptian public opinion.'[14]

Here Cromer was guilty of deliberate exaggeration, or, at best, of failing to gauge native feeling about the Khedive. Abbas was no more callous to Egyptian public opinion than Cromer himself. He was very popular personally with the people, and the fact that, although only nineteen years old, he was able to influence public opinion, was proved by subsequent events. Newspaper articles of the period were full of eulogy for the young ruler—a tribute that they had not paid his father. For the first time in over ten years, someone was opposing the British, someone who seemed eligible to rid the country of its foreign yoke. But Cromer refused to see matters in that light, and even maintained that native public opinion appreciated his efforts to get a Muslim premier appointed. Whereas public opinion actually thought the whole struggle with Cromer implied a depreciation in British prestige, and was delighted with the Khedive.*

Cromer felt strongly about this act of insubordination, because he rightly interpreted it as a struggle for power between himself and the Khedive. He told Rosebery that he had been tempted to threaten the Khedive with the removal of Tigrane from Egypt, on board a British ship of war, if the Khedive did not give up his

---

* Educated public opinion was relatively limited, since the literacy rate was only 10·5% for men and 0·3% for women according to the census of 1897 as reported in Cromer's yearly report for 1901, Cd. 441.

intention of nominating him, but that he had realized that this was too strong a measure to take.[15] 'The young Khedive is evidently going to give a great deal of trouble,' he wrote to Rosebery. 'He is an extremely foolish youth. It is difficult to know how to deal with him . . . I think he will have to receive a sharp lesson sooner or later—and the sooner the better. The difficulty consists in finding the proper occasion for giving him a lesson and the proper manner of giving it to him. I do not think persuasion will be of much avail . . . if the youth gets his head up in the air, and thinks he can do just as he pleases, things in general will go wrong here.'[16]

The last sentence pointed to the Khedive's real danger. If he was going to attempt to rule as well as reign, then he would put the Veiled Protectorate in jeopardy. Cromer talked the situation over with Tigrane, who, realizing how precarious his position as premier would be if he had to contend with Cromer's ill will, advised the Khedive against his own appointment. Meanwhile Mustafa Fahmi's health had taken a turn for the better; and as there seemed to be no immediate need for a new premier, the matter, as far as Cromer was concerned, was dropped. Rumour, as expressed in the long and illegible letters that Malortie (an Austrian adventurer-cum-author who had lived in Egypt for a long time and who was Director of the Press Bureau) scrawled to Milner, claimed that Abbas had been left with the impression that he could appoint whichever premier he pleased, so long as the man was a Muslim. This was confirmed by Cromer's saying that, 'with the exception of Tigrane Pasha, whom I do not wish to see named, it matters little whom the Khedive appoints.'[17]

Although Mustafa Fahmi was out of danger, Abbas was none the less determined to get rid of him, for he thought him weak and too pro-English for his liking.[18] His determination was strengthened when, on January 10, a police circular was sent round to the Governors of provinces, signed by Coles Pasha, the Head of the Police, and not, as it should have been, by the Egyptian Minister of the Interior. This usurpation was caustically commented upon both by *al-Ahram*, and by *Le Bosphore*

Egyptien. Here was the proof that Abbas needed for the weakness of Fahmi's cabinet.

Seizing on this event as an excuse for getting rid of Fahmi, Abbas sent on Januray 15 one of his men to ask Fahmi to resign, and to assure him of the Khedive's goodwill towards him. It was alleged that Fahmi refused to accept assurance of goodwill in exchange for his cabinet post, and expressed 'regret' at his inability to resign until he had consulted Lord Cromer.[19] This response so infuriated Abbas that he immediately dismissed Fahmi and appointed Fakhri Pasha, a former Minister of Justice who had previously come into conflict with Cromer, as Prime Minister. He also changed two other cabinet ministers, the Minister for Finance and the Minister for Justice, and then sent the news to Cromer. The act was as good as a coup d'état.

Needless to say, Cromer was indignant at this high-handed procedure, and at once sent a telegram to Rosebery saying: 'I have little doubt that the Khedive has taken this step in order to show his complete independence. I beg to refer to Lord Granville's despatch of January 4, 1884, on the subject of English advice being followed whilst the occupation lasts.' If the Khedive were allowed to act as he has done in this matter, said Cromer, the whole situation both of the English government and the English officials would be changed, and great trouble would ensue. 'I have very good reason for believing that the Khedive's present attitude is due in a great degree to the belief that I shall not be so fully supported by Her Majesty's present government as I was by the last government,'[20] he ended caustically.

Cromer's reading of the Khedive's motives was shrewd and correct. Cromer's proclaimed objections to the change of cabinet were that it was carried out without his being consulted, that it had happened because Fahmi was known to be pro-English, and that Fakhri was unfit to be a premier. The last two reasons were minor details. Fakhri had once been Minister of Justice, and had been dismissed because he had opposed Judge Scott's judicial reforms; therefore according to Cromer, he had 'shown himself to be unfit for office by his opposition to the policy of reform introduced into Egypt during the British Occupation'.[21] This was, however, only a pretext, for Nubar had resigned office over a similar issue, but was still considered worthy of office. Cromer's real objections to Fakhri's appointment were set out subsequently in a book he wrote in 1915: 'It was not so much the fact of his nomination, as the manner in which he had been nominated, which was open to objection. If the Khedive had consulted me previously I should not . . . have made any strong objections to his nominating Fakhri, or, indeed, any other Pasha. But the whole affair had been planned and executed without my being taken into council.'[22] It was also the chance to administer the lesson that Cromer felt the Khedive needed. Cromer was insistent that the Khedive be cowed there and then, so as to prevent future trouble in the shape of a European intervention. He warned Rosebery that 'unless we insist at whatever cost on the Khedive's yielding, the work of the last ten years in Egypt will be thrown away and we shall have an Egyptian question on our hands possibly more serious than any we have had before'.[23]

Rosebery's answer to the incident was a message sent on January 16, that 'Her Majesty's Government expect to be consulted in such important matters as a change of ministers. No change appears to be at present either necessary or desirable. We cannot therefore sanction the proposed nomination of Fakhri Pasha.'[24] The purpose of this message was to show the Khedive how little independence of action he was likely to be allowed by the Liberal cabinet. Yet Tawfiq had been allowed to dismiss his premiers, and there was never any question of consulting Cromer, perhaps for the simple reason that he only dismissed them after they had fallen out of favour with Cromer. Be that as it may, Tawfiq had established the precedent of dismissing his own ministers without previously obtaining Cromer's permission, and his son was, overtly, merely following the father's practice.

To improve on his argument of the imminent danger of foreign intervention, Cromer sent two further telegrams carrying the information that the incident had been managed in connivance with Turks acting on behalf of the Porte, and of the deposed Khedive, Ismail; that it was also pre-arranged with France and

Russia, and that if it proved successful, would be followed by the wholesale dismissal of British officers in the Egyptian government.[25] Ismail Pasha, the deposed Khedive who lived at Constantinople, was known to be constantly intriguing in an attempt to return to Egypt. Cromer knew that Abbas admired his grandfather, and suspected that they were both plotting together against Britain. He also suspected that Mukhtar Pasha Ghazi, who remained in Egypt as the Sultan's representative-cum-spy after the failure of the Drummond Wolff Convention, was involved in the plot. Thus the incident, from being an internal struggle for power, acquired international ramifications and subtle under-tones of intrigue on a grand scale. Or so the British government was led to suppose by Cromer's telegrams. Whether Cromer deliberately meant Rosebery to come to that conclusion is a matter for conjecture; but the references to the Sultan, France and Russia were sandwiched in between definite statements that the coup was the Khedive's own idea, and were sent by Cromer at a time when London did not seem likely to take any step other than Rosebery's telegram of disapproval. As a matter of fact, Rosebery had explicitly instructed Cromer to 'take no measures beyond communicating my telegram without referring back to me. What means of pressure do you possess and what steps do you propose to take in event of Khedive's refusal?'[26]

In answer, Cromer suggested that General Walker, Commander in Chief of the army of occupation, should take military possession of the Ministries of the Interior, Finance and Justice, to prevent the newly appointed ministers from entering their offices, and that the British Advisers in the Ministries in question should then take charge of the respective departments.[27] But Rosebery considered this suggestion 'too violent, and such as might constitute a breach of international law . . . and would necessarily lead to the intervention of the Powers'.[28] With this point of view Cromer begged to differ, for he had already sent British troops to the press which published the *Journal Officiel*, in order to prevent the decree appointing Fakhri from appearing in print. Although Cromer had asked the Khedive to withhold publication until he conferred with London, and the Khedive had assented to this request,

Cromer still did not trust him to keep his word, and sent a few soldiers to the press as an added precaution.

On January 18 Cromer was empowered by London to give the Khedive twenty-four hours in which to reconsider his answer to Rosebery's telegram of January 16. The Khedive sent for both Riaz and Nubar and asked their advice. Riaz advised the Khedive not to yield, while Nubar told him to give in. The following day the Khedive capitulated. He dismissed Fakhri, or rather, allowed him to resign; and both he and Cromer agreed on appointing Riaz as Prime Minister. Furthermore Cromer extracted a verbal promise from the Khedive that in future he would follow the British government's advice on all important matters—a promise which was not kept.

The crisis was over, but who had won the round? In spite of the fact that the Khedive had had to bow to British pressure, yet he and the Egyptian public considered the whole affair a victory. The press spoke of Abbas in most flattering terms. And even the British Consul in the Delta reported that the action of the Khedive was openly approved without reserve, and the highest hopes were now entertained that the country would soon be rid of the English.[29]

Cromer's blood boiled, for he realized that his lesson had been worse than useless. He therefore asked the British government to increase the garrison in Egypt. 'I understand that Riaz Pasha has recently taken a strong religious turn,' he wrote to Rosebery a day after Riaz had been appointed, in justification for his request. 'This would predispose him to fanaticism and opposition to Europeans . . . the ultra Mohammedan press is very violent and mischievous . . . General Walker and I both think the British garrison is not sufficiently strong';[30] and he urgently recommended that it be increased in size. Cromer's message to Rosebery contained two of the bogeys calculated to frighten the British government most: the threat of a fanatical uprising, and its support by the Egyptian army. This could not fail to conjure up an image of the Indian Mutiny, or even of the Alexandria riots.

The necessity for the adoption of Cromer's suggestion was rendered more acute by his adding, 'from all I hear I have no doubt that the sympathies of the Egyptian army are with the Khedive. It appears that all the young officers are in favour of Egypt for the Egyptians.'[31] Even Riaz had thrown in his lot with the Khedive; for he claimed that the latter had gained immensely in popular esteem by his recent conduct, and that all the Egyptians were now behind him—'so far as the Pasha class are concerned this is probably true',[32] added Cromer ruefully. But the Pasha class was not the only one supporting the Khedive, for there were popular demonstrations by students, and by the populace who unhorsed his carriage when he went to prayers on Friday at the Sayidna al-Husayn mosque, and pulled it themselves; while on January 20 there were hostile demonstrations in front of the offices of *Al-Muqattam*, the Agency's mouthpiece. 'It was probably got up by the Khedive, or his surroundings,'[33] commented Cromer, and he may well have been right. But it showed the new spirit abroad, for ten years ago nobody would have dared behave in such a fashion.

Cromer's request for more troops was unwelcome to two members of the cabinet, Gladstone and Harcourt. Gladstone said that they might as well ask him to put a torch to Westminster Abbey as to send more troops to Egypt.[34] Harcourt, just as violently, said; 'We are now able to understand what Lord Cromer means by "at all cost", viz. a conflict with France. The means that he proposes is a military coup d'état by England . . . that amounts to the annexation of Egypt . . . and is an entire breach of the European understanding on which our occupation rests.'[35] But Rosebery was determined to back Cromer, although he was annoyed by Cromer's 'tumultuous storm of sinister telegrams that rained on the Foreign Office.'[36] But he felt that the moment was not yet wholly propitious for such a serious move as an increase of garrison, unless there was sufficient reason. So he asked Cromer if he expected any disturbance of public order, for only such a contingency would justify the despatch of troops to Egypt. Cromer answered: 'If no fresh political incident occurs I think any disturbance is improbable, but in the present frame of mind of the Khedive and his ministers not only have I no confidence that he will not create any fresh incident but I think there is a great probability unless timely measures are taken that he will do so.'[37] He then added that an Egyptian friend of his had remarked that the whole incident savoured of the Urabi movement, except that it had the Khedive at its head.

Thereupon Rosebery threatened the cabinet with resignation unless Cromer got his troops, and a stormy cabinet meeting followed, with Harcourt, Morley and Gladstone strongly against the move. 'If Rosebery stuck to his agent, Cromer, the government would inevitably break up',[38] was Harcourt's estimate of the situation. Naturally this was unthinkable, and West, Gladstone's private secretary, had to do much canvassing to get various members to change their minds. West was convinced of the wisdom of sending troops to Egypt because he had been much impressed by Cromer's messages about the Egyptian army and its loyalty towards the Khedive, and the inadequacy of the British garrison if action became necessary. Morley would not consent to an additional regiment because he said that he distrusted Cromer. West then replied that the government was bound to support Cromer, or recall him, and was it 'worth while to throw up Home Rule for this?'[39] As usual, Ireland was again used as a makeweight. After all, continued West, 'all Cromer's messages tended to evacuation afterwards'—a sop to the conscience of the ministers which seemed to work. Eventually West talked Gladstone round to his point of view, and Rosebery got his way. Whereupon West commented that 'Cromer had no doubt lost his head, but my view was that he must be supported'.[40] Cromer was informed that 'in view of the recent occurrences which threatened to disturb public security in Egypt',[41] he could have his increase in the British garrison.

But had Cromer indeed lost his head, or had he merely chosen the argument best calculated to influence the British government into following the line of conduct that he desired? Fear of an outbreak of fanatical violence was largely Cromer's invention. Rather the other way about, the native press, which Cromer claimed was violent and virulent, abounded in exhortations to the Egyptians to avoid giving the Europeans any provocation. For if England remembered the Indian Mutiny, Egypt remembered the Alexandria riots and their after-effects. A specific article that Cromer castigated as 'very violent', one written by Abdallah Nadim in *al-Ustadh*, was the very article that warned people to beware of a second Alexandria, to treat the Europeans as well as possible, to put their faith in the Khedive, and to let him handle politics while they went peacefully about their business.[42] In fact the article was so moderate that it was reprinted in the pro-British *al-Muqattam*. But 'fanatical outbreak' was always an effective plea. Cromer was determined that the Khedive should not be allowed to score a victory over him—the Khedive was to be forced by all available means into an awareness that his country was occupied by a foreign army, and that he was not the sole ruler of Egypt.

On the other hand, the Egyptians, convinced that the Khedive had won the duel, were ready to minimize the importance of the incoming troops, and it was rumoured that when Riaz was informed of their impending arrival, his sole comment was a sarcastic one: 'Les soldats Anglais se sont toujours si bien conduit qu'on a toujours plaisir à les voir.'

The incident had considerable repercussions on the international level. France viewed it in the light of an attempt by England to show Europe that it claimed the right to nominate Egypt's ministers. This was the interpretation put on the incident and communicated by her Ambassador in London, Waddington, to Rosebery. Rosebery replied that England merely claimed the right to give authoritative advice as to the choice of ministers.[43] This answer did not satisfy France, and the French Ambassador formally objected again to the action taken by Lord Cromer with regard to the nomination of Fakhri Pasha as Prime Minister in Egypt. Furthermore, France objected to the 'high-handed nature of the proceedings' as an event 'unprecedented in the history of the Occupation ... one which went far beyond the terms of Lord Granville's despatch', and would, His Excellency feared, 'be taken throughout Europe, as in France, to be a long step in the direction of actual annexation'.[44]

In another letter, Waddington told Rosebery that the French government 'believed that the Khedive had been moved to this serious action by irritation at hearing that Lord Cromer had assured Mustafa Fahmi of his support even against the Khedive, his master'.[45] Cromer's reply to this was terse: there is 'no foundation to such an allegation'.[46] But it is interesting to note that Baron Malortie, who played the part of a Mme. de Sevigné with his letters to Milner, claimed that Cromer had sent Hardinge, the First Secretary, to Mustafa Fahmi to assure him that he had Cromer's support if he wanted to continue in his position as premier. But Fahmi had turned down this generous offer with the remark that his position would become untenable in such circumstances.[47]

Turkey was also much disturbed over the incident, especially when Mukhtar Pasha Ghazi (the Turkish Commissioner) advised the Sultan to take action, otherwise the Khedive would be deposed by the British. The Sublime Porte immediately sent back a message: 'L'Angleterre n'a aucun pouvoir ni de le réprimander ni de le congédier et de l'éloigner de l'Egypte. Sans le consentement des Grandes Puissances, l'Angleterre ne saurait établir en Egypte un nouvel état de choses.'[48] Brave words: but the Sultan had, first, to sound out the Powers and see with which party to a dispute, if dispute there was to be, they would side. Berlin, Vienna and Rome all said that they would side with England, and the Sultan was left with France—a weak reed in the face of such opposition. The Sultan then decided to play his usual game, and do nothing. The odds were too high, and he could not afford to antagonize England.

The end result of the coup was that although, on the international level, some fuss was made, nothing concrete occurred; on the local level, the population became more pronouncedly anti-British and pro-Khedive, as even Cromer was forced to admit. It would seem then that the Khedive was fully justified in saying that he could take care of public opinion in Egypt. Even though he was only nineteen years old, he emerged from his struggle with sixty-year-old Cromer as a courageous patriot, in the eyes of his people. From then on they regarded him as a leader at the head of a reawakened nationalist movement.

Cromer, not unnaturally, viewed the whole incident with pessimism. On January 30 he wrote Lord Rosebery a long despatch, in which he set forth his views of the situation in Egypt. He said that the Khedive would not be easily intimidated, or yield to

Mustapha Kamil

Dr Ahmad Lutfi al-Sayyid

Saad Zaghlul Pasha, at his country residence outside Cairo

threats, and that though he was a 'well-mannered youth with a very respectable private life, he was extremely arbitrary, vindictive and untruthful'. As for the Egyptians, 'when once their sentiments of religious animosity and to some extent of patriotism are evoked, considerations based on material interests are almost certain to be thrown temporarily in the background . . . the whole machine has now to a great extent slipped out of my hands . . . I do not feel the least confidence that I can control the Khedive, and it is on his action that the development of future events mainly depends.'[49] He added that, given the situation, they must either withdraw the British garrison and relax English administrative control; or accentuate interference, and devise some means for coercing the Khedive in case of need. In the first contingency, the evacuation of Egypt would mean a fulfilment of England's pledges to Europe, and would avoid the serious risk of trouble with France. England would get rid of a heavy and irksome responsibility, and avoid the odium of forcing on the people of Egypt a foreign rule which would be represented as hateful to them, and which, in reality, was hateful to certain classes amongst them.

As for the arguments against evacuation, these were the usual ones, that all the reforms would be wrecked, and the dervishes would invade Egypt from the Sudan; and since Egypt was too important to Europe to be left alone, France would not hesitate to step into British shoes once Egypt was evacuated.

The pivot of the situation was the Khedive, concluded Cromer; if he were removed from power, all the difficulties would disappear. Cromer hastened to add that he was not advocating that the Khedive be deposed, for he had not, as yet, done anything to call for such a drastic step; but such a contingency had to be envisaged, and the British government had best be prepared for it—an argument which evoked memories of Malet's despatches with respect to Urabi.

In another long despatch, the same plea was repeated. Cromer had been put out by Abbas; he had been forced to interfere openly before Europe. This was the greatest sin, for although the Egyptians well knew who was governing Egypt, Europe had been lulled by Britain's discreet administration. But now 'the reality which before was only known to a few behind the scenes, becomes patent to all the world. This is enough to shatter the system. I fear we must devise something else. We must either go backwards and withdraw from the country, or forwards and assert ourselves more strongly than heretofore . . . The worst course of all is to drift on without any positive idea of what we want.'[50]

Rosebery agreed with Cromer that the Khedive's recent acts aimed a blow at the whole basis of the occupation, and that if the Khedive had his way, it might preclude a return to a life of tyranny and anarchy, when all thought of reforms would be forgotten. Therefore 'England had to force the Khedive's hand in order to bring reform to Egypt'.[51] And yet the whole basis of the occupation according to the Dufferin report had originally been a desire to restore 'the stability of the Khedive's authority, and for the judicious development of self-government'. But in spite of Dufferin's statement that the British government did not propose arbitrarily to impose its views on Egypt, or to hold her in an irritating tutelage, and in spite of her ruler and her people, Egypt after all was to have British rule and reforms imposed on her.

The device of rousing Europe's fear of a massacre of the Christians by fanatical Muslims was especially effective at the moment when the Armenian massacres of 1894 were taking place in Turkey. Without taxing the imagination, public opinion in England could be led to fear the same happenings in Egypt. Here was a convenient excuse for justifying the occupation. Cromer had no compunction about playing on this fear, sometimes with ludicrous results. Thus on March 25, 1895, he sent a despatch reporting on an alleged secret society called the Muslim Benevolent Society, which aimed at 'promulgating pan-Islamic views, and notably to drive the English out of Egypt'.[52] This society had the following pashas amongst its members: Riaz, Mahir, Mazlum, Shawarbi, Saad Zaghlul, al-Hilbawi, al-Sharif, al-Minshawi, Fakhri—a list of the names of all the rich and prominent pashas in Egypt. A few days later the bubble burst, and it was discovered that the man who had supplied the Agency with the information was a crook. The society, founded by Shaykh Muhammad Abduh, and which indeed had all the men listed as members, along with an impressive list of Egyptian notables, was exactly what it claimed to be—a charitable organization. But rather than wait until he made sure of the veracity of this damaging information, Cromer, a prudent man in most things, seems to have had no hesitation in reporting such alleged pan-Islamic intrigue as soon as he heard of it.

The lesson administered to the Khedive had not been sufficiently sharp to deflect him from his original plan, the more so when the Khedive saw how popular his acts were amongst his people. Cromer was apt to blame Abbas for arousing Egyptian public opinion into expressing antagonism towards England, but this antagonism had always been latent. It only needed strong stimulus in order to come into the open. Wingate, as Director of Military Intelligence, appreciated this, and said: 'We have to deal with a turbulent and headstrong youth—the foreign backing still continues and the boy has got his head turned by the popular adulation he receives on all sides—I believe he goes as far as to say that if he does not get his way he will abdicate . . . the native press and public opinion is just as strong now as it was in the midst of the crisis in applauding His Highness' action.'[53] More important, Wingate was aware that the Khedive had succeeded in gaining the affection of the Egyptian army, and indeed, he added, why should it be otherwise?

The first step towards the new, more stringent policy, was taken in the matter of the attendance of the British Advisers in the cabinet councils. Under Tawfiq the practice had been that the Adviser attended cabinet meetings on invitation, and sat in during that part of the discussion relative to his department. For example, Scott attended the council only when judicial matters were discussed; Grenfell, the Sirdar prior to Kitchener, attended only when the Prime Minister presided at the Council, or else at the special invitation of the Khedive when he himself presided; Scott-Moncrieff, of the Public Works department, was the only one who attended the whole cabinet meeting, but only when the Prime Minister presided. In March 1893, Cromer reported a change in this procedure. The Ministers of Justice, War and

Public Works were now under an obligation to show to each of the English functionaries concerned any proposal which they were sending up for discussion in Council. The Advisers could express a wish to be present at the discussion, and the President of the Council was then under obligation to invite to the Council the official concerned. The English officials were also to be present when any draft of a law or regulation was discussed which concerned their own department, even if not instigated by it. Should any discussion take place without the presence of the British Adviser, and on a matter in which he was concerned, then, added Cromer, 'I should be obliged to condemn it as null and void.'[54] More changes were to follow, but these came after another series of incidents had occurred.

By now anti-English feelings had increased so noticeably that Anglo-Egyptian officials commented on it. Garstin, the head of the Public Works department, wrote to Milner: 'There is no doubt that the anti-English feeling is spreading and increasing. Even with us [in the irrigation department] it is becoming more difficult to carry out measures.'[55] This was just what the Khedive wanted, in order to render England's stay in Egypt too uncomfortable to maintain.

Wingate once more wrote to Milner: 'You have no notion how completely changed are the relations between the Egyptian and English officials. Personally I confess to having lost sympathy with the Egyptian and can it be wondered at when he looks askance or obstructs everything we do to try and help him—we have created a huge Frankenstein and now we must do our best to stifle the monster.'[56]

That was how the rising nationalist movement was regarded, but the monster was not to be stifled so easily. The native press urged Egyptians to rally in support of the Khedive, but warned them that their aims could only be achieved through peaceful means, through patience and moderation.

In July 1893, the Khedive went on a visit to Constantinople, and there were various rumours that he intended to request the Sultan to send a Turkish garrison to take over from the British army. Several delegations of *ulama* and notables followed the

Khedive to Constantinople, some at the Khedive's instigation, others on their own initiative, to show the Sultan how solidly public opinion stood behind the Khedive. Gossip, reported by the ubiquitous Malortie, claimed that when Cromer heard the rumour of the Khedive's desire for a Turkish garrison, he pronounced himself not averse to such a plan so long as England kept control of the finances; and added that it would serve Egypt right, since he did not see why England should continue to sacrifice herself for such an ungrateful people.[57] Although what sacrifice was involved was not clear to the Egyptians, since they even paid the cost of the army of occupation.

The Sultan did not give the Khedive much encouragement, but Abbas was planning more trouble. There followed a series of minor disturbances that culminated in the 'frontier incident'. The first of these minor skirmishes came from the Legislative Council, that normally self-effacing organ. In December an article appeared in the *Bosphore Egyptien* accusing a member of the Legislative Council of reporting to Cromer the decisions of that body, which were meant to be secret. Ali Pasha Sharif, the President of the Council, was constrained by his colleagues to go round to Cromer and ask him if Shaykh al-Bakri, the member in question, had indeed been telling tales. Cromer, who had been expecting such a visit, informed Sharif that it was contrary to the rules of diplomatic procedure for him (Cromer) to communicate directly with Ali Pasha Sharif, but that he would give his answer through the official channel of the Minister of Foreign Affairs, Tigrane Pasha. Cromer then sent a strongly worded letter to Tigrane, and inquired whether it was customary for the Egyptian government to investigate his private affairs, and, stressing the complete liberty of any individual to visit him, he declined to give any information as to his visitors' topics of conversation. Tigrane had no recourse but to write him a letter of apology.

The incident was a slight one, but it was indicative of the line that the Legislative Council meant to take.

The next incident was also instigated in the Legislative Council. The Council had ordered a commission to report on the 1894 budget, and the commission had presented a report which contained such provocative sentences as: 'Les Egyptiens sont dans un état de pauvreté et de gène qui tend à augmenter d'un jour à l'autre,' because of excessive taxation—when it was Cromer's boast that taxation had been greatly reduced. On the basis of the items investigated in the report, the Council decided not to approve the item on the budget paying the expenses of the army of occupation.[58] This was another way of saying that they wanted Britain to go.

Cromer suggested to Rosebery that someone should be put up in the House of Lords to ask a question relating to that report; and that the British government's answer should be that—as the Legislative Council was mainly composed of government nominees —it was not an altogether independent body, and that one need not attach as much importance to it as if it were a really representative organ.* In the House of Commons, Gladstone said that the Council represented the opinion of private individuals, and was not representative of Egypt. Yet was not this the organ that Dufferin had assured the British Government was to represent the most intelligent men in the country, was to represent the 'strong and almost irresistible force of public opinion', and was to satisfy Egypt as an organ of representative opinion? In private, Cromer was upset by the incident and wrote to Rosebery that 'the Egyptian government backed by an Assembly, which although not representative of the whole country, does really represent some influential classes, has publicly and officially declared that they want us to go, and all this is done under the inspiration of an inexperienced headstrong boy of no particular talent, who would probably not be able to maintain himself in power for six months without our assistance.'[59]

That this incident rankled in Cromer's mind can be deduced from the way the subsequent episode of suspected slavery was handled. In August 1894, Ali Pasha Sharif, the President of the Legislative Council, and Shawarbi Pasha, a rich notable, were accused of buying slaves and were to be tried by a court martial.

* B.P., Cromer to Rosebery, December 17, 1893. The council had eighty members of whom sixteen were elected by the Provincial Councils, and the rest were nominated by the Government.

Both Pashas denied the accusations, and, as a complication, Ali Pasha Sharif, in a fit of panic, claimed to be an Italian national, in order to benefit by the Capitulations. Ali Pasha's defection from Egyptian nationality created a tremendous scandal. Cromer, who was away on leave at the time, was informed of the facts of the case, and was asked what should be done. His answer was that he could understand that a Pasha of the old school could not be made to see why he should not buy slaves, and could not really be expected to understand the ramifications of the Slave Act, especially as buying a slave was, in Islam, considered tantamount to a good deed, since it freed the slave from the clutches of the slaver. But, added Cromer from his pinnacle, the law must be respected, and an example must be made of these culprits. He added: 'The episode will discredit the Legislative Council, which, considering all things, is perhaps not a bad thing, for they thoroughly deserved to be discredited.'[60] And yet, two years earlier, in his yearly report for 1892, he had said that, 'what they [the Legislative Council] most of all require for the time being is a little sympathy and encouragement'. But that, of course, was before the Council had shown its opposition to Cromer. Dare one assume that this was one way of punishing the Council for its insubordination, especially since Cromer knew that no actual evidence could be produced to inculpate the Pashas, and that they would be pronounced innocent by the court? The trial was allowed to proceed, and it discredited the Pashas, as it was meant to do. Ali Pasha Sharif's cowardly action in claiming foreign protection killed him politically, and almost physically, for the shock brought on a stroke. He had to throw himself on the clemency of the court, which dropped the case.

The last of the series in Abbas' policy of calculated pinpricks came in January 1894, when the Khedive tried his hand with the army, while on a tour of inspection of the frontier posts. During the tour he was accompanied by Mahir Pasha, Under Secretary of State for War, who was regarded somewhat suspiciously as a potential trouble-maker and Anglophobe. Kitchener, the Sirdar, was particularly suspicious of Mahir, for they had once quarrelled, and had since remained on bad terms. During a large parade of

troops at Wadi Halfa, the Khedive made some disparaging remarks to Kitchener concerning the performance of the troops.
Abbas was alleged to have said: 'To tell you the truth, Kitchener
Pasha, I think it is disgraceful for Egypt to be served by such an
army.'[61] Kitchener at once tendered his resignation. The Khedive
was taken aback and asked Kitchener to withdraw his resignation,
since nothing personal was meant by the remark. After some
discussion, Kitchener withdrew his resignation, but sent a telegram to Cromer with full details of the event, and added that the
Khedive had embarked on a deliberate policy of belittling the
English officers, and praising the native ones.

On the last day of the tour, Kitchener asked the Khedive to
say something to the officers that would minimize the effect of
his unfavourable remarks to them; but the Khedive categorically
refused, saying that it was his army and he had every right to
criticize it. Kitchener then said that the British officers, *en masse*,
might see fit to resign from the Egyptian army, and that he,
Kitchener, would not be able to find others to serve in their place.
Under this implied threat, the Khedive answered that the matter
would then create a stir in Cairo, and left it at that.[62]

Cromer, who had been waiting to give the Khedive a much
sharper lesson than the last, immediately seized the chance now
offered. 'This,' he said, 'was the opportunity for which I had been
waiting . . . the Khedive richly deserved to be punished.'[63] He
claimed that the Khedive, by his actions, was seeking to undermine the authority of the British officers in the army, and that this
would lead to a mutiny such as had occurred under Ismail Pasha;
that, in fact, it meant nothing less than an attempt at inciting the
army to insurrection. Cromer had exaggerated the importance of
the incident because he was bent on cowing the Khedive; but he
also set great store by the army, and felt that the British officers
were the sole guarantee against chaos in the country, in the event
of any outbreak of violence. In later days he accused the Khedive
of constantly making a 'number of frivolous and often impertinent
complaints against British officers'.[64] Though the term impertinent
was hardly the correct one to use in referring to a monarch's
criticism of the officers in his own army—even if they were

British officers; yet it was an indication of the degree of importance that Cromer gave them. The Khedive was requested to make reparation to the army on pain of dethronement.

A letter from Rosebery informed the Egyptian government that 'it has become the practice of His Highness to inflict slights on British officers ... should His Highness refuse to give just satisfaction, it will become incumbent on Her Majesty's government to consider stringent measures which will place the Egyptian army under more direct control and which will protect British officers from injurious treatment'.[65] Moreover, he added, the various incidents which had formed the subject of the recent conflicts would then be published in order that the true facts of the situation should be made known in England. 'I can scarcely doubt that publication would produce a deep effect on English public opinion.' This threat of the effect of the Khedive's actions on British public opinion implied that it might then demand that the British government annex Egypt or declare a protectorate over it, in view of the Khedive's lack of co-operation. The reparations which Cromer was instructed to propose were that the Khedive should publish an order of the day in commendation of the army, especially of the British officers, and that Mahir Pasha be dismissed from office.

In Fayyum, the Khedive (who had not been informed of the furore that he had raised) was met by a distraught Riaz, who, according to the Egyptian version, pleaded with the Khedive on bended knees to accede to the British government's demands. The Khedive gave in, but he never forgave Riaz for his pusillanimity, and he never forgave Kitchener. Once again Abbas was foiled by Cromer, and to his chagrin was let down by his own government. Some of the men in his entourage had urged him to follow that policy and had assured him that he would be fully supported by everybody; yet at this moment of real need for support by a response from Cairo, none was forthcoming, and his government were the first to ask him to retract. He thereby learnt that the army, like the government, was not his own, and that he had little authority over it. More important, and for the first time, he was threatened, by implication, with an upsurge of

British public opinion against him which might demand his deposition for his apparent persecution of British officers. Had the Khedive been threatened by *Egyptian* public opinion it would not have been so serious, but the fact that he was threatened by the *British* public was an indication of the relationship which England bore towards Egypt. And when he was forced to publish a commendatory order of the day, many of the army officers, and of the elite among the Egyptians, realized that he did it under constraint. They wondered, as did Abbas himself, whether he was a 'monkey on a stick to dance to the British Consul-General's tune?'*

After the frontier incident, relations between Abbas and Riaz were strained, and on April 14, 1894, the cabinet resigned, and Nubar was chosen as Prime Minister. He eventually proved to be too pro-British for the Khedive's liking, and the latter decided to remove him from office. The Khedive bluntly informed Palmer, the Financial Adviser, that Nubar was to go because 'il est bon pour vous, mais il n'est pas bon pour nous'.[66] Dawkins, Palmer's assistant, who recounted the incident to Milner in a letter, added that it had been rumoured that when that remark was reported to Cromer, he decided to send a telegram to the British government proposing that, should the Khedive persist in his evil ways, he should be deposed. He had then hinted to Nubar that if he made a stand against the Khedive, he would be backed. For some reason, Nubar refused the offer, and the telegram was never sent. Dawkins commented that 'the experiment of governing Egypt through this Khedive is not succeeding. There seems no doubt that he is resolutely hostile to us, and that his inactivity and passive acquiescence during the last few months is to be exchanged for an active campaign.' Then Dawkins went on to ask Milner what the position would be in England, and internationally, if Abbas were deposed—adding that the great difficulty lay in the fact that the Khedive had given no good ostensible cause for strong measures. 'If he would do something outrageous, English, and possibly European opinion, would justify us in deposing him.

* Abbas was alleged to have complained to Valentine Chirol in these terms, *Fifty Years in a Changing World*, London: 1927, p. 45.

But he won't . . . you will see that the position is a very difficult one, but that a crisis may break out at any moment, and that what is badly wanted is some light as to the support which could be got out of the Ministry from a vigorous policy. Can you give some?'[67]

This illuminating letter received the following reply from Milner: 'People here are thoroughly sick of Abbas, who has lost all sympathy, and beyond this, they are prepared for and would welcome any decided action in Egypt which would put an end to the present melancholy impasse. A bold act of usurpation, if forced, or even if only apparently forced on you, would be instantly condoned, and even applauded by almost everybody here. The only thing needful is that there should be, or seem to be, a state of things sufficiently critical to justify it. Disturbances at Alexandria, even if they are not very bad disturbances, are quite good enough and they have the additional advantage of frightening the European "colonies" [residents], the most timorous aggregations of human beings in the world, and inducing them and their governments to look leniently on any action which may avert the danger, largely imaginary, of a repetition of the events of 1882.' Milner added that the Foreign Office was irresolute and cowardly and that it would be vain to ask it for permission to depose the Khedive. As for France, though it might bark, it would not bite. If, however, 'a coup d'état became necessary, I suppose the thing would be a deposition and a provisional government by a native Ministry entirely in our hands . . . or an English "Ministry of Affairs" under Palmer, consisting of him, Kitchener, Scott, Garstin, Gorst and you . . . I am not advising a *coup*. All I say is, if you are driven to it, and don't bungle it too hopelessly on the spot, which you will not, there is nothing to be afraid of. But the lead must come from you. Never in my recollection was everybody here so willing to accept that lead. Cromer's prestige is immense, and if he was convinced that a bold stroke was necessary and acted upon his convictions, he would have nine-tenths of the English public of all parties behind him.'[68]

This interesting correspondence is revealing as to the British Adviser's attitude towards Egypt. It is couched in the proprietary

tone of people with vested interests, and not in the tone of dis-
interested advisers. Neither man was in the slightest degree
affected by any effect the deposition might have on the Egyptians
(which, to judge by their silence on the point, did not seem to
matter); but both were preoccupied with the effect it would have
on Britain and Europe. It clearly reveals the change, in British
eyes, that had occurred in Egypt's status, from that of a sovereign
state to a British dependency. It also underlined how convenient
was the sabre-rattling device constituted by fear of a European
massacre. Cromer had already sounded the British Government
several times on deposition, but had received no satisfactory
answer to his inquiries, so could not follow Milner's advice;
while the Khedive was shrewd enough to realize how precarious
his position was becoming, and to refrain from pushing Cromer
too far.

The Nubar incident finally ended in a telegram from Rosebery
informing the Khedive, through Cromer, that there were no
grounds to justify any change in the present Egyptian ministry,
and that Nubar's removal from office at present would be regarded
by the British government, not merely as a wanton blow to good
government in Egypt, but as a measure practically directed
against Great Britain. 'If, therefore, a change does take place, His
Highness must be prepared to take the consequences, which may
be of a more serious nature than he imagines . . . Your Lordship
should let the Khedive understand clearly that he has to deal with
the British government, and not with his government only.'[69]

Thus within three years of his accession, in 1895, Abbas found
British rule in Egypt changing from covert to overt. The British
Advisers, no longer made to act in the background through the
ministers, now had a seat in Cabinet Councils. The Khedive could
neither appoint nor dismiss his ministers without British consent,
on pain of dethronement; neither was he allowed to exert any
influence on the army. Abbas was shorn of all power, and did not
even have that support which Cromer had given his father. Moreover, he constantly laboured under threat of deposition. Fully
realizing the precariousness of his position, from 1895 onwards
Abbas pursued his pinprick policy against England through the

medium of other people, young journalists who were placed in a less vulnerable position than he was.

The antagonism between Cromer and Abbas was more than just a political struggle for power between two different countries; it had all the hallmarks of a clash of personalities as well. Cromer was an autocrat by nature. 'Whiggery, inborn and confirmed by his career, convinced him of his right to lead';[70] and his ten years of unopposed rule in Egypt, added to his years in India, had not diminished this belief—especially since, with age, an inevitable hardening of the arteries occurs. This hardening became apparent to Cromer's subordinates and colleagues by 1904, when it became increasingly more difficult for them to convince him of such straightforward matters as the nomination of a candidate for a position. The habitual and established methods of doing things became, with time, the only conceivable way, and any opposition, which at an earlier age might have been given due consideration, at sixty was regarded with intolerance and irritation—the more so when it originated from a youth of nineteen.

Cromer had always been a difficult man to deal with, as his nicknames indicated. 'His air of conscious superiority and his habitual disinclination for small talk made him appear somewhat difficult to approach.'[71] His manners were often brusque and abrupt, and—as most of his colleagues testified—he could be very stern. These characteristics were not likely to endear him to a young and similarly imperious person such as was Abbas. In Egypt, the British government had entrusted Cromer with an important mission, that of restoring Egypt from the after-effects of a revolution. This he had done; furthermore he had restored Egypt's finances, and given her prosperity. At the same time that Egypt's condition improved materially, her political importance to England increased, and so did England's determination to prolong the occupation, so that Cromer's position acquired a quasi-permanent status that was different from that of the early days of uncertainty. The longer he stayed in Egypt, the more attached he grew to his position, and the more he felt that he could improve Egyptian affairs. As Salisbury put it: 'If the world was falling to pieces around his ears, but Egypt was left intact,

Lord Cromer would not ask for more.'[72] This affection for Egypt, and for his accomplishments in Egypt, was the source of Cromer's resentment against Abbas. For here, he thought, was an upstart, questioning the established methods that he had devised, aiming at changing the order of things, and thereby posing a threat, both to Cromer's position, and to the reforms which had become his life's work. Thus Cromer could only regard Abbas in the light of an obstructionist who would revert to an autocratic and tyrannous rule if he were given a free hand in Egypt.

His resentment against Abbas increased as he blamed him for the rise of anti-British feeling in Egypt. 'He is really making himself impossible, and I cannot help thinking that his deposition sooner or later is inevitable,' he wrote to Kimberley, the Foreign Secretary. 'He is an incorrigible youth, and is the sole originator of all the trouble in the country.'[73] And again: 'If we have another serious flare up, the deposition question will very likely be forced on us.'[74] Complaints poured forth against the Khedive. From being a 'very gentlemanlike and healthily minded boy', Abbas had now become a 'true successor of Ananias'—irresponsible, tyrannical, crooked and incapable of telling the truth. Cromer went so far as to write: 'The Khedive plays with lunatics and is scarcely sane himself according to his doctor.'[75]

Cromer had never seen Abbas in his true light, as a young man eager to try his wings, but who saw himself baulked at every step by a domineering foreigner. Too early in his reign Abbas had been shown the iron fist in the velvet glove by Cromer; but ten years of experience with Tawfiq had worn the velvet thin, so that too much iron showed through. There was unwisdom in such treatment, for it only made the young, crowned king see the old, uncrowned king in the role of the wicked step-mother in the fairy tale, who had to be destroyed before the young prince could become free. In his turn, Abbas's extreme youth, coupled with his pretensions to authority, rankled with Cromer, who scarcely ever referred to him save as 'a self opinionated boy of an arbitrary disposition',[76] or as a 'petulant boy',[77] or a 'foolish youth'.[78] The rest of the British colony in Egypt soon followed Cromer's lead, and referred to the Khedive in the same disparaging terms. This eventually reached Abbas's ears, and did nothing to endear the English to him.

Abbas's upbringing in the Theresianum was not calculated to teach him to bow to authority—especially an authority that had usurped his power. Thus the two autocrats could not fail to clash. Unfortunately for Abbas, Cromer was too strong for him as a person. Backed by the British government and its growing interests in Egypt, Cromer won the battle for supremacy, and the Khedive had no recourse but to intrigue against Cromer and hope to effect changes by this indirect method. In this process, he came to encourage the rise of a nationalist movement, and secretly recruited young men into forming an articulate opposition to Britain in Egypt through the press. In March 1894, a young British official in the Ministry of Finance wrote to Milner: 'As I wrote to you after the first "incident" of a year ago, a national party does exist, its members are the young and educated, their intentions are pacific, they mean to make the most of our presence here to learn all they can from us, the better to run their country themselves when left to themselves. They are by no means ripe yet: but no one can blame their aspiration, and no Englishman especially for we are here ostensibly to lead them to such an end; but will their dream ever be realized?'[79] We are not likely to know to what specific group he was referring, for many such groups were growing in Egypt; and, among the young and the educated, the Khedive served as an example of the true patriot. Later, they were to change their opinion of him; but for the time being any nationalist aspirant saw his fortunes bound to those of the Khedive.

Abbas, though young and tyrannical, was also intelligent, and a capable administrator who could have worked constructively for Egypt had he been given the chance, or had he been surrounded by different advisers than those he had, and so followed a different line of conduct. Cromer estimated that 'the Khedive if he knew it, is in reality much more master of the situation than he imagines ... Fortunately he is very timid, and his timidity constitutes our best guarantee against a collapse of the present system.'[80] Abbas's timidity may have been another name for caution. He had been threatened with deposition often enough to believe in its possibility. He was aware that it was fairly easy to depose him, for he was not a favourite at Constantinople; and if his illustrious grandfather could be deposed without fuss, so could he. Abbas was not wrong in his assumptions, for on December 11, 1897, an informant of Cromer's in Constantinople had written saying: 'The Sultan is quite prepared to agree to a permanent British occupation of Egypt if, on our side, we will consent to set aside the whole family of Mohamed Ali in favour of a Turkish *Vali* [Governor] to be appointed for five years.'[81]

Abbas had to fight the influence of the British Empire as well as its manifestation in Egypt—his was a losing battle. By the time he came to the throne, Egypt had become indispensable to England, and all his efforts could not have shifted England from its position. Cromer thus proved a true prophet when he said that 'deposition is at present the *ultima ratio* in Egyptian affairs, and it is as well to bear constantly in mind, looking to the personal character and political views of the present Khedive, that a moment may come when we shall be obliged to resort to it. It would cause a splutter, but if the political status of Egypt were not changed, I do not think that it would be anything more than a splutter.'[82] With time, Cromer was to cow the Khedive so completely that this treatment became a by-word in English political circles, and the tale was told that once, when Cromer countered a summons from King Edward VII by a somewhat brusque alternative suggestion, the latter muttered: 'He seems to take me for the Khedive.'[83] But three events were to take place before Abbas was finally defeated. These were: the reconquest of the Sudan; the incident at Fashoda; and, lastly, the signing of the Entente Cordiale with France.

We have seen how Salisbury in 1888 had sensed the shift in the focus of British power from Constantinople to Cairo, and had begun to think in terms of one day reconquering the Sudan as an added measure of Egyptian security. Salisbury was capable of biding his time until the propitious moment when Egypt's finances made possible such an undertaking. In 1895 rumours were rife of an impending French advance into the Sudan from the south.

This prospect once more revived the question of the Sudan, for the advance, if it materialized, posed a double threat. First it posed a threat to Egypt in that 'it is obvious that if any civilized power holds the waters of the Upper Nile, it may in the end be in a position to exercise a predominating influence on the future of Egypt'.[84] For it was then wrongly supposed possible to divert a portion of the water-supply that was so vital to Egypt. In the second place, it posed a threat to the projected plans for the reconquest of the Sudan. Cromer, who necessarily saw things from an angle narrower than that of the British government, did not advise an advance into the Sudan. He was planning to build a dam at Aswan, and knew that Egypt had not the necessary funds for an expedition in the Sudan. In November 1895 London informed him that it was not contemplating an invasion just yet.

Suddenly, on March 13, 1896, Salisbury sent a despatch to Cromer informing him that a cabinet meeting, held on the previous day, had decided to advance to Dongola, on the Nile. This decision was undertaken quite deliberately as a calculated act of policy, and for reasons that had little to do with rumours of a French advance. On March 1, 1896, the Italians had been defeated at Adowa in Ethiopia, and it was rumoured that the Ethiopians and the dervishes were combining forces. When the Italians asked Britain for help, the British government agreed to undertake a diversionary campaign which would help the Italians, but which above all aimed at the reconquest of the Sudan. The real reasons for the Dongola campaign, as Salisbury explained to Cromer, were 'a desire to help the Italians at Kassala, and to prevent the dervishes from winning a conspicuous success which might have far-reaching results. In addition, we desired to kill two birds with one stone, and to use the same military effort to plant the foot of Egypt rather farther up the Nile. For this reason we preferred it to any movement from Suakin, or in the direction of Kassala, because there would be no ulterior profit in these movements.'*

---

* Salisbury to Cromer, March 13, 1896, Zetland, *op. cit.*, p. 223. Suakin is a port on the Red Sea while Kassala is a province lying between the Nile and the Red Sea.

The Italians had first laid claim to Kassala in 1889. But since this commanded the Atbara tributary of the Nile, Cromer had convinced Salisbury that 'whatever Power holds the Upper Nile Valley must, by the mere force of its geographical situation, dominate Egypt'.[85] Italy was therefore warned off. In April 1891, the British government and Italy reached an agreement whereby Italy was permitted to occupy Kassala, if the military situation demanded it. This Italy had done when, in 1894, it started its colonial campaigns in Ethiopia. In September 1895 the dervishes attacked Kassala, and matters looked so serious for the Italians, that Cromer suggested a relief expedition, so that Kassala should not fall into the hands of the dervishes. But Salisbury would not hear of it, and said: 'Whenever we are masters of the Valley of the Nile Kassala will be easily dealt with. Till then it has little value'[86] —for the dervishes had no technical knowledge of any kind that could threaten Egypt's water-supply.

The Italian situation gradually grew more desperate. Finally, on March 10, the government in Rome suggested that Salisbury undertake a diversion 'du côté du Nil',[87] to help them out. This suggestion met with Salisbury's approval, for though he was not willing to help the Italians by other methods, this diversionary action would be a way of planting 'Egypt's foot up the Nile'.

The British cabinet did not object to the Dongola expedition, since neither British money, nor British soldiers, were to be used. The Egyptian government was expected to defray the costs of the expedition out of funds held by the Caisse. After all the plans were worked out, and orders to advance had been issued, Cromer suddenly realized that the Egyptian government had not been informed of the impending reconquest of the Sudan that was being undertaken in its name, and with its army and money; and he hastened to inform the Khedive. But though the Khedive gave no trouble over the Sudan, the Caisse did so. When the Egyptian Government 'borrowed' £800,000 from the Caisse, the French and Russian Commissioners at once sued the Egyptian government before the Mixed Courts and won the case, for a reconquest did not come under any category of 'authorized' expenditure. The money therefore had to be returned, and Britain advanced Egypt the equivalent sum at $2\frac{3}{4}$% interest. Later it was to remit that sum. The whole Dongola campaign was run on a shoe-string, and Kitchener's parsimony was to become a by-word among his troops. Hangings and floggings as a means of keeping discipline were remembered even longer by the soldiers.[88]

When Dongola was captured, there were no funds to allow the expedition to go on to Khartum. Salisbury said that if it were done, it must be done with English money, since there was no Egyptian money available, and he was under the impression that the House of Commons would not be disposed to authorize the expenditure.[89] But the House eventually did provide the funds, and Kitchener pushed on south and eventually made his triumphal entry into Khartum in September 1898.

On reaching Khartum, Kitchener heard rumours of a certain foreign expedition stationed at Fashoda. Suspecting that it might be the much publicized French Marchand Mission, he himself pushed on to Fashoda, where he found Marchand ensconced in a fort, flying the French flag. Kitchener requested that the Egyptian flag be hoisted, and claimed that he was restoring the Khedive's authority on Egyptian land. Marchand at first demurred, but later agreed to fly the Egyptian flag. Since his force was greatly outnumbered, he finally withdrew from Fashoda, without instructions from France. For a while it looked as though Britain and France would go to war over Fashoda. According to Freycinet, 'c'était bien de guerre qu'il s'agissait. Durant cette période [September 1898–March 1899] nous avons été à deux doigts des hostilités. Un peu par notre faute . . . beaucoup par la faute des Anglais'.[90] Many of the members of the British Cabinet were bent on war, and, although Salisbury counselled moderation, the government authorized naval preparations on October 24. Fortunately, both countries chose to exercise caution, and on March 21, 1899, they signed an Anglo-French Declaration which delimited the spheres of influence of the two powers in the area.

Fashoda was a grievous blow to the Khedive; for all his hopes of using France as a lever with which to oust Britain from Egypt were destroyed. Only too clearly, he saw proof that France was not prepared to take any effective action against Britain. The second blow came with the form of government that was adopted in the Sudan.

As early as November 16, 1896, Salisbury had warned Cromer to 'avoid as far as you can using any official and formal phrase which can be quoted as proving that Dongola is part of Egypt.'[91] After the conquest of Khartum, the British and Egyptians flags were hoisted, side by side, 'as a visible expression of a *de facto* situation . . . The Khedive knows perfectly well that neither in Egypt nor in the Sudan can he take any important step without the consent of the British government.'[92] This condominium rule, which Cromer, helped by his legal adviser, drew up, was a device that Cromer had invented because he did not want to see the Sudan crippled by the Capitulations as Egypt had been for so long. But Salisbury's reasons were that it was intended to emphasize Britain's predominant voice in all matters concerning the Sudan. Britain had helped conquer the Sudan by sending British troops to assist Kitchener in the conquest of Khartum, and out of a total cost of the campaign—which amounted to £2,354,000—had contributed £800,000, the remainder being supplied by the Egyptian government. The British government maintained that Egypt could never have conquered the Sudan without British assistance. The Egyptians concomitantly believed that England could not have conquered the Sudan without Egypt's initial claims on the territory as a justification for its re-occupation. In signing the Condominium Agreement, Egypt signed away her rights to a country which she had helped reconquer with her money and her men. Egypt continued to support the Sudan financially, from the date of its reconquest until 1936; and even Cromer could wax indignant over Britain's reluctance to contribute towards the administration of a country where the British flag was flying, when the market value of the Suez Canal shares was £26 million. When Wingate became Governor of the Sudan, he estimated that England's financial share in the Sudan administration amounted to the cost of the bunting for the flag.[93]

The Sudan campaign showed Egypt that England was preparing to stay in the area, rather than to evacuate it, for it could now establish legal title to a half share in the Sudan. The Egyptian nationalists, who by 1898 were growing vociferous, denounced England for her actions in staking claim to a territory that belonged to Egypt. They were equally indignant over the funds provided for the expedition, and for the subsequent administration of the country—when all Egyptian demands for reforms in such fields as education were constantly met with the reply that there was no money available.

The last event that killed any remaining hopes that the Khedive might have cherished with regard to England's evacuation of Egypt, was the signing of the Entente Cordiale with France in 1904. From the standpoint of finance, France had been a constant thorn in Cromer's side, by showing antagonism towards England in periodic quibbles over the funds in the Caisse. Cromer's ambition was to effect a reconciliation between the two countries which would give him a free hand in Egyptian finances. This ambition was eventually fulfilled; and, in the estimation of Lord Sanderson, the Permanent Under-Secretary of State for Foreign Affairs, 'the actual determining cause of the Entente was Lord Cromer's anxiety for an arrangement with France which would let him place Egyptian finances on a more satisfactory footing, and pave the way for abolishing the Capitulations. The proposals relating to Egyptian finance formed a sort of nucleus from which the further agreements developed themselves.'[94] A reconciliation with France also implied an acceptance of the occupation, which was of great moral significance to Cromer. While negotiations for the Entente were under way, Cromer wrote to Gorst: 'Gloss it over as we may, it is certain that very distinct pledges to withdraw were given, and that we cannot, and do not intend to redeem our pledges. Hence we are to a certain extent in the position of political pirates. I want to remove that taint, and moreover to render it impossible for the French at any future time to summon us to withdraw.'[95]

Cromer suggested that Britain should attempt to negotiate with France on the basis of a virtual abolition of the Caisse, although this could carry on in a purely nominal manner until France and Britain had convinced the other Powers of its redundancy. If the Powers refused to be convinced, then England could resume her liberty of action and unilaterally abolish the Caisse. He believed that if this happened the Powers were likely to bring the question before the Mixed Courts, and that those would have to be abolished as well. In fact, Cromer's suggestions amounted to a proposal that England should virtually annex Egypt, although not in actual legal terms.[96] During the early days of the negotiations Cromer suggested that France's assent to the occupation of Egypt should be given in terms which implied that the occupation had acquired a character of permanency. However, this was not included in the final text of the Entente, which merely declared that France recognized Britain's dominant position in Egypt, and stated: 'Her Majesty's Government declare that they have no intention of altering the political status of Egypt.'

When the terms of the Entente Cordiale were made public the Khedive knew that he was beaten by England, and realized that the only alternative was for him to become 'oppressively pro-British'. But by then the struggle for the independence of Egypt had passed from his hands and into those of men who were less fettered by public position—those of the nationalists.

CHAPTER VII

The Rise of the Second Nationalist Movement

The first nationalist movement arose in antagonism to the Khedive Tawfiq and his method of government: the second nationalist movement was stimulated by the Khedive Abbas and directed against the British occupation.

During the early days of the occupation it was generally believed in Egypt, and also in England, that Britain's intervention would bring about immediate and pronounced improvements in the country. This promise seemed justified at first, when real reforms took place in the administration, in the system of taxation and its collection, and in justice. But a decade later the Capitulations still functioned, the Caisse continued to exert its stranglehold over Egyptian finances, and, worse still, the same men continued to be used in governing the country. The Drummond Wolff Convention, which had offered promise of hastening the day of evacuation, never reached the stage of ratification. The first impetus of reform slowed down. A change of Khedive had not provided Egypt with a change in the methods of government— quite the contrary: Cromer's treatment of Abbas during the incidents of 1893 and 1894 seemed to denote a stricter hold on the Egyptian government than ever before. People in general, and the new generation in particular, began to feel disillusioned, and by 1895 to mistrust England's intention towards Egypt.

Abbas encouraged the rise of a nationalist movement, and allowed it to become articulate, through his financial assistance to the press. During the early days of his reign he had placed himself at the forefront of the movement, and when he could no longer act in the open, he found recruits who were willing to carry on the struggle against Britain. For by 1896, nationalism had become synonymous with opposition to British rule in Egypt, and to a demand for the evacuation of the British troops.

Unlike the older generation, the budding nationalists were no longer frightened by thoughts of bankruptcy, for the country was enjoying an unprecedented run of prosperity that was to last till 1907. Cromer's financial policy, based on his Indian recipe for reform—low taxation, efficient fiscal administration, careful expenditure on remunerative public works, and minimum interference in the internal and external traffic of goods—plus Egypt's powers of recuperation, due to her fertile soil, had by 1890 brought prosperity to the country.[1] The real *per capita* income during the first decade of this century was higher than at any time in modern Egyptian history, with the possible exception of the early 1920's.[2] Cromer believed that this prosperity would act as a bond between Egypt and England, one based on admiration and gratitude for British achievements. But it did nothing of the sort. The Egyptians took their prosperity for granted, and England's role in bringing it about was forgotten, or assumed to have ended. The nationalists who had appeared on the stage pointed out how pernicious were England's reforms in Egypt, for they lulled people into the acceptance of the occupation by appealing to their self-interest, making them forget the greater interests of the nation. The nationalists pointed out the errors they saw in Cromer's policy, and often magnified them beyond measure. Cromer was accused of keeping Egyptian industry in check by imposing an 8% customs duty on imported coal: he was said to have killed the tobacco industry in order to increase the government revenue through high duty on the imported product; and to have killed the textile industries by imposing an 8% excise duty on them, to put their products on a par with Lancashire goods.[3]

In Cromer's defence it must be said that he was a Free Trader, and could not conceive of protective tariffs. He believed that if an industry could not thrive without protection, then it must die. Moreover, since the main sources of government revenue came from the land tax, the State Railways and customs duties, Cromer assumed that taxes on these items were necessary and justifiable. Without them he could not have managed to balance the budget during the early days of the occupation, when his primary pre-occupation had been to find means of saving Egypt from bankruptcy. With affluence, the Egyptians acquired assurance, and England's financial policy came to be regarded with hostility.

Meanwhile, a group of young intellectuals had appeared on the scene. These were the university graduates who had never known the insecurity of Ismail's last days, or the autocracy of Khedivial rule as perpetrated by as strong a hand as Ismail's. They formed a new stratum that was becoming familiar with modern social and political theories. Many of them had travelled and studied abroad, had been introduced to Western principles of liberty, to the ideas of the Enlightenment, the French Revolution, and the Romantics. Others learnt these concepts in the secondary schools, through translations, or from newspapers. The old Egyptian society with its religious restrictions and strict code was breaking up, bringing in its wake a period of restlessness. A group of disorientated youngsters needed a *raison d'être*, and they found it in the nationalist movement. A modern writer on nationalism explains that though nationalist movements were ostensibly directed against the foreigner, they were also the manifestation of a species of civil strife between the generations. 'National movements are children's crusades; their very names are manifestoes against old age.'[4] That was the feeling that pervaded the young nationalists: if the old generation in Egypt was unfit to rule, and had to be protected and guided by England, then the young educated generation was willing to take over and rule in its place. Over and above this feeling of restlessness, a deep chasm had opened between the English officials and the Egyptians. The number of British officials had greatly increased, so that where in 1896 there were 286 officials, in 1906 there were 662. This was part of a natural self-perpetuating process that sought to ensure the existence of a continuous supply of British officials for the administration; and was also due to the fact that Egypt, like any of the colonies, had become a place where officials could make a name for themselves, or even try out their wings. Humphrey Bowman, who was a teacher in one of the secondary schools in Cairo, described the relationship between the English and Egyptian teachers by saying that 'as soon as their work was over, the English masters escaped on their bicycles to the Sporting Club at Gezira . . . they referred slightingly to their pupils as the "walads" and hardly less so to their Egyptian colleagues as the "effendis" . . . they even had separate common rooms'.[5] With the increase in the number of British officials, their bonds of friendship with the Egyptians had weakened, for they now formed a colony of their own, and did not need to mingle with the natives. The new British officials had little knowledge of the Egyptians, and even less contact with them.

The canker of dissatisfaction lay in the civil service. As yet there was little inclination among the Egyptians for free enterprise, and since most of the business enterprises were in the hands of the foreign community, the civil service was the only area of advancement that lay open to the average Egyptian. As more and more Egyptians acquired university degrees, they expected to be given more posts in the government; instead of which, they found that an increasingly large number of young British graduates were being imported into the country to fill these posts. (When the Milner Mission came to Egypt in 1921, it estimated that in 1905 only 28% of the higher government posts were occupied by Egyptians, while 42% were occupied by British officials, and the remaining 30% by Armenians and Syrians.[6]) Previously Britain had followed the policy of 'British heads and Egyptian hands', and only highly skilled and experienced men had been imported because of their expertise, and because no trained Egyptians could be found to fill these posts. But this policy had gradually changed when England decided to continue the occupation; untrained men were being recruited from England, and trained in Egypt. Ronald Storrs, who was later to become Oriental Secretary at the Agency, gives a humorous account of his first few months in Cairo, when he was shunted from department to department, because none of them had a vacancy or needed him for any purpose, until finally a position was found for him. This was no laughing matter to the Egyptian. He resented this discrimination, and thought that if anyone was to be trained on the job, then surely it should be the Egyptian, who had been repeatedly told that the occupation was there only until he was taught to rule himself, so that he could eventually take over the whole government of Egypt. How could he learn when he was not even appointed to the administration?

The increase in the number of British officials coincided with a diminution of ability; and the relationship between the newly trained, young British officials, and the older Egyptian officials, gave rise to a great deal of dissatisfaction. It was one thing to receive suggestions from an expert irrigation-engineer, and another to be put under the tutelage of a man who was still learning the ropes—especially when this occurred in realms which called for knowledge of the local customs, such as in the Ministry of the Interior. The Governor of a province, the *mudir*, who was often twice the Inspector's age, resented any suggestions coming from a foreigner who barely spoke his language, and who could scarcely have mastered fallah folkways and mores (even had he been so inclined) during his brief period of training. No amount of tact or self-effacement on the part of the Englishman could gloss over the knowledge that he represented the occupation, and that his was the word that reached the Adviser's ear.

Sometimes the Egyptians had to deal with British Inspectors who were completely ignorant of the areas they were supposed to inspect. Husayn Haykal, one of Egypt's foremost men of letters, one-time president of the Senate and several times a cabinet minister, recounts in his memoirs a ludicrous incident when the Inspector for Agriculture in his area of the delta turned out to be the geography teacher who had taught him at school. Mr Swift had not gone home to England for the summer holidays, so he was delegated to inspect the countryside. As he knew less than nothing about agricultural conditions in the Sharqiyya province he accepted Haykal's word that all was well, and happily returned to Cairo, so to report.[7]

This may have been an extreme example, but the Egyptians maintained that many of the Inspectors were sufficiently ignorant and tactless to warrant native displeasure. Haykal for one bitterly commented on the situation, saying that the British Inspector considered himself superior to the highest Egyptian official by virtue of the fact that his only superior was the Adviser; and that this led the Inspector to believe that to be English was a sufficient attribute to warrant an automatic superiority.

The reasons for the decision to use British officials fresh from university in the Egyptian administration had its origins in Cromer's belief that government in Egypt depended more on persons than on institutions. When he was sure that England had no intention of evacuating Egypt, he decided that the policy of teaching the Egyptians was not the most efficient one, for he contended that Egyptians lacked 'character'. And since he was particular about the sort of men he wanted for the administration, he looked elsewhere than in Egypt for them, mostly in India. But as the demand for officials increased, the recruiting system became less discriminating, and the calibre of officials was much lowered. In a memorandum which Cromer had prepared for the instruction of these budding officials, he informed them that it must always be kept in mind that Egypt should be ruled, whenever possible, by the Egyptians themselves, but that this principle had not proved successful. Therefore young Englishmen were recruited in order to keep an eye on details as well as on broad lines, and the object they should keep in mind was one that verged on pure altruism: their job was to *'confer benefits and privileges and to endeavour to the utmost of our power to train up, by precept and example, generations of Egyptians, who in future may take our place and carry on the traditions of our administration* . . . the Englishman is in Egypt as a guide and a friend, not as a master'.* The arrogant notion underlying this memorandum—that young Englishmen just down from the universities could teach Egyptians how to run their administration—was galling to the Egyptian officials.

How successful could a relationship be if based on an altruism that was combined with a sense of superiority on the part of one of the parties? In the event it produced a widening rift between the two groups. For how were the English ever to become guides and friends, when their social lives were so wide apart from the Egyptians'? Cromer himself set the pattern, for in spite of his

* Memorandum found in the *Harry Boyle Papers*. This Memorandum was never finished because Cromer thought it might create trouble if it fell into the wrong hands; the italics are his.

assertions of accessibility, he was an aloof figure. He paid dutiful calls on the high and the mighty, on the *ulama* and the political figures, and even called some of them his friends; but that was in the line of duty, and not from personal choice. He was even aloof from the British community, and after 1885 his constant companion was Harry Boyle, his Oriental Secretary, who was facetiously referred to by his colleagues as the keeper of the Pro-Consul's conscience.[8]

If aloof with the English, then how much more aloof must Cromer have been with the Egyptians, especially since he despised the Egyptian mind, and believed that it, 'like that of all Oriental races, is naturally inaccurate and incapable of precision of thought and expression'.[9] These were the opposite of qualities which he prized, and for that reason he approved of the Syrians in Egypt, who seemed to him to have the 'power of inductive reasoning' and a certain 'strength and virility of character'.[10] Part of this dislike for the Egyptians Cromer had acquired from Harry Boyle, who had a great respect and admiration for the Turks and for their military discipline, and who despised the self-effacing Egyptians. It is therefore not surprising to find that the Egyptians detested Cromer. Antipathies are usually mutual.

How could Cromer expect gratitude from people who, after nearly twenty years of occupation, were less far along the road to self-government than when they started? In 1896 Alonzo Money, the British Commissioner on the Caisse, wrote an article on his views of the occupation which stressed that point. The article was not meant for publication, but for restricted circulation amongst his closest friends. In it Money said that the reasons Britain was giving for prolonging the occupation in Egypt were spurious: in India, England had a free hand—there were no Capitulations, and no France to hinder reform—yet after a century of the rule of order, the reforms there instituted would collapse were Britain to leave. Therefore to say that Britain had to continue the occupation in Egypt until the desired reforms took root was a weak excuse. The British presence, far from creating a new ruling class, was undermining and weakening whatever power of self-government existed in Egypt. 'We are emasculating the governing classes,' said Money. 'During our years of occupation I do not see a single new man of any mark who has made an appearance.'[11]

Unfortunately for Money, a copy of the article fell into Cromer's hands, and he sent it to Salisbury, dubbing Money a fool who did not know what he was talking about. But Money was stating a fact. England was not teaching Egypt to rule itself; on the contrary, it seemed to be grooming Egyptians for permanent occupation. This assumption was discerned by several Anglo-Egyptian officials. Thus P. G. Elgood, who was an Inspector in the Ministry of the Interior, wrote to Wingate that 'of all whimsical ideas, commend me to that which protests that our *raison d'être* in Egypt is to teach the Egyptians to govern themselves. Perhaps some wise person invented that phrase in order to avoid awkward questions concerning the continuous occupation of Egypt. I can't think of any other possible reason; and certainly such a policy will defer our departure until the Greek Kalends'.[12] Elgood's scepticism was mirrored by the Egyptians', for that was exactly what they suspected that British policy aimed to do.

As the occupation continued there was a perceptible shift in the reasons given for sustaining it. It had first taken place to restore the Khedive's authority over a rebellious army; then the occupation was pursued until it supervised the administrative reforms that Dufferin suggested; then it was needed to defend Egypt from an invasion by the dervishes, and when that was no longer a valid excuse, Salisbury added that England would continue to occupy Egypt until the Sudan had been restored to it. Finally the British government announced that it would remain in occupation until it had taught the Egyptians self-rule, at a time when all its actions pointed to turning Egypt into a British colony. Such a procession of excuses could no longer be accepted by the thinking Egyptian. Although the real reason for the occupation, which had nothing to do with Egypt, was not revealed to the Egyptians, eventually those with any knowledge of world affairs came to realize that England's interests in Egypt as the key to India were permanent.

This then was the mental climate of Egypt at the turn of the century. It was the perfect atmosphere for the growth and flowering of a nationalist movement among students, civil servants, and the upper classes: in fact among all the articulate groups. All they needed was a leader. The only group that was apathetic to this ferment consisted of the fallahin, numerically the majority of Egypt's population. It was customary for fallah mothers to frighten their children with the *Injilizi*, 'Englishman', as a variant to the time-honoured bogey, the *afrit*. But apart from such comment, the occupation, when thought about at all, was regarded as an infliction from the Almighty, similar to a flood, to punish the faithful for their iniquity.* The only articulate social elements who were actively opposed to the nationalist spirit were the Levantine and European communities, who were the richest groups in Egypt, and the ones to benefit from the Capitulations and the occupation.

Abbas during the early days of his reign had seemed to be the leader the nationalists were looking for. It seems strange that a monarch who, theoretically, ruled his country in an absolute fashion, should deliberately encourage liberal nationalists—men who aimed at goading the apathetic Egyptians into becoming an active population capable of expressing forceful public opinion, and who agitated for a constitution and full parliamentary life. Both Ismail and Tawfiq (to a lesser extent) had encouraged a limited liberalism to appear as a sop to Western criticism of their autocracy. But whereas they supported pliable politicians who could be contained, Abbas encouraged the young intellectuals. This apparent anomaly may possibly be explained by Abbas's Austrian experience. Very little is known about Abbas's stay at the Theresianum, but it is worth while to speculate on the probable effects it had upon him. Perhaps Abbas had witnessed the effect of nationalism on the Hungarians and the Austrians, and had seen how it could inflame and mould men into becoming an active pressure-group. He may have then decided to rouse the same force in Egypt as an adjunct to his plan for levering the English out of position. Abbas might also have realized that this was a relatively safe policy to follow in protecting his own position; for to make a show of encouraging liberals does not necessarily

* That was the explanation given Ahmad Amin by his father in *Hayati*, Cairo: 1958, p. 87.

mean an intention to concede authority to them or to shift the centre of power from his hands into theirs. Especially since the men Abbas used were not members of the governing class, but were mostly native Egyptians who might have been satisfied with reforms which, while they gave the outward appearance of responsible government, still left the reins of power in the Khedive's hands. Abbas felt capable of handling such details if the problem arose in the distant future, but his immediate necessity was to find allies who would bring the occupation to an end: and the only allies he could find who could be of any practical use, were the liberals. If subsequent events can be used as an indication of Abbas's original purpose, he had had no real intention of ruling as a constitutional monarch; for when the *Umma* party, and the other political parties in 1907, raised the cry for a constitution, he refused to grant them one. And although various excuses have been given to justify his reluctance to do so, the basic reason remains that, when the policy of conciliation with England took place, he saw no reason to saddle himself with constitutional rule. Abbas's sincerity in espousing the liberal cause eventually became suspect in some eyes. But at first, the only group of nationalists to question his motives was the group of Shaykh Muhammad Abduh and his friends and followers. Their eyes were opened to the Khedive's motives by stages—first by his venality, then by his increasing opposition to certain reforms, and lastly by his stand against granting Egypt a constitution.

Financing the nationalist movement called for a long purse, and Abbas's early incursions into the *Waqf* funds* were occasioned by this need. But gradually, as Abbas lost all hope of winning the unequal match with Cromer, he turned his considerable talents to making money: partly by way of compensating his frustrations at not being able to rule Egypt; partly out of an acquisitiveness which seemed to be a family trait, for Abbas I and Ismail both had it; and partly in readiness for the day when he would be sent into exile. The Khedive constantly expected deposition, whether by Turkey or by Britain, and bought large tracts of land in Anatolia

---

* The *Waqfs* were religious endowments held as mortmain for charitable purposes.

and other areas outside Egypt, in preparation for this contingency.* This fear of deposition led him into acquiring riches in the most blatant manner. He had no scruples about selling titles and decorations to the highest bidders through the intermediary of such people as Shawqi, the famous poet, and even through Shaykh Ali Yusif and Mustafa Kamil (the founder of the nationalist movement) if we are to believe Shafiq's words.[13] Shafiq also alleged that Abbas helped the Sultan against the Young Turks in Egypt, in exchange for the concession to mine minerals on his island of Tashyuz (Thasos)—a concession which the Sultan promised but never granted. When Abbas could not get the concessions he wanted from the Sultan, he turned to Cromer, and—through Wingate—informed him that he was ready to co-operate with him, if Cromer helped him to get the concession.[14]

This venal side of Abbas's character shocked many people, especially Abduh and his group. Various rumours grew about the Khedive's methods of acquiring land and money—methods which though technically legal, were often devious. A rumour also went the rounds that Gorst, when he was Financial Adviser, helped Abbas, quite legally, in his financial transactions. Blunt, in his diaries, notes the information: 'Abdu tells me that Gorst has been certainly helping the Khedive in his commercial speculations, and there has been a quarrel between him and Cromer on the subject.'[15] But venality was not the sole reason for the disenchantment of some of the moderate nationalists with their would-be leader. Even Mustafa Kamil, whose early nationalist activities had been encouraged and financed by the Khedive, disowned him with maximum publicity in 1905. But coolness had appeared between them as early as 1901, after Mustafa Kamil had sent the Sultan a report on increasing Young Turk activity in Egypt,[16] just when the Khedive was assiduously endeavouring to show the Sultan that he had smothered the Young Turk movement in Egypt.

In 1905, after twelve years of his reign, Abbas witnessed the total revulsion of the nationalist movement against him and, together with the occupation, he became one of its major targets of

* Rashid Rida, *Tarikh*, I, p. 597, recounts a conversation he had with the Khedive, during which he inquired why the Khedive bought so much land abroad, and received the answer that it was in preparation for the day when he would be deposed.

attack. Abbas had all of Ismail's autocratic proclivities, but did not develop sufficient strength of character to make autocracy palatable, or to help camouflage his less savoury traits. Times had changed, and acts which might have been condoned in the past, under Ismail, were now questioned and attacked by a more active and enterprising group of nationalists. However, if one aspect of nationalism is to help in the regeneration of a people and to evoke in them the desire to rid themselves of foreign domination, irrespective of the motives behind the actions, then Abbas can be counted among the nationalists, and credit is due to him for having helped to recreate the nationalist movement in Egypt.

The Khedive's connections with the nationalist movement rendered it suspect to Cromer. He was convinced that Abbas had manufactured the whole movement for his own ends, and that it was spurious. To the very last he never admitted that there was a spontaneous nationalist movement in the country, with a desire to see the British occupation at an end. He persisted in ignoring it, claiming that no sensible Egyptian supported it. Egypt was not a nation, so how, he asked, could anyone advocate Egypt for the Egyptians? Who is a true Egyptian, when people of so many different origins live in Egypt—Greeks, Armenians, Syrians, Copts, Bedouins, etc.?[17] Today one can smile at such a remark, especially when we realize that the native Egyptians were over 9 million out of a total population of 9,734,000; but then it was accepted at face-value by many people, including Egyptians themselves. One of the tasks the nationalists set themselves was to convince the Egyptians that they did in fact form a nation, and that they were capable and indeed deserving of self-rule.

It would be misleading to say that the nationalist movement was a single movement with a leader at its head, since there were several men who influenced several tributaries of thought that only in the end, in 1919, flowed into a single stream. These men were often in opposition to each other, but they all raised a nationalist spirit. Thus Shaykh Muhammad Abduh inspired Ahmad Lutfi al-Sayyid and the moderates—Girondists, as Cromer dubbed them—who formed *Hizb al-Umma*. And though Lutfi expounded the ideology of the *Hizb* it would be misleading to call him its leader. Likewise, Shaykh Ali Yusif, though he founded a political party, was not really a leader. The only man who had the aura, or charisma, of a leader was Mustafa Kamil; yet he too did not appeal to all the nationalists involved. Perhaps then we should say that several men of completely different background, temperament and technique, came into contact with the Khedive, and that the interplay of these personalities gave rise to the currents of national thought.

Shaykh Muhammad Abduh's dearest wish was to reform al-Azhar University. Since it was the centre of Islamic learning, he believed that if it were reformed, then the whole of Islam would be reformed also. He wanted, he said, to turn al-Azhar into a beacon that would enlighten the whole Muslim world not only on matters of religion, but in secular affairs as well, so that it should come to resemble a European university as much as possible.[18] When Abbas ascended the throne, Abduh approached him with his plan for reforming al-Azhar, and he succeeded in convincing the Khedive of the necessity for this move. In 1895 the Khedive appointed Shaykh Abduh and his friend Shaykh Salman, as government representatives on the Administrative Committee of al-Azhar which was in charge of reforming that institution.

Unfortunately the intellectual reforms in al-Azhar that Shaykh Abduh hoped for never took place. Only the material reforms were successful, for the *ulama* were more interested in their material welfare, than in the spiritual fare they served. Abduh's reforms were judged as too revolutionary by them, for he wanted to broaden the curriculum and to improve teaching methods. Gradually the Khedive also became Abduh's opponent, for reasons we shall discuss later, and balked his attempts at reform, until Abduh was forced to resign from the Committee of al-Azhar on March 19, 1905, not long before he died.*

One of the reasons for the Khedive's disaffection with Abduh is attributed by Shafiq to the intrigues of Shaykh Ali Yusif and Mustafa Kamil, who set the Khedive against Abduh.[19] Another,

---

* Abduh resigned after the Khedive made a speech in which he hinted that he would accept Abduh's resignation if it were offered. Ahmad Amin, *Zuama al-Islah*, Cairo: 1948, p. 442.

and more potent, reason stems from the time Abduh opposed the Khedive over his use of funds from the benevolent foundations, the *Waqf*. In 1899 Abduh, on the Khedive's recommendation, had been nominated Mufti of Egypt. This appointment automatically put Abduh on the Superior Council of the *Waqf* administration. One of the items that the Council had to examine was a suggestion from the *Maiyya Saniyya*, the Khedive's cabinet, that the *Waqf* should give the Khedive a piece of land near Cairo, in exchange for one of his farms. When the Council examined the transaction in detail, its members discovered that the *Waqf* would have to bear a loss of £E50,000; naturally, the Council refused to allow the transaction to go through. The Khedive never forgave Abduh for this refusal, and from then on lent a willing ear to his detractors, encouraging them to sabotage Abduh's projected reforms. One of Abduh's disciples and his biographer, Rashid Rida, recounts that on one occasion Khalil Pasha Hamada, who was a friend of both Abduh and the Khedive, had begged Abduh to let the Khedive have his way with the *Waqf*, and he would guarantee Abduh a free hand with his reform in al-Azhar. Abduh, however, refused, saying that he could not follow the path of evil, even if it led to the good.[20]

Abduh's connexion with Cromer was a third reason for the Khedive's antagonism towards him. Cromer had helped the Mufti* on several occasions. He had prevented Tawfiq from acting vindictively towards him when he returned from exile, and had been instrumental in recalling him back to Egypt. The relationship between the two men was one of mutual respect. They often met, sometimes at Princess Nazli Fazil's salon. Had Cromer been an Egyptian, Abduh might have wholeheartedly supported him, for in an article entitled, 'Should a benevolent despot appear in the East'—written after Abduh returned from exile, and in answer to an article entitled 'Should constitutional rule invade the East' —Abduh said that, should such a just despot appear in the East, then he could, within a period of fifteen years, do more for Egypt than the intellect—unaided by coercion—could perform in fifteen

* Mufti and Imam were titles applied to Abduh by virtue of his position in the religious hierarchy.

centuries. Obviously Abduh was thinking of some of the qualities that Cromer possessed, qualities which unfortunately from Abduh's point of view were marred by the fact that Cromer was an Englishman and a Christian. Furthermore, Cromer did not display *all* the qualities necessary for such a despot—one of which was willingness to rule in consultation with men of authority.

Abbas, who disliked and distrusted anyone connected with Cromer, seized on this relationship as a basis for spreading calumnies, through his suite, to the effect that the Imam had sold out to the British, and was a supporter of the occupation. Once the Khedive had shown his antagonism to the Imam, his entourage redoubled its energy, and accusations rained on Abduh. He was accused of being a heretic, a Mutazilite, and a Wahhabi,* because he advocated a return to the pristine purity of Islam, and the use of reason in questioning those traditional tenets which formed, in his opinion, non-essential elements in religion. The Imam had to put up with much petty persecution from the Khedive and his suite. Since many people did not know him personally, they were willing to believe the libellous rumours spread about him, so that they rejected his teachings. It was only after his death that most thinking Egyptians realized what a genuine loss he was to Egypt as a patriot, a scholar, a teacher and a reformer.

The Imam's followers tried to carry on his good work, but with a fundamental difference. For whereas Shaykh Abduh had seen religion as the basic bond of society, one group among his pupils 'replaced the religious impulse by the national impulse',[21] while yet another of his pupils, Rashid Rida, tried to carry out religious reforms. These young men, the Imam's party as they came to be known, formed the nucleus of the moderates in Egyptian political life. They adopted a secular line, and were more interested in expanding his plans for social reform, and his line of social criticism than his religious principles. Among them were three men who were instrumental in awakening Egyptians to the need for social

---

* The Mutazilites were members of a heterodox rationalist movement under the Abbassid Caliphs, while the Wahhabis were members of an extreme orthodox sect which appeared in Arabia in the eighteenth century. Orthodox *ulama* disapproved of both sects, and used the names almost as insulting epithets.

reform: Ahmad Fathi Zaghlul, Qasim Amin, and Ahmad Lutfi al-Sayyid.

The first of these men, Ahmad Fathi Zaghlul, was the younger brother of Saad Zaghlul, and Under Secretary of State for Justice. Little is remembered about Fathi today save the stigma of having served as one of the judges in the Dinshwai trial. But Fathi's translations of European political theory were the start of Egypt's intellectual renaissance along political lines.[22] He translated works by Spencer, Bentham, Rousseau and Gustave le Bon. The book which, at the time, had the greatest effect on thinking Egyptians was a translation of Demolins's *A quoi tient la Supériorité des Anglo-Saxons*. This book led to a 'cult of British education and a flood of books attempting to prescribe for a society that needed reform in nearly every aspect'.[23] In his introduction to the translation of Demolins's work, Fathi analysed the weaknesses of Egyptian society. He accused it of lacking 'will and determination. Even our personal relations lack warmth and intimacy. There is no chivalry (*nakhwa*) among us any longer . . . we are so weak that we do nothing ourselves; we ask the government instead.'[24] The Egyptians, he said, had no faith in themselves, and were therefore unaware of their rights as individuals and as a nation. This argument was often used by the nationalists, but gained in effectiveness when presented in the introduction to a book that showed how people who have developed the very qualities that Fathi found lacking in Egyptians had become superior. And yet, sadly enough, he himself seemed to lack these necessary qualities, and through moral weakness acquiesced in the judgments of Dinshwai, and ruined his standing in the eyes of his countrymen.

Another of Abduh's followers, Qasim Amin, was a Magistrate in the Court of Appeal. By writing a small book with the help of Abduh and Lutfi al-Sayyid on the *Emancipation of Women* he raised the most violent controversy of the period, one which provoked no less than thirty books and pamphlets in answer. It roused the *ulama* to such anger, that the Khedive—who constantly tried to please them—would no longer receive Amin at his levées. Qasim's book advocated that women should receive a modest degree of education, and that they should no longer be secluded from society. The uproar that his book occasioned caused Amin to write a second one entitled *The New Woman* to refute the charges made against him. In the second book, which he wrote on his own, he advocated stronger measures, and claimed that a change in Egypt's mental attitude was necessary—that is, a mental and intellectual revolution. He said that women were held in bondage by their ignorance, and could not fulfil the role they ought to play in society. Hence the moral basis of society had decayed, and had caused the whole of Islam to decay. This bondage of women, he claimed, was not an Islamic trait, but one introduced to it from outside, and therefore one that needed to be set aside. The heart of the social problem lay in the position of women in society, a position which could be improved only by allowing them to become educated. Towards the end of the book, Qasim wrote: 'We want definite ends and means, and we need to prepare the young for the new life. No amount of talking from pulpits or orders from authorities can transform us, nor can magic or intercession from above. To change, we have to work.'[25] While treating Islam with respect, Qasim claimed 'the right for civilization to develop its own norms and act in the light of them'.[26] Here he differed from his master, the Imam; for while Abduh sought to reconcile civilization and Islam, Qasim sought to separate them into two different spheres.[27] Although Qasim's aspirations for the emancipation of women are, by modern standards, very modest, yet they were the first expression of such an attitude towards women; and though they roused controversy, others picked up the same idea. Soon the emancipation of women became one of the tenets of nationalists such as Lutfi al-Sayyid and, in the 1919 revolution, Saad Zaghlul.

The third reformer was Ahmad Lutfi al-Sayyid, who set on one side the religious aspect of society, and, instead, sought an answer to the question of what made for the rise and decay of any society.[28] His ideas call for the fuller description that is given in the next chapter. Lutfi al-Sayyid and Mustafa Kamil were the two men who exerted the greatest amount of influence on the political thought of the period, although along different lines and by different methods. But every nationalist movement needs a combination of different types of leaders—it needs orators to rouse the emotions of nationalism, and intellectuals to supply the people with an ideology. Mustafa Kamil and Lutfi al-Sayyid filled these distinctive roles.

CHAPTER VIII

The Orator, the Pro-Consul, and the Intellectual

Mustafa Kamil wanted to preach nationalism to a new Egypt. One of the earliest letters he wrote to his brother Ali Fahmi in 1894, when he was still a student, suggests that he had deliberately chosen nationalist agitation as a career. In his letter Mustafa informed his brother that he had decided to enrol in the Faculty of Law because he wanted to defend the rights of the Egyptian people before the world. For Egypt, he added, in a burst of rhetoric, did not deserve to have her honour sullied by the stigma of a foreign occupation, nor did she deserve to see her children treated as strangers in their own land.[1] This intense letter, written by an eighteen-year-old youth to his own brother, supplies the key to Mustafa's character. It hints at the vehemence and the sense of theatre to which he was prone, and which in future days were occasionally to degenerate into bombast, but which were useful qualities in a politician. It also provides the leitmotif that ran throughout Mustafa's political philosophy: the evil of a foreign occupation, and the feeling of resentment that this aroused.

This dream, at the age of eighteen, of becoming a national leader, was perhaps shared by young men of his years; but to die at the age of thirty-four after having turned these dreams into reality presupposes qualities of leadership. To these qualities he added the gift of eloquence, of true oratorical powers. But no matter how gifted Mustafa Kamil's oratory, he would not have found many followers had not the temper of the age in which he lived been favourable to his gospel.

Physically Kamil was well endowed. He was a handsome man, slight and dapper, with large velvet eyes, and the luxuriant moustaches fashionable at the time. In manners and looks he was an elegant dandy. Nothing in his outward appearance denoted the feverish patriot—until he started to talk: then he appeared bold, arrogant, impervious to criticism, completely dedicated to a cause that was to absorb all his energy. It was at Ali Pasha Mubarak's house that Kamil met the famous men of the day, and it is not unlikely that it was through one of them that he made his initial contact with the Khedive. Abbas was known to be on the lookout for young men who were willing to preach the nationalist gospel, and Kamil was an obvious choice. So it was with the moral and material support of the Khedive that Kamil began his nationalist campaign.

An Egyptian historian, Abd al-Rahman al-Rafii, said in his biography of Kamil that Kamil had sought out the Khedive because of a piece of advice that Abdallah Nadim had given him in 1895, on how to become a successful nationalist. Nadim, a wit and poet, who had been sentenced to exile for his share in the Urabi revolution, had gone underground when the revolt collapsed, and for ten years had wandered in various disguises all over Egypt. He was eventually discovered and sent into exile for a year. Kamil had met Nadim on his return to Egypt, and Nadim had given him three rules to follow if he wished to meet with success as a nationalist. These were: never to use the army in a popular movement, for subsequently it would become too difficult to control; never to antagonize the Khedive, for he was bound, in order to save his throne, to join forces with the Powers against the nationalists; and never to give way to despair, for that was the sure way to defeat. Jurji Zaydan, another writer, claimed that Nadim also added that Kamil ought to get in touch with the Khedive because he would finance his nationalist activities.[2]

Kamil did get in touch with the Khedive, and the Khedive did finance his agitation, and even gave him his plan of action, especially in the early days of the movement. This is apparent in the correspondence that took place between Mustafa Kamil and Abd al-Rahim Bey Ahmad, the Khedive's private secretary.[3] Kamil's plan of action was two-fold: it proposed first, a campaign to convert European public opinion into favouring nationalist demands to evacuate all British troops from Egypt, and to put an end to British influence. Second, a simultaneous campaign aimed at the Egyptians themselves, and calculated to create a public opinion that would become sufficiently vocal and powerful to make matters so awkward for England that it would be forced to evacuate the country. Since the mass of the Egyptians were not sufficiently aware of the issues at stake, this was the more difficult part of the programme.

The first part of Kamil's campaign took place in Europe in 1895, where, armed with generous funds supplied by the Khedive, he succeeded in getting articles published in many of the French newspapers. But his efforts gained momentum with a letter he wrote to Mme Juliette Adam. Mme Adam was the editor of the *Revue des Deux Mondes*, a periodical that was well known for its anti-British leanings, and she was also a powerful figure in French literary and political circles. Kamil, in a rather theatrical letter, written in not quite correct French, asked to be allowed to meet Mme Adam and to present Egypt's case to her. He wrote: 'Je suis encore petit, mais j'ai des ambitions hautes. Je veux, dans la vieille Egypte réveiller la jeune. Ma Patrie, dit-on, n'existe pas. Elle vit, Madame, je la sens vivre en moi avec un amour tel qu'il dominera tous les autres et que je veux lui consacrer ma jeunesse, mes forces, ma vie.'[4] Mme Adam invited Kamil to meet her, and from their first meeting he won her completely. She adopted him as her protégé, and opened for him the doors of the French press and French political salons.

With the help provided by Mme Adam's introductions, Kamil published articles in most of the important French papers—*Le Figaro, L'Eclair, Le Journal des Débats*. The French press was only too glad to continue its policy of pinpricks against England, and Kamil was of nuisance-value to the editors. In the face of France's requests that England set a date for evacuation, England had always temporized with an allegation that Egypt did not wish for evacuation; yet here was a young Egyptian brought up in the shadow of the occupation, and clamouring loudly for evacuation in the name of the new Egypt. Cromer had repeatedly informed the world at large that the Egyptian nation did not exist, that Egypt was a conglomeration of different races living together;

yet here was Kamil maintaining that an Egyptian nation did exist, and speaking in the name of that very nation. The French press could not have hoped for a more sensational figure than Kamil. Young, handsome, speaking fluent French, 'Caramel Pacha' (as the French press was later to nickname him) was a newsworthy novelty as the first Egyptian to attack British policy coherently and consistently in the European press. Kamil did not limit himself to appeals to the French; he also published articles in Austrian and German papers. He even directed some of his agitation towards the British public—but there he met with far less response. The British government did not relish this journalistic agitation, for it was bringing Egypt back into the international limelight. As far back as 1888 Salisbury had warned Cromer against bringing Egypt to the attention of the French elector, who might embarrass his government into taking action; and French opinion, if excited, might turn to war.[5] This advice was repeated at later dates and was especially applicable to years of crisis such as was 1895.

The Khedive had instructed Kamil to put his faith in the political group in the *Chambre des Députés* that was headed by Etienne Deloncle, known to be anti-British. Deloncle had visited Egypt in that year, and had convinced the Khedive that France was ready to back any bid for independence that he was prepared to make. Encouraged by these words, the Khedive had advised Kamil to get into touch with the Frenchman and collaborate with him. But Kamil distrusted the man, and warned the Khedive against placing too much faith in him. In a letter dated June 8, 1895, he said that Deloncle was dangerous because he was indiscreet. The Khedive was apt to place his trust in anyone who promised him support; but Kamil, more canny, soon reported that the French deputies were not interested in the Egyptian question as such, but were more interested in using it for their own ends. Yet he too believed that France would support a bid for evacuation—albeit for French reasons—and in a letter he sent on September 19 he said optimistically that he did not expect the occupation to last for longer than six months.[6] This optimism was wholly unjustified, for though Kamil's articles roused much interest in Europe, interest was all they roused. France, with colonies of her own in North Africa, was not won over by his arguments for self-rule, nor was she ready to go to war with England over Egypt, as Fashoda in 1898 was to show. This incident delivered a blow to both Kamil's and the Khedive's expectations of French assistance for the Egyptian cause. France was willing to annoy England, but would go no further.

Although his work outside Egypt was an important feature of Kamil's campaign, it was his work within Egypt that really counted. This took the form of numerous speeches and articles in the newspapers of the day, *al-Ahram*, *al-Muayyad* and (in 1900) *al-Liwa*, a newspaper that he founded. His agitation rapidly bore fruit, and he soon gathered round him a group of nationalists who called themselves *al-Hizb al-Watani*. Correctly translated this would be the Patriotic Party, but it has always been known as the Nationalist Party. Starting as a secret society, this expanded into a grouping that regarded itself as an 'emanation of the national consciousness', rather than as a political party. Its members became a political party, officially speaking, only in 1907 when other political groupings also began to form themselves into parties.

The press became the main channel for nationalist agitation, and Kamil was fairly free to write as he wished, for although a press-censorship law existed from 1881, it was seldom applied. Cromer believed that the native press was not of sufficient importance to warrant censorship. He looked upon it as mendacious and mischievous—at best a safety-valve, but harmless so long as the army of occupation remained in Egypt. For that was the only guarantee that inflammatory writing would not lead to any serious disturbance of public order.[7] And yet by 1898 there were fifty Arabic dailies, and around 200 periodicals and newspapers had been founded, though many were short-lived.[8] In 1900 the circulation of *al-Liwa* alone was said to have reached 10,000. These figures offer some indication of the increasing importance of the press of the day, especially when we know that the literacy rate was only 10·5% for men and 0·3% for women, according to the 1897 census. Its significance called for more attention to public demand than those in authority were ready to pay. Cromer in particular dismissed press-comment in the belief that no sensible person paid any attention to it, and dismissed the nationalist movement as spurious and artificial.

Kamil's campaign in Egypt was based on three interdependent ideas: the need to break down local rivalries and unite all the elements of the population into a nationalist front; the need to develop a national education in order to strengthen patriotic sentiments; and the need to support the Khedive. The tone of his many speeches, and that of his articles, as well as their subject-matter, differed from the tone he used in Europe. And though he often talked as though to a European audience, yet where in Europe he used logical arguments designed to convince a sceptical and rational audience, in Egypt he pitched his appeal at the emotional level—therefore it was sometimes illogical. Whereas in Europe he tried to convince, in Egypt he had to rouse an apathetic and submissive mass into realizing that it formed a nation worthy of self-rule. Every Egyptian, whatever his religion or origins, had to be pressed into the service of Egypt; for the rise and fall of the nation was, said Kamil, the collective responsibility of the population both Copt and Muslim. Some of the prominent Copts were encouraged by this attitude, but the Taba incident (which will be discussed later), and Kamil's support of Turkey on religious grounds, savoured too much of pan-Islam for their peace of mind, and frightened many of them away. Education was the cure for Egypt's lack of unity, added Kamil, for the spirit of independence could not hope to take root in an ignorant nation. To this end he founded a model school in Hilmiyya as an example for other Egyptians to follow. But Kamil was not really interested in social reform, and was too impatient to wait until a new generation had been educated; he wanted to educate the present generation.

Many Egyptians did not believe that evacuation was possible. Britain, they maintained, was too powerful to oppose: struggle was useless in the face of such odds. Others said the occupation was the will of God. Both were typical Egyptian reactions to adversity, for in the face of centuries of oppression the Egyptians had learned to present a blanket of apathy and submission as the sole means of survival. Kamil had to combat their defeatism. The average Egyptian had lost pride in himself and in his nation. The Capitulations and the occupation had increased his sense of inferiority. Confidence in himself and in his race had to be restored. Kamil had to recreate the myth of Egypt's past grandeur, to show that Egypt was worth serving, that Egyptians were capable of great things; and to this task he brought ingenuity, putting to good use his invaluable gifts of oratory. His short, catchy slogans such as 'had I not been born an Egyptian, I would have wished to become one', and 'there is no sense in life when it is coupled with despair, and no sense in despair so long as there is life', are still popular today. Above all, Kamil wanted to instil a love of Egypt into the Egyptians. His own attachment to Egypt was so intense that one modern author detected overtones of Sufi mysticism in his use of terms like *tafani*, 'to lose oneself', in the service of one's country.[9] His speeches and articles abounded in such sentiments, some of which became national songs sung to the present day, such as 'My country, to you my love and my heart, my life and existence . . . For you, you are life, and there is no life without you, O Egypt.'

When some Egyptians sought to justify the material benefits of the British occupation, or maintained that social reforms must precede self-government, or (like Cromer) said that good government was better than self-government, Kamil countered with: 'There is no level of prosperity that can make a man set aside his dignity, his mission in life, the freedom of his country.' Acceptance of material benefits was the greatest evil, he thundered at the complaisant; it meant selling the future for the benefits derived in the present. Nothing England did for Egypt was good, for it merely served to gild the chains that bound Egypt to dishonour. 'The chains of slavery are still chains whether they be forged of gold or of iron,' he wrote on September 14, 1907, in an open letter, published in *Le Figaro*, to Campbell-Bannermann, the British Prime Minister. Independence must precede all other considerations, for it was of paramount importance, and all Egypt's energies must be directed to that one goal.

Kamil's speeches electrified his audience. His personal magnetism and, above all, his gift of oratory, were of the rare kind that hypnotized and dominated his listeners, and fired people to espouse his cause. He inspired them with an ideal; but he also antagonized a section of the educated Egyptians by his relationship with the Khedive, and by his pro-Turkish attitude. And whereas they agreed heartily with the patriotic feelings that he generated, they disapproved both of his approach and of much of the content of his speeches and articles, as we shall see later. Because of the emotional content of the nationalist movement, which is characteristic of all nationalist movements, Cromer attempted to equate it with fanaticism, and sent home reports to that effect. Kamil was determined to prove the falsity of this allegation, hence his constant exhortations to his countrymen to treat foreigners residing in Egypt with the utmost regard. He even coined an epigram which became his motto: 'Free in our country, hospitable to all.' To his credit be it said that he conducted the whole of his campaign without an appeal to force.

An important element of Kamil's campaign rested on the need to rally round the Khedive, whom he described as the source of patriotism and the focus of loyalty. He argued that Europe had guaranteed the existence of a Khedive in Egypt by treaty, and so long as a Khedive remained on the throne, Egypt could not be made a part of the British Empire. Further, a nationalist movement that was sanctioned by a strong Khedive was more likely to produce concrete results than a movement that was not sanctioned by the head of state. Abbas and Kamil therefore continued to cooperate for a long time; and though Abbas seemed to be the mastermind in the early days of the nationalist movement, Kamil eventually took over and acted on his own initiative. Occasional conflict between the two men broke out, but their differences were always patched up. With the passage of time Abbas became discouraged by an opposition that brought no tangible returns save a constant threat of deposition and the curtailment of much of his prerogative. Fashoda was such a grievous blow to him that he never quite recovered from it, and from then on his ardour for the nationalist cause cooled. In 1900 we find Kamil writing in commiseration: 'Poor Khedive, Fashoda has reduced him to utter despair, and with the attitude of Europe in the affair of the Transvaal, who could counsel the Khedive seriously to resist England?'[10] The Entente Cordiale of 1904 almost threw Abbas into the arms of Cromer, and soured Kamil against France so completely that he said: 'I would be an imbecile were I to believe for an instant that France can be the friend of Egypt or of Islam.'[11]

As the Khedive's hopes of evacuation waned, so did his friendship with Kamil; and although in January 1904 Kamil wrote an article in *al-Liwa* which abounded in fulsome praise for the Khedive, the break was not far off. On March 9 an article in *al-Liwa* made no mention of the Khedive, and said that the sole guarantee of Egypt's freedom lay in a parliamentary life. On October 25 Kamil published an open letter to the Khedive in which he put an end to the connection between them. He said that since Abbas was blamed by the British authorities for nationalist agitation, the nationalists and the Khedive had better sever their connection, so that the Khedive could no longer be accused of plotting with them. Some people believed that this break had been engineered, with the maximum publicity, in order to protect Abbas from British accusations that he was fomenting troubles in the country, and to save him from the threat of deposition; and that in secret he continued to collaborate with the nationalists. There is some truth in that allegation; but, at the same time, at this stage of the game neither the Khedive nor Kamil needed each other. Kamil no longer relied totally on the Khedive's financial backing; by now, money for the nationalist movement was pouring in from various sources. Neither did he need the stamp of legitimacy that the Khedive gave to the movement, since it had come to be accepted by large masses of the population. On the other hand, Abbas had become discouraged by the attitude of the Powers towards his bids for independence, and more than ever feared deposition. In 1904 he made the first gesture of accepting the occupation by appointing a British aide-de-camp, and in November he made the further gesture of reviewing the troops of occupation on King Edward's birthday. This was such a pro-British move for him to make, that he felt constrained to issue a public explanation through his cabinet. A statement was issued to the press that on that day the Khedive had merely happened to be at Abdin Palace by 'accident', and that Cromer had asked him to review the troops. But this 'accident' was repeated in each following year.

Rashid Rida claimed that Muhammad Farid, Kamil's lieutenant, had told him that Kamil was befriending the Khedive in order to obtain funds for the nationalist cause, but that he was determined to set him aside once Egypt had become independent and the nationalists were in power.[12] Ronald Storrs, the Oriental Secretary, also believed this to be the case, and said that both the Khedive and the nationalists were making use of each other, 'each firmly believing that the moment the Occupation ceases, he will boot the other out'.[13] That may well have been; but though Kamil and the Khedive were estranged, their estrangement was only temporary. They soon effected a secret reconciliation, and the Khedive continued to finance Kamil's newspapers.

Cromer was convinced that Kamil was a creature of the Khedive's, and that all the nationalist agitation in Egypt was fomented by Abbas. He regarded Kamil's break with Abbas as a charade, designed to hoodwink the British authorities and to safeguard the Khedive from British wrath. For this reason, Cromer underplayed the importance of Mustafa Kamil on the Egyptian scene, and—despite the large following that the Nationalist Party had acquired within a few years of his agitation—Kamil was rarely mentioned by name in despatches. In one of his yearly reports, Cromer had accounted for the rise of the nationalist movement by asserting that in a country where reforms were sponsored by an alien race, '. . . a slight, but nevertheless pernicious tendency could exist to regard the action of government as somewhat out of harmony with legitimate native aspirations if not wholly antagonistic to them'.[14] But he believed that such a tendency could be overlooked, or treated with the contempt it deserved; for the nationalists were nothing but 'ambitious young men with a very superficial acquaintance with public affairs, and with very little serious sense of responsibility'. And since the material benefits of the British occupation in Egypt were so obvious that 'criticism in that direction save on some minor points of detail is barred', he did not see that nationalist demands were at all justified. He later added that the attempt to create a national party by demanding an extension of parliamentary institutions had been made, but 'had not met with a hearty response', because the intelligent portion of the native population realized that 'any radical change of system would be premature if not absolutely dangerous'.[15] And yet the demand for an extension of parliamentary institutions to which Cromer referred, and which he described as meeting with 'no hearty response', was a motion made in the General Assembly and carried unanimously by the members, who certainly represented a good cross-section of intelligent Egyptian society.

There may have been some justification for Cromer's statement that the young nationalists had a superficial acquaintance with public affairs, and there was certainly justification in his refusal to recognize Kamil as sole leader of the nationalist movement in Egypt, since there were other groups who did not support Kamil. But there is little justification for his refusal to recognize that there was a *bona fide* nationalist movement in existence. His disregard for the nationalists stems from several causes, not the least of which was his concept of the way to rule 'subject races', and his low opinion of the Egyptians and their governing abilities. But he also met the men who were in opposition to Kamil; the Egyptians he frequented were moderates who feared Kamil's extremism, or were anti-Khedive, and who either distrusted Kamil by reason of his connections with Abbas, or else were pro-occupation. All of these groups tended to encourage Cromer in his belief that Kamil was a charlatan, and a creature of the Khedive's. But even if Cromer had accepted that Kamil was a genuine leader of a genuine movement, he would still have relegated him and his movement to the realm of ignorant opposition. He was so sure that Egypt did not need a change of government, that he convinced himself that the 'intelligent' Egyptians likewise wanted no change. Refusing to open his eyes to any proof to the contrary, he countered all complaints with the argument of material benefits. He had completely missed the point of the nationalist movement. The fact that the British occupation had brought material benefits to the Egyptians was irrelevant to the problem; for, as Albert Hourani succinctly put it, 'the essence of imperialism is to be found in a moral relationship—that of power and powerlessness—and any material consequences which spring from it are not enough to change it'.[16] The need the nationalists felt for a change of government was a need for recognition of their very existence as thinking and intelligent men, capable of sharing in the government of their country. It was Cromer's humiliating disregard of them that drove them to become intransigent and virulent.

Kamil reaped a harvest from his campaign in 1906—a busy year for him—a year of crises for Egypt. Incidents followed each other in disastrous succession. In January the trouble with Turkey over Taba took place. In February, all the students of the Faculty of Law went on strike. In May came the incident of Dinshwai.

Taba was a desert spot at the head of the Gulf of Aqaba and had never roused anybody's interest until, in 1906, a Turkish force landed there and proceeded to set up posts. The British government strongly objected to this action, claimed Taba as part of Egyptian territory, and asked for a delimitation of the frontier to determine title. The Porte refused on the ground that the whole of the Sinai Peninsula was Ottoman territory. Aqaba and its environs had acquired importance for Turkey since the start of a plan to bring the Hijaz railway from Maan to Aqaba.[17] In Cromer's eyes too, the Sinai Peninsula was important because it formed a protective barrier between Turkey and the Suez Canal. But the British government's main concern over Sinai stemmed from a fear that the Taba landing might have been inspired by Germany, in order to deflect Britain's attention while Germany attacked France. This fear was supported by an intelligence report that, on December 31, a steamer, supposed to be German, had been seen discharging a cargo looking suspiciously like arms and ammunition, at Ras Mallop on the Sinai coast.[18] Suspicion of Germany increased when two Germans, one of whom was Military Attaché in Tokyo, attempted to go to Sinai without applying for passes, on the pretext that they were going ibex-shooting on their way to Palestine.[19]

Rumours spread in Cairo of an impending Turkish advance towards Egyptian territory. Egyptian editors and columnists, headed by Mustafa Kamil, came out in support of Turkey. The line they took led Cromer to report that pan-Islamic influence was rife, and he feared that in case of an actual attack the Egyptian army might not fight against Turkey. Owen, the Director of Intelligence, disagreed, maintaining that '. . . the vast majority would do all in their power to assist the Turk out of the place—religion or no religion'.[20] But Cromer and Wingate—who was then Governor of the Sudan, but who for a long time had served as Director of Military Intelligence—thought otherwise. Wingate maintained that Draconian measures should be applied, and suggested to Cromer that '. . . if the Turks persist we shall declare a British Protectorate over Egypt'.[21] The British Ambassador in Constantinople therefore presented a Note to the Porte requiring it to comply within ten days with the British government's demands for evacuation and delimitation of frontier, and threatened that in the event of non-compliance 'the position will become grave'.[22] Turkey complied.

Meanwhile Mustafa Kamil published on April 22 an editorial in support of Turkey in which he claimed that Egypt had no jurisdiction over the area, and that the firmans had given Egypt administrative authority over Sinai simply as a temporary measure. This was in answer to Cromer's claim that Sinai was included, both in the firman of 1841 and the firman of Abbas's investiture in 1892, as part of Egypt's 'privileged territories'. On May 8 Kamil wrote another article saying that the incident at Taba should be judged as occurring between a country that had occupied Egypt by force, and a country that had rights of suzerainty over Egypt. Every Egyptian must support the rights of Turkey in the face of British allegations. A further article on May 13 was entitled 'Support your brother whether he be in the right or the wrong', which afforded Cromer the opportunity to accuse the nationalists of pan-Islamic tendencies and of religious fanaticism.

For the previous few years Kamil had adopted a policy of rapprochement with Turkey. The Sultan looked benevolently enough on him, and in 1904 decorated him and made him a Pasha. This pro-Turkish policy alienated some Egyptians, for they suspected that Kamil had been bought by the Sultan, who was in the throes of his pan-Islamic movement. Kamil knew the appeal that Islamic arguments held for the masses, and, since the Sultan was Caliph of the Muslims, and the occupying power was a Christian one, the Sultan could become an asset as having a nuisance-value. His arguments did not convince Shaykh Muhammad Abduh and his friends, and they continued to be suspicious of Kamil's friendship with the Sultan. The incident at Taba, and Kamil's attitude of cutting off Egypt's nose to spite the British government's face, alarmed some of Abduh's followers—so much so that they decided to form a newspaper of their own.

At the invitation of Ahmad Lutfi al-Sayyid, a young lawyer, a group of men of substance—Muhammad Mahmud Sulayman, Hasan Abd al-Raziq and Umar Sultan—met together to discuss the situation. The Egyptian press, said Lutfi, was filling the public's ear with nonsense, and dragging in appeals to religion without explaining the real issues at stake. Was Egypt to give up a large part of her territory just to annoy Britain, who was fighting Egypt's legal battle for her? Umar Sultan, one of the richest notables of Egypt, a man who had donated vast sums of money to Mustafa Kamil's movement, then suggested that they should join together and found an independent newspaper, one that did not have to curry favour either with Turkey, the Khedive or the British Agency, one that could afford straightforward newscoverage without pandering to the public's liking for scandal and sensation. As a result of this meeting *al-Jarida* was born nearly a year later, on March 9, 1907, with Ahmad Lutfi al-Sayyid as its editor, and a list of shareholders that read like a *Who's Who* of the notables of Egypt.

Cromer looked on *al-Jarida* with a benevolent eye. He believed that so long as people were prosperous they would be satisfied with British rule in Egypt; and were not the shareholders of the new paper some of the most prosperous men in the land—many of them known to him personally? Cromer approved of the paper because he believed that it would temper the extremism of the other newspapers with its moderate approach, that it would be the voice of reason and good sense. Eventually, the shareholders in *al-Jarida* were to form the first official political party in Egypt, the party of moderate nationalists, *Hizb al-Umma*, the People's Party.

The next crisis to follow Taba in 1906 was the strike of the law students. This was the first manifestation of its kind, and reached such proportions that the Director of the School threatened to expel every student who did not break the strike and return to the Faculty at once. The students, who were all ardent followers of Mustafa Kamil, had been urged to go on strike by *al-Liwa* when they complained of unjust treatment by their Director. When the students would not accept the Director's ultimatum, Cromer had to intervene and mediate between the two parties before the students would go back to their studies.

During the month of April, the British press reported 'symptoms of unrest' in Egypt, and the *Daily Mail* of April 20 claimed that these were due to Turkish influence, and to the effect of the Russo-Japanese War. The victory of Japan had so affected Kamil that he wrote a book called *The Rising Sun* in which he attributed Japan's spectacular rise to its spirit of nationalism, and exhorted Egyptians to look upon it as an example to follow. According to the *Daily Mail* of April 25, 'the native press in Cairo is adopting a very inflammatory tone . . . it is being instigated to violence by leading officials of the Sultan's household'. One leading official was Mukhtar Pasha Ghazi, who was accused of plotting with Kamil to rouse pan-Islamic feelings against the British over the Taba incident. Kamil could be accused of rousing nationalist emotions, or even religious sentiment; but it was patently untrue to accuse him of incitement to violence, since his whole activity was precisely aligned on pleas of non-violence. A week later the *Daily Mail* again reported 'great excitement in Cairo among the better class natives'. Thus when the incident of Dinshwai happened, coming as it did after a period of unrest, it was treated by the British authorities in Egypt with a total lack of proportion because of the tension that had preceded it. Hence the degree to which it became a turning-point in Anglo-Egyptian relations.

Briefly, the facts of the Dinshwai affair were as follows. A group of British officers went pigeon-shooting near the village of Dinshwai at the invitation of one of the notables. When they arrived at the village, they failed to find the village headman, but went ahead with their sport. While they were shooting, a barn caught fire; and the villagers, angered at the shooting of their pigeons, which were a means of livelihood, and blaming the officers for the fire in their barn, rushed out with their wooden staves and, while attempting to disarm the officers, belaboured them heartily. During the fracas, a gun belonging to one of the officers went off. A woman fell wounded, and was assumed to be dead by the villagers; four men were also peppered with shot. The villagers became even more incensed and, joined by the woman's male relations, they beat the officers violently. One officer, Captain Bull, finally managed to escape, and ran all the way back to camp in the heat of noon, to fetch help. Just outside camp, Bull fell dead, and an Egyptian peasant—finding him lying there—tried to help him. He was found so doing by British soldiers from the camp, who, assuming that he had killed Bull, beat him to death. Back in Dinshwai the remaining officers were detained by the villagers until the police arrived. They were found to be suffering from various wounds, contusions and broken limbs. The medical verdict on Bull was death due to sunstroke aggravated by concussion.

The British authorities took a serious view of the affair, and set up a Special Tribunal to try the villagers of Dinshwai on a charge of murder. It is interesting to note that no one was prosecuted for the death of the Egyptian peasant who had tried to help Bull. The Tribunal was set up according to a law passed in 1895, when it had been reckoned that the Egyptian Criminal Code was inadequate in cases of 'crimes of violence against officers and men of the Army of Occupation'—although adequate enough for dealing with crimes of violence against Egyptians. The Tribunal's function was 'to administer justice more promptly and inflict punishments of greater severity than is possible if the Egyptian Criminal Code continues to be applied in its integrity'.[23] The law in question was of the kind that caused deep resentment against Britain among the nationalists, for the court set up under its term had the power to pass sentences of death, the defendants having no right of appeal. The Tribunal had never before had occasion to sit, and the only approach to a precedent had happened in 1887 when a Special Commission had been set up to examine the case of British army officers who had been attacked by villagers near the Pyramids, while quail-shooting. On that occasion sentences of flogging not exceeding fifty lashes had been passed, and Cromer's sole comment on that incident had been: 'I think the latter [flogging] carried out on the spot was very necessary.'[24]

The Special Tribunal which was set up to try the villagers of Dinshwai was by way of being a court-martial, and was composed of Butros Pasha Ghali, a Copt who was acting as interim Minister of Justice; Mr W. Hayter, acting Judicial Adviser; Mr W. Bond, Vice-President of the Courts; Fathi Bey Zaghlul, President of the Native Courts; and Colonel Ludlow, Judge Advocate, representing the army of occupation. The native press was quick to point out that only two of the men on the bench knew sufficient Arabic to understand the testimony of the peasants, or indeed of the lawyers; and only one Muslim was to be found among the five judges. During the trial tempers ran high. The prosecution tried to establish premeditated murder, while the counsel for the defence, one of whom was Ahmad Lutfi al-Sayyid, attempted to show that the attack on the officers was an accident due to fortuitous circumstances, the motives for the crime arising at the moment. From the beginning, the British authorities were determined to make an example of the villagers, and to turn the trial into a show of force. Fifty-two accused were examined within thirty minutes; i.e. 34 seconds per man—just enough time to give his name and age. Out of a whole village of several hundred persons, the British officers were able to identify twenty-one men as their assailants—an impossible achievement. If only on these two counts, the trial, if trial it can be called, was a gross miscarriage of justice.

On June 18, several days before the end of the trial, and before sentences had been passed, *al-Muqattam*, the mouthpiece of the Agency, announced that orders had been issued to send several sets of gallows to Dinshwai. It looked as though the court intended to be as harsh as possible. And, indeed, on June 27 the court established premeditation and concerted action, and the following sentences were passed on twenty-one men out of fifty-two accused, ranging in age from seventeen to sixty: four men were sentenced to hang, two men were sentenced to penal servitude for life, six men to seven years' imprisonment, three men to one year's imprisonment and fifty lashes, and five men to fifty lashes. Although public executions had been stopped two years previously, the sentences were to be carried out in public on the site of the attack on the officers in Dinshwai, and the whole village was forced to watch the executions.

The severity of the sentences can only be explained by British uneasiness about the state of feeling among the Egyptians. Cromer had left Egypt on his summer vacation before the sentences were passed; and Findlay, the Chargé d'Affaires, was left to manage the proceedings. He intended that Dinshwai should serve as an example. In his report he said: 'I do not believe that this brutal attack on British soldiers had anything directly to do with political animosity. It is, however, due to the insubordinate spirit which has been sedulously fostered during the last year by unscrupulous and interested agitators.'[25] Then he added: 'The conduct of the villagers is looked upon as casting discredit on the whole Egyptian people, as well as being indefensible in itself.' This outrageous statement is not only notable for its smugness, but pinpoints clearly how completely ignorant of public opinion Findlay was; it serves to underline the gap that by now existed between the British officials and the Egyptians. Never had feeling run so high in Egypt as over this affair. The court's version of premeditated murder seemed entirely indefensible to the Egyptians. An angry fallah will not hesitate to split a man's skull with his axe, but between that and premeditation there is much difference. The man in the street asked why, if the fallahin were planning murder, they did not carry out their plan, instead of sitting round the officers and waiting for the police to appear? Why did they go armed with wooden staves if they intended to murder men carrying fire-arms? Above all, why were so many men punished for the accidental death of one man? The answer was that it was because the man who died was an English officer. The public had reason to be shocked.

The emotional impact of Dinshwai was so profound that Mustafa Kamil said that it had done more to awaken people's feelings against the occupation than the passage of ten years could have done.[26] Ahmad Amin, who in later years became Dean of the

Faculty of Letters, and who was a distinguished author, recounted that when news of the sentences reached him, he was at a dinner party, and most of the guests wept when they heard the verdict.[27] Qasim Amin said: 'Everyone I met had a broken heart and a lump in his throat. There was nervousness in every gesture—in their hands and their voices. Sadness was on every face, but it was a peculiar sort of sadness. It was confused, distracted and visibly subdued in the face of superior force . . . The spirits of the hanged men seemed to hover over every place in the city.'[28] Poets wrote odes on Dinshwai, and even the fallahin created a folk-ballad recounting the cruelty of the English to the Egyptians, and sang it throughout the countryside. Freely translated it runs:

> They fell upon Dinshwai
> And spared neither man nor his brother.
> Slowly they hanged the one and flogged the other.
> It was a gloomy day when Zahran was killed,
> His mother from the roof watched, while
>   tears from her eyes spilled,
> His brother, O you People, stood by him
> And gazed till his eyes grew dim.[29]

This peasant song was an indication of the depth of feeling the trial aroused even among the Egyptian fallah—of all sections of the population the most apathetic. The three Egyptians involved in the trial—Butros Ghali, Fathi Zaghlul, and Ibrahim al-Hilbawi, the Public Prosecutor—were despised, and the public never forgave them their share in the trial. When Zaghlul was later nominated Under-Secretary of State for Justice, a poem was written about his appointment implying that it was his reward for complicity, for his betrayal of the 'pigeons' to feather the nest of the 'chickens'—a pun on his name which means a chick. Many years later, at a public meeting at which Hilbawi was to speak, he was greeted by an unfriendly audience that released pigeons over his head; while one of the reasons al-Wardani gave for assassinating Butros Ghali in 1911 was, that he had passed a treacherous sentence over Dinshwai.

Dinshwai had repercussions in England. Speakers in the House said that they had never heard of a more brutal, barbarous exhibition—that it would remain a stain on the history of the British occupation in Egypt.[30] Sir Edward Grey, who was at the time Secretary of State for Foreign Affairs, made a statement in the House saying that throughout the year fanatical feeling had been increasing in Egypt, and that further measures to protect Europeans in Egypt might have to be taken: 'If the House of Commons questions the decision of a tribunal composed of the highest English judges and the highest Egyptian judges, it is bound to have the effect of weakening the authority of the Egyptian government, and if the House does so then the fanatical feeling in Egypt will get the better of the constituted authority and you will be left to face the use of force.'[31]

This answer put a stop to any further embarrassing questions about the incident, but it made the Egyptians even angrier by adding insult to injury. Not only were they being treated as an occupied country by the imposition of extraordinary tribunals which had no connection with the laws of the land, but they were now being accused of plotting massacres and of fanaticism.

The Egyptian press was quick to take up the challenge of Dinshwai, and Ali Yusif wrote twenty-three articles on it. Mustafa Kamil published a long article in the *Figaro* of July 11 in protest at the verdict: '. . . I ask the British nation whether it is worthy of them to allow their representatives, after twenty-four years of occupation, to use extra-ordinary measures and barbarous procedures to govern Egypt and to teach the Egyptians human dignity.' (That was the question that Sir Charles Dilke had put to the House, albeit in different terms.) Kamil added that the accusation of fanaticism was unjust, for, if it were true, how could a court composed of four Christians and one Muslim dare sit in judgment on fifty-two Muslims? Cromer had always defended his autocratic ways in Egypt by saying that his actions were controlled by the House of Commons and the force of public opinion in England, yet when the House put questions to the government, it was silenced by stories of massacres and fanaticism. If Dinshwai happened because a woman was wounded, then the judgment was hideous and must rouse the whole world to indignation,

Kamil wrote; if it was due to a national and religious sentiment, then Cromer must perforce admit that all Egyptians hated the occupation.

Undoubtedly Dinshwai was a blunder on the part of the British officials. To this day, whenever it is mentioned, it serves to arouse indignation among the Egyptians. Why then was this blunder allowed to happen? One explanation is that offered by Lord Lloyd, who succeeded Allenby as the High Commissioner in Egypt. He said that it was an example of the 'kind of barbarity which is generally dictated by panic'.[32] Grey in his memoirs claimed that his defence in the House had been based on telegrams sent by Findlay, and admitted: 'When the full facts were before me I felt that what had been done was open to question.'[33] It is possible that, had Dinshwai happened twenty years earlier, sentences would not have been as severe. But the incident came as the culmination of a series of events: the agitation of the nationalist press for evacuation; the loss of British contact with native public opinion and the consequent inability to gauge correctly the results of measures taken; the feeling on the part of British officials that the situation in Egypt was now less secure; the concomitant need for a show of force to cow the population into submission. A combination of these developments changed England's position from that of friend and protector into that of colonizer, requiring protection from the natives.

As the incident of Dinshwai made the Egyptians forget Taba and the Turks, and once more focus their resentment on British rule, a tone of pessimism creeps into Cromer's reports. 'Although matters are outwardly quiet, there is an undercurrent of bad feeling here which causes me some little anxiety.'[34] It would appear that people in London realized the time had come for a change of policy. Once the hubbub had died down, the Liberal government, which had come to power in 1905, began to see the need for a modified policy. Its leader, Campbell-Bannermann, accordingly arranged a meeting with Kamil, and asked him to supply a list of names of men whom Kamil considered capable of forming an Egyptian ministry. Kamil gave the Prime Minister a list of over thirty names, some of whom were his political opponents, and more than half of whom were subsequently to become cabinet ministers. Among the names that Kamil cited were Muhammad Said, Saad Zaghlul, Husayn Rushdi, Ismail Sirri, Ismail Sidqi, Abd al-Khaliq Tharwat, Yahya Ibrahim, Adli Yaghan, Aziz Izzat, Ahmad Lutfi—all but two of whom later became prime ministers.[35]

The first step towards change was the appointment of Saad Zaghlul as Minister of Education. Zaghlul was perhaps the only Egyptian whom Cromer wholeheartedly admired. He described him as 'not only by far the most able, but also by far the strongest Egyptian with whom I have yet had to deal'.[36] This was a serious attempt at nominating an Egyptian to a responsible position. 'He is a real working man,' added Cromer in a letter to Grey, 'and not a mere dummy. He belongs, not to the nationalist party, but to the school of *bona fide* Mohamedan reformers to whom I alluded in a memo which you saw before I left England.'[37] The reformers that Cromer had in mind were the group of moderates who were later to form the People's Party, *Hizb al-Umma*, and who were at the time the founders of *al-Jarida*. Saad Zaghlul was appointed for two basic reasons. In the first place the students were becoming too rowdy: they were all followers of Mustafa Kamil, and their English head masters had little hold over them. The strike of the law students had indicated that a strong hand was needed over the students in general, and preferably an Egyptian hand. In the second place, education was one of the sorest points with the Egyptians, every one of whom accused Cromer of deliberately neglecting education so that he could continue to claim that the Egyptians were incapable of running their own administration. The man in charge of educating the Egyptians was a dour Scotsman named Dunlop who worked as Adviser to the Ministry of Education. He had no sympathy with the Egyptians, and was even alleged to have told Professor Browne of Cambridge that he would not accept men from Cambridge who had passed an examination in Arabic, as teachers in Egypt, because this gave them 'romantic ideas about the natives'.[38] He believed the Egyptians should be made to learn English. Unfortunately Saad was not able to do much to improve education, for the whole system needed radical overhaul. The standard of education was low, it aimed at turning out clerks or petty civil servants, and was certainly not geared to develop a new class of leaders.

The second step came with Cromer's tacit encouragement to the moderates to form a political party, his purpose being to counteract the effect of the extreme nationalists. In 1909 he wrote: 'When I was in Egypt I did give a certain amount of encouragement to some of the Moderates, who I thought might be a set-off against the extremists.'[39] What exactly was the relationship between Cromer and the moderates? Had he been in communication with them? These were questions which the Egyptians asked. Saad Zaghlul was often regarded as the link between the two groups; he was *persona grata* at the Agency and a friend of most of the moderates. Zaghlul had started life as an obscure Shaykh from al-Azhar, a disciple of al-Afghani's and of Abduh, who had made him an assistant editor on the *Journal Officiel*. He was implicated in the Urabi rebellion, and was imprisoned. He then practised law at the instigation of Princess Nazli Fazil, and became famous and successful, eventually marrying the daughter of the Prime Minister, Mustafa Fahmi. This alliance, and his friendship with Nazli, gave him entry to the circle that frequented the Agency, and he became a friend of Harry Boyle. It is also reasonable to assume that he first met Cromer at the salon of the Princess, where both men were welcome visitors. In spite of these connections, Zaghlul was regarded by the rest of his countrymen as a moderate who was not averse to helping nationalists, although he himself took no part in the movement. For example, he financed Shaykh Ali Yusif when the latter needed money for his newspaper. There was nothing uncommon about this seeming paradox, for many Egyptians frequented the Agency and also wished for England's eventual evacuation. Perhaps a sycophantic element entered into their attitude, in that they wished to become identified with the party in power while claiming to disapprove of it in principle, or perhaps they approved of British reforms, or perhaps they were simply realists accepting a *fait accompli*. Zaghlul approved of British attempts at reforming Egypt. He believed that his country's salvation lay in preparation for an eventual evacuation through education, and a better system of justice; that it was futile to depend on French pressure to evict Britain, and dangerous to depend on Turkey. Hence he regarded Kamil's approach to the problem as a waste of energy, and told him so, although he was on friendly terms with him. Rashid Rida has tried to make out that Abduh and Zaghlul disapproved of Kamil, and he even claims that Zaghlul said Kamil was a lunatic.[40] His statement is, however, open to question, since it was well known that Kamil visited Zaghlul, and had great respect for him, while Saad tolerated Kamil. When Zaghlul became Minister of Education, Kamil was one of the first to visit him and speak of him in eulogistic terms before the rest of the gathering. Then he left, before meeting Saad's brother, Fathi, because—as he explained to Saad—he would not shake the hand of the man who had sat on the court of Dinshwai.

Although many of the moderates were friends of Saad Zaghlul, he refused to join *al-Umma* party when it was founded, because he felt that any political party in Egypt just then would be useless. But the Khedive, who was abroad when the party was founded, suspected Zaghlul of having a hand in creating it. Abbas anxiously inquired of Ahmad Shafiq, his Arabic Secretary, on two separate occasions, whether the Zaghlul brothers were involved. Shafiq answered that Saad did not seem to have any connection with the party, but that his brother Fathi was one of its members.[41] Abbas was not convinced, and in his memoirs recorded that in 'October 1906 there arose a group which aimed at combating the nationalists and which was inspired by Cromer and probably subservient to him. This party was *Hizb al-Umma*, and Saad Zaghlul was the brains behind it.'[42]

Abbas was wrong on all counts. The group did not aim at combating the nationalists, since in fact its members were themselves nationalists who simply chose to adopt a different language; and Saad was not the brains behind the party—he was not even its link with the Agency. It was Fathi Zaghlul who led the moderates to believe that Cromer was contemplating a new departure, was planning to use a new group of men as administrators, and would look with favour upon a party of moderate nationalists. This was later borne out by Cromer's assertion that he had encouraged those who were in favour of a 'moderate, reasonable, and gradual extension of self-governing institutions'. Cromer's successor, Eldon Gorst, was even more explicit, writing in 1911 that for some years before his departure Cromer had been 'considering what steps were possible for the purpose of associating the Egyptians more directly with the conduct of their own affairs'.[43] And though 'years' is a slight exaggeration, it was nevertheless plain that Cromer was contemplating a new line of policy and hoped that the moderates would help him. Like Cromer, the moderates measured Egypt's welfare in terms of reform, of the greatest good of the greatest number. They realized that blind antagonism to England would lead nowhere, and hoped that a policy of co-operation, though not subservience, would bring about an extension of parliamentary rights and some measure of self-rule. Unlike Kamil, they believed that reforms would necessarily have to precede evacuation, and the vital reform was to curb the Khedive's arbitrary powers.

The third step came with Cromer's resignation in March 1907. Resignation was forced on him by a nervous affliction of his digestion so serious as to produce the medical verdict that six more months' work would kill him. In his letter of resignation Cromer wrote to Grey: 'If I were younger I should rather enjoy fighting the Khedive, Mustafa Kamil and their English allies [referring to Liberal Members of Parliament], and moreover, I think I should beat them.'[44] But perhaps there was more than illness behind his resignation; possibly the accumulation of disasters had become too much for an ageing man. Harry Boyle hinted as much in a letter to Rennell Rodd in which he wrote, '. . . the political situation here is simply damnable. The Nationalists . . . are very active and intensely virulent . . . You would not believe the language they use, even now about the Lord in their papers.'[45]

1907 was a year of economic crisis, and many people lost money through speculation. This crisis confronted the British administration with awkward criticisms on financial grounds, whereas Cromer had prided himself on the financial achievements of the occupation. At the same time there was a breakdown of public security and an increase in the rate of crime. Cromer had commented on this phenomenon in his yearly report, and called it 'the most disquieting feature in the whole Egyptian situation'.[46] But he failed to interpret it as a symptom of social disorganization. The idols of the past, the symbols of power and authority, had been destroyed by the British reforms. As a result of a new law passed in 1895, the once all-powerful village headman was now replaced by men of straw who had no authority over the villagers. The fallahin did not understand the new laws; and the police officer, with his new-style western education, had lost contact with the villagers and could no longer understand them. Until the new system of laws had penetrated to the grass-roots of the country, Egypt was bound to go through a period of malaise. Cromer must have realized that the Liberal government would not continue to support him as previous governments had done, especially when the unrest of the past few months showed that his policy was not as successful as he would wish people in England to believe. He must have known of Campbell-Bannermann's meeting with Kamil, which was tantamount to a negation of all he had reported about Kamil and the nationalist movement. Very wisely, he realized that the time had come for him to go. The Liberal ministry was indeed disenchanted with him, and he was never asked to serve again, even in an advisory capacity.

When news of Cromer's resignation was announced in April 1907, Mustafa Kamil claimed that it was the agitation of his party that had brought it about. He wrote an article in *al-Liwa* of April 12 asking what Egypt would remember about Cromer, and answered his own question with a diatribe. Egypt, he wrote, would remember that Cromer had usurped Khedivial authority, that he had conquered the Sudan with Egyptian men and money, and then denuded Egyptians of every influence in that land; that he had deprived the executive of every power; that he had attacked the Muslim religion; that he had denied the Egyptian his right to education, and, accusing him of ignorance and ingratitude, had insisted that Egypt be ruled by England; that he had attacked nationalism and attempted to stifle it; above all, that he had turned Egypt into a British colony.

The Orator, the Pro-Consul, and the Intellectual

In a more objective vein Lutfi al-Sayyid wrote an article in *al-Jarida* on April 13 entitled 'Lord Cromer in the light of history'. In it he paid tribute to Cromer as an economist and financier, and a great patriot. Cromer, said Lutfi, had rendered England great services, but in so doing had deprived Egypt of its right to the kind of political life to which every nation aspired. Though Cromer gave the average Egyptian personal freedom, he had deprived the civil servant of all the freedom of initiative—making that a prerogative of the European employees. Through his educational policy Cromer had kept the Egyptian subservient to British interests; for the inevitable result of a low level of education, fit only for turning out government clerks, was a dearth of capable administrators, giving Cromer an excuse to import Englishmen to fill the posts. Had Cromer not insisted on retarding Egyptian education, and had he made use of Egyptian talents instead of denying the very existence of the Egyptian nation (the article ended), he would have earned praise from the Egyptians for his good works, and for introducing justice; and he would have won Egypt's friendship for England. This article was followed by another written on April 14 and entitled 'What qualities make a man great?'—the answers being a devotion to the interests of his own country.

The joy of the nationalists at Cromer's resignation was soon damped by three subsequent events; the first of these was Cromer's yearly report; the next was his farewell speech; and the third was the appointment of Eldon Gorst as his successor.

In his yearly report on the situation in Egypt, which appeared in April, Cromer spoke of the moderates in favourable terms, while castigating the Nationalist Party. He said that the programme of the nationalists was incapable of realization, that the party was harmful because tinged with pan-Islamic sentiment which could easily rouse fanatical manifestations, and cited the Taba incident as an example of what he meant. He then referred to the moderates whom he called the 'Girondists of Egypt' and the 'Imam's Party', and said they were the main hope of Egyptian nationalism. In particular he referred to Saad Zaghlul's recent appointment as Minister, explaining that this move was made in a 'desire to associate an able man and enlightened Egyptian of this particular section of society with the work of Egyptian reform'. Should this experiment prove successful, then 'some encouragement will be afforded to move further in the same direction'. These words were greeted with pleasure by the moderates, but the rest of the report was less pleasing, for Cromer set out an alternative to the nationalist programme by describing what he considered to be the 'only possible Egyptian nationality'. This must consist of all the inhabitants of Egypt, irrespective of race or religion—and so far the nationalists agreed with him. But he added that an International Legislative Council should be formed in Egypt which would combine the Egyptians and the resident Europeans, who, while maintaining their foreign nationalities, were to govern Egypt side by side with the Egyptians. And though the European residents formed a numerical minority, Cromer proposed to give them a majority of voices in his projected council. To make quite sure that no one misunderstood his meaning, Cromer wrote: 'Can any sane man believe that a country which has for centuries past been exposed to the worst forms of misgovernment at the hands of its rulers . . . is capable of suddenly springing into a position which will enable it to exercise full rights of autonomy.' He ended on a note of warning to the nationalists: 'It is essential to show that British policy in Egypt . . . is not liable to be influenced, nor the British occupation disturbed, by any passing wave of local opinion.'[47]

If the moderates still retained some illusions as to Cromer's intentions, these were completely dispelled by his farewell speech, given on May 6 at the Royal Opera House. Once again Cromer repeated that he was opposed to any rapid change in the form of government in Egypt. He said: '. . . The British occupation is to continue for an indefinite period . . . So long as that occupation continues, the British Government must of necessity be responsible, not indeed, for the details, but for the main lines on which the administration is conducted.' This refrain was familiar to Cromer's hearers, but he went on to add: 'I shall urge that this wholly spurious and manufactured movement in favour of a rapid development of parliamentary institutions should be treated for what it is worth, and gentlemen, let me add, that it is worth very little.' This came as a shock to the moderates, for although Kamil had advocated constitutional rule in his campaign, he had done so only at the later period when he had become temporarily estranged from the Khedive; it was rather the group of moderates who were strongly behind the move for a constitutional government and an assembly, as a means of restraining both British and Khedivial autocracy. After this speech they realized that Cromer's encouragement to them was not genuine, or was at best based on a misconception of what their function in the body-politic was to be. He was using them as new wine in old bottles.

The appointment of Eldon Gorst as Consul-General even further alienated the moderates from the Agency. Gorst was given instructions to follow a policy of rapprochement with the Khedive as a change from Cromer's policy of opposition; this came to be known as the policy of conciliation, and basically aimed at wooing the Khedive away from the Nationalist Party. The Agency did not believe that Kamil had severed his relationship with Abbas, and planned to sow discord between the two. Kamil realized the implications of Gorst's appointment, and, in a letter to Mme Adam, wrote indignantly: 'La diplomatie Anglaise croit jusqu'a présent que nous suivrons toujours la volonté du souverain et que nous n'avons pas de volonté personnelle.'[48] Kamil gave practical effect to his 'volonté personnelle' by turning *al-Hizb al-Watani* into an official political party in October 1907, a month after the moderates had founded their party, *Hizb al-Umma*.

In February 1908 Mustafa Kamil died at the age of thirty-four. Ronald Storrs gave him the following obituary: 'Though he was a charlatan of the first order, discredited in his private life and backshished up to the eyes by all parties, it was evident that he had a great hold over the town "effendis".'[49] The town effendis felt Kamil's loss keenly. Qasim Amin, who neither liked nor admired Kamil, said that he had sensed the heart of Egypt throb on two occasions: the first was when the sentences of Dinshwai were carried out, and the second was on February 11, 1908, the day when Mustafa Kamil died. Many a hero has feet of clay, and Kamil was no exception. He accepted money from any source a shade too easily, and thereby laid himself open to charges of backshish. His attempts to dabble in pan-Islam gave Cromer the chance to accuse him of fanaticism, alienated the Coptic community from his party, and earned him the reputation of being retrograde. His arguments were often illogical and contradictory—for instance, his claim that the Sudanese would surrender to Egypt once England evacuated Egypt, since they were all fellow Muslims. His pan-Islamic approach was a contradiction of the nationalist line. His advocacy of the Khedive's authority vis-à-vis the British authorities did not tally with his statements as to the people's right for constitutional life. The list of Kamil's shortcomings as a political thinker is substantial; but such an assessment would be unjust to him, for his was not the role of the political thinker, his role was to act as a goad. His function was to be the ritual-maker, the spell-weaver, who should awaken Egypt from its sleep of centuries. He succeeded in making the thinking Egyptian conscious of himself as a nationalist. He created activity out of apathy, he stimulated nationalist feelings in the young. These were the Egyptians who were most influenced by Kamil, for his message was based on an emotional appeal that could not fail to strike the imagination of the young, whereas at times it roused cynicism in the old. On the other hand, Kamil galvanized the other politicians into action, albeit in opposition to himself. He tried to instil self-respect and hope into the Egyptian, and in this lay his greatness. The Khedive said that Mustafa Kamil was the man who revived the national movement in Egypt through sheer personal magnetism, because its people believed in him perhaps even more than they believed in his ideas. But Kamil's friend and political opponent, Lutfi al-Sayyid, said that Mustafa Kamil had broken through Egypt's apathy and indifference, and had made the nation busy itself with its political life. Here was Kamil's function: to supply the ferment that is necessary to the political renaissance of any country. His efforts were a hyphen that linked the nationalist movement under Urabi with the movement under Saad Zaghlul in 1919—an abortive revolution with a successful one.

If nationalist movements gain impetus through the efforts of orators and agitators like Kamil, they also gain substance through the efforts of intellectuals and theoreticians like Ahmad Lutfi al-Sayyid.

The son of a wealthy *umdah* (village headman) in the Delta, Lutfi was destined for a career in al-Azhar; but a timely visit from a family friend convinced his father that he should send his son to a government school, from which he eventually went on to the School of Law. It was in the School of Law that Lutfi met the men who were to become his friends and political associates: Abd al-Aziz Fahmi, who was to be one of the founding-members of the Wafd, and a cabinet minister; Abd al-Khaliq Tharwat, who was to become a prime minister; and Ismail Sidqi, one of Egypt's most outstanding political figures, who also later became a prime minister. It was there too that Lutfi met Shaykh Muhammad Abduh, who was one of his examiners. Lutfi came to the Imam's notice through an essay he wrote in 1892 on the right of the government to punish a criminal, in which he maintained that a government had no such right, because governments were founded on force, not contract, and force did not confer a right. Having written thus, Lutfi believed that he would be failed in the examination. Great was his surprise when Shaykh Abduh congratulated him on his essay, hastening to add that it was not Lutfi's political ideas that were of value, but the excellence of his prose style. Encouraged by this remark Lutfi, together with Tharwat and Sidqi, founded a magazine called *al-Tashri*, 'Legislation', which aimed at teaching people the workings of the law by examining and commenting on the legal decisions of the day. Lutfi was a keen journalist, he had worked for *al-Muayyad*, translating telegrams, and had even been asked by Abdallah Nadim to proof-read *al-Ustadh*; in this way be came into contact with the leading journalists of his day, and with the intellectuals, many of whom were also journalists.

In 1893, while in his third year at the School of Law, Lutfi went to Istanbul on a holiday with his friend Sidqi. This was the year in which the Khedive Abbas had gone to pay his respects to the Sultan, and a large number of Egyptians followed suit. While there Lutfi ran into Saad Zaghlul, and was taken by him to meet Jamal al-Din al-Afghani who, in spite of being kept under close surveillance by the Sultan's spies, still held court for his friends and followers. Lutfi was so captivated by al-Afghani that he paid him a visit every day for the rest of his stay. He later said that al-Afghani had widened his horizons and had taught him to hold himself to account for every word and deed, as the beginning of self-education.

When he graduated from the School of Law in 1894, Lutfi joined the government ranks as a Deputy Public Prosecutor. Two years later, in 1896, together with Abd al-Aziz Fahmi, he formed a secret society with the object of liberating Egypt from the occupation. The Khedive and Mustafa Kamil, who were on the lookout for potential propagandists for the nationalist movement, soon heard about this secret society, and got into touch with Lutfi. Kamil, who knew Lutfi, told him that the Khedive had suggested that he join another secret society, having the same aims as his own, and headed by the Khedive. Lutfi accepted the offer and was taken to meet the Khedive. This new secret society turned out to be *al-Hizb al-Watani* which was still in its infancy, and which had only five members: the Khedive, Mustafa Kamil, Muhammad Farid, a pharmacist from Zagazig, and Lutfi. They all had code names: the Khedive was known as 'al-Shaykh'; Kamil as 'Abu-l Fida', after a famous historian prince; Lutfi as 'Abu Muslim', the propagandist of the Abbassids. The aim of this society was to discover how to contend peaceably with British strength; but it soon ceased to remain secret, and (since the Khedive could not advertise his connection with it) became a political grouping identified with Mustafa Kamil. But while it still remained a secret society, the Khedive suggested that Lutfi live in Switzerland for a year, thus becoming eligible for Swiss nationality, after which he was to return to Egypt and found a newspaper, financed by the Khedive. To understand the implications behind this move, one must bear in mind two points. Under the Capitulations, foreigners in Egypt enjoyed many advantages over Egyptians; and whereas an Egyptian journalist could be prosecuted by a decree issued by the Minister of the Interior for writing articles that did not meet with the approval of the government, a foreign journalist was immune from such prosecution. And although Cromer rarely censored the press, the Press Censorship Law could theoretically be invoked at any time. Secondly, this was an era of journalistic nationalism: the press was the most powerful way of disseminating ideas and stirring up agitation. Hence men like Kamil and Lutfi had been recruited by the Khedive precisely for their journalistic ability.

While in Geneva, Lutfi met Shaykh Muhammad Abduh, Saad Zaghlul and Qasim Amin, who were on holiday there, and it is said that Qasim's book *The Emancipation of Women* was written there with Abduh's ideas and Lutfi's stylistic corrections. Together with Shaykh Abduh, Lutfi attended lectures at the University. In spite of the disparity in age between the two men, a strong bond of friendship was forged. Lutfi's affection for Abduh was deep, perhaps not only because of the man himself, but also because Abduh bore an amazing resemblance to Lutfi's own father—so much so that the two men were always mistaken one for the other. Whether as a result of his conversations with Abduh and Zaghlul, or whether of a decision on his own initiative, Lutfi wrote Kamil a letter in which he said that they must never lose sight of the fact that they were patriots serving Egypt first; thus they must not become too closely identified with the Khedive. For if by any chance the Khedivial throne were to become an obstacle in the path of the nationalists, then it would be their duty to remove such an obstacle. Mustafa Kamil was later to use this letter. When, shortly afterwards, a misunderstanding broke out between him and the Khedive, and Abbas spoke slightingly of Kamil saying that Lutfi was the only genuine patriot among the whole lot of them, Kamil in a fit of pique showed the Khedive Lutfi's letter. He then wrote to Lutfi apologizing for his act. Lutfi at once resigned from the party, thus severing his connection with the Khedive, and returned to Egypt.

On his return, he resumed his work with the government, although he was growing increasingly discontented with its nature. The higher he rose in rank, the more he came into contact with the British employees, and the more keenly he felt the restrictions that were placed on the actions of the Egyptian officials. For instance, unlike their British colleagues they were never allowed to examine important cases without first referring to the Public Prosecutor. Lutfi believed that all spirit of initiative was being stifled in the government service. This view emerges in many of his later articles which attack British policy for keeping Egyptian officials on a leash.[50] Finally in 1905, after a disagreement with the Prosecutor over a legal point, Lutfi resigned, even though the Prosecutor admitted that Lutfi had been in the right. Under the influence of Tolstoy's works Lutfi thought of retiring to the country, but Abd al-Aziz Fahmi, who had also resigned from government service and had set up a law practice, soon induced him to join forces. This Lutfi did for a little over a year. The most important political case that he and Fahmi handled during that period was the defence of the peasants of Dinshwai. But long before that, Lutfi had decided to take up journalism, as the result of the incident of Taba; he therefore became editor of *al-Jarida*.

The first issue of *al-Jarida* on March 9, 1907, stated the aims of the paper and said that it was a purely Egyptian paper which aimed at defending the rights of the Egyptians, and their interests, by publishing whatever was conducive to the country's moral and material progress, and by encouraging the growth of an enlightened public opinion based on a foundation of truth and reason. The editorials of the next few issues were devoted to a discussion of what constituted nationalism.

Cromer favoured *al-Jarida* because he thought that it would temper the extremism of the other newspapers with its moderate approach; that it would be the voice of wisdom and good sense. But because of its moderate approach it became the butt of the pro-Khedivial press. Kamil accused it of being an apologist for British rule: and once, Shaykh Ali Yusif even accused Lutfi of being a rebel against the Sultan.[51] Yet in time *al-Jarida* came to be respected for its moderation. It never acquired the wide circulation or the popularity of *al-Liwa* and *al-Muayyad*, but it had a more solid reputation. These three newspapers each portrayed a discernible current in Egyptian politics and each was to become the organ of a political party. They were mainly addressed to a small, literate section of the population—although a new type of Arabic language that soon evolved produced eventually a reformed language more easily understood by the man in the street than the purely classical language. Lutfi in particular perfected this new style of Arabic.

When in September 1907 the stockholders of *al-Jarida* formed a political party, *Hizb al-Umma*, the People's Party, they hoped that this could become a third estate standing between the Agency and the Palace. It would co-operate with both and likewise check their excesses. The programme of *al-Umma* called for the creation of an Egyptian personality, for without it Egypt could not achieve real independence. It stressed the importance of agricultural reforms, having to do not with land tenure, but with irrigation and drainage schemes; it pointed out the need for a system of education that would turn out capable administrators; and finally insisted on an increase in the powers of the Provincial Councils and the Assembly, in preparation for eventual constitutional rule. When this programme was made public the wrath of other nationalist groupings poured on its authors. Kamil claimed that *al-Umma* was advocating co-operation with the British, which was an act of treachery. His thesis was that evacuation must be immediate, and that only after Egypt became independent could it start to think in terms of social reforms. Lutfi, as spokesman for the party through his editorials in *al-Jarida*, maintained that, once social reform was under way, evacuation could not fail to be its logical and inevitable conclusion; that immediate evacuation was not as important, or even as feasible, as social reform. England would evacuate Egypt, but only as an act of goodwill, not through force. Part of Kamil's anger may well have been sour grapes, for the *Umma* had stolen a march on him by forming the first official political party. To men like Rashid Rida, founder of *al-Manar* magazine, and follower and biographer of Muhammad Abduh, the creation of *al-Umma* was an important milestone in Egyptian political life. If it failed, he wrote in an article, it would prove that Egypt had not yet reached political maturity.[52]

In October 1907 Kamil published the programme of his party, which now became official. The programme was a repetition of a manifesto that he had published in *Le Figaro* of May 8. It demanded the autonomy of Egypt as guaranteed in the 1841 treaty and in the firmans; representative government responsible to a parliament; the furtherance of education; the development of agriculture, commerce and industry; propagation of a national spirit, and the strengthening of ties of friendship between Copts and Muslims. The last item on his agenda stressed the need for closer ties between Egypt and the Ottoman Empire.

Shaykh Ali Yusif, with encouragement from the Khedive, likewise founded a party, *Hizb al-Islah ala-l Mabadi al-Dusturiyya*, the Constitutional Reformers. Though similar to the other two parties, it differed in that the first item on its programme called for the maintenance of Khedivial authority as guaranteed in the firmans. Then followed the familiar items asking for representative institutions, free and general education, and so on. The party was set up to bolster the Khedive's authority, as opposed to the other two parties, which were bent on diminishing it.

There were three basic issues on which the parties diverged: relationship with Turkey, the occupation, and the Khedive. Kamil followed a policy of rapprochement with the Sultan. The members of *al-Umma* suspected that this allegiance was motivated by bribes from the Sultan, and were firmly anti-Ottoman. Kamil construed their stand as pro-British. He argued that so long as Turkey remained Egypt's suzerain, Britain could not legally annex Egypt. *Al-Umma* retorted that it wished for independence from both Britain *and* Turkey. This was a bold statement to make, for independence from the Porte had never been propounded before. Shaykh Ali Yusif at once accused Lutfi of rebellion against the Porte. Lutfi parried the charge with a jesuitical argument that to demand 'full independence' (istiqlal tam), did not mean 'complete independence' (istiqlal kamil). The quibble silenced Ali Yusif, but Lutfi regretted having advanced it, for he had really meant total and complete independence; and later, at a more propitious time, he reiterated his demand for independence from Turkey. The bond between Turkey and Egypt was quite strong, so strong that when in 1908 the Young Turks carried off their revolution and a parliament was set up, many Egyptians suggested that they should be represented in the Turkish Assembly since Egypt was a part of Turkey. The suggestion was violently attacked by Lutfi who repeated his wish to be rid of Turkish suzerainty for ever.

The second issue between the parties was their relationship with England. All three parties were opposed to the British occupation, but with varying degrees of virulence. Kamil denounced all co-operation with Britain as treachery, while the members of *al-Umma* believed in making use of what Britain had to offer pending the day of evacuation. For while Kamil maintained that once evacuation had taken place, the Egyptians would automatically establish reforms, the moderates believed that reforms would lead to evacuation.

The last divergence of view has to do with the attitude of the parties towards the Khedive. The moderates saw the Khedive as an obstacle to reform: to them, he was the epitome of autocracy, and undesirable simply because absolute rule of any kind was undesirable. Mustafa Kamil, who had backed the Khedive's authority, eventually gave up supporting it, and called for constitutional government as the sole safeguard of the population. Shaykh Ali Yusif was the only person who remained faithful to the Khedive's interests, and his party became an apologia for the new policy of reconciliation between Khedive and Agency.

One can thus see that the differences between the parties were fundamental. Differences both of approach and of method found expression in these issues. The ideology of *al-Umma* party was expounded by Ahmad Lutfi al-Sayyid in *al-Jarida* from 1907 until 1914, when he resigned from the life of journalism. Though his ideas show the inevitable contradictions that arise from concepts when these are treated piecemeal over a number of years, yet they were the first coherent expression of a socio-political ideology of nationalism based on liberal principles derived from Aristotle, Rousseau, Spencer and others. Thus many of the ideas propounded were familiar to the West, but were new to Egypt. Lutfi, unlike Kamil, no longer needed to labour at proving that the Egyptian nation existed. By the time he was writing his articles (and in spite of Cromer's assertions to the contrary) the Egyptian nation was an already established entity in the minds of educated

Egyptians. Lutfi's function, then, was to dissect Egyptian society, point out its ills, and show the way to political regeneration.

Inspired by Rousseau, Lutfi began with the idea that man was by nature good and free, and that it was a bad society that had corrupted and enslaved him, through the rule of tyranny. Lutfi traced many of Egypt's defects to the rule of tyranny, whether exercised by Khedives, British Representatives, or even Mamluks and Pharaohs. Any form of enslavement was evil, for it was built on fear and led to the degradation of mankind. Personal government was therefore the most despicable form of rule, for it was founded on the worship of force. Tyranny taught people to act servilely through fear of reprisal on the rulers' part; it taught them to present an outward façade of submission while nursing inward feelings of hatred. The result was that virtues turned into vices, the virtue of forgiveness became the vice of *maalish*, 'never mind'—a word that Lutfi abhorred. The population grew to suspect every action of the government, for the nation was not familiar with the motives underlying government decisions. Only by allowing the nation to participate in the governing process, that is by putting an end to the rule of tyranny, could the antagonism between government and people be allayed.

But before a nation can progress it must rid itself of its social diseases, said Lutfi. It must learn to put aside its feelings of inferiority vis-à-vis its rulers. It must learn to develop a sense of its own worth, and stop idealizing power. The nation must accustom itself to habits of independence; it must teach itself 'constitutional behaviour' before it can acquire a constitutional government, for an absolute government can exist only if the character of the nation is such as to encourage absolutism.

The diseases of Egyptian society could be checked through education, he wrote, but the whole process of education in Egypt was geared to turning out government clerks—cogs to fit a bureaucratic machine. Schools taught by rote, without attempting to instil comprehension. If a proper system of education were introduced in Egypt, it must take into account all the elements of which the population was composed, including women; for by relegating women to a position of inferiority, society encouraged them to develop tyranny and intrigue within the household. A free society could rise only if all women were emancipated: a free mother would raise free children. These were the ideas that Qasim Amin had expounded in his books. Lutfi put the ideas into practice by making his father send his sisters to school, to the horror of an uncle who asked if he intended to make government officials out of the girls.

Lutfi was worried by the lack of common culture as between man and man, or man and woman, in Egyptian society, which was fast becoming a major problem. The gaps between husband and wife, between the Western educated intellectual, the kuttab-trained shaykh and the uneducated fallah, were creating schisms in society. This problem was to exercise other social writers: al-Muwailhi's satire, *Isa ibn Hisham*, was an illustration of it. Many writers realized that lack of a common education would inhibit national unity, and only such unity was capable of creating a public opinion fit to act as a check on tyranny. Unity in society meant the co-operation of all the elements that formed the population, both Copt and Muslim. That was one reason why Lutfi regarded the pan-Islamic movement with distaste, for it led to divided loyalties amongst the Muslims, and alienated the Christians. Unlike Kamil, Lutfi was fully aware of the contradictions inherent in a nationalist movement that also owed loyalty to another territorial unit on grounds of religious sentiment. Religion could not be used as a political device in Egypt, for it would end by checking the nationalist movement. Cromer had indeed used the pan-Islamic movement as a stick with which to beat the nationalists, by saying that the nationalist movement in Egypt was simply a desire to merge into a larger Muslim whole, and this was a retrograde sentiment that had nothing to do with a need for independence. Lutfi's rejection of pan-Islam, therefore, did a great deal to unite Copts and Muslims; Salama Musa, for instance, a Coptic man of letters, said that Lutfi had made it possible for him—a non-Muslim—to become a nationalist in Egypt.

But apart from the local diseases in Egyptian society, there was always the bane constituted by foreign occupation, Lutfi wrote. British rule in Egypt was bad because, though it introduced many worthwhile reforms, it retained the worst features of absolute rule. It ruled Egypt by means of a tyranny, which was none the less despotic for being benevolent. It expected blind obedience on the part of the people simply because it told them that it was working for their good. But people can only believe in the good intentions of a government if they participate in that government. Egypt thus needed a constitution, not from a desire to emulate the West, but from a belief that a constitution and a liberal government are the only safeguards against personal rule. An absolute government can never lead to moral development and cannot educate people towards self-government. Cromer's oft-repeated cliché that Egypt would be granted a constitution when it was ready for it, rested on a false premise—namely, that the grant of a constitution hung on the testimony of an absolute government. The right of a nation to rule itself was a natural right, born simultaneously with the birth of that nation; and the theory that people should be lengthily prepared for self-rule was simply a British import from India, designed to postpone giving Egypt its rights.

Lutfi's cry for a constitution was soon picked up by all the other nationalists, and became the password of Egyptian politics. Haykal records that when he was a student in a secondary school, the boys would stand on the roof of the school, which was adjacent to the palace, and shout '*al-dustur ya Effendina*' ('the constitution, Your Highness'); or they would lie in wait for the Khedive's carriage and yell the same slogan as it passed by.

But perhaps Lutfi's most important gift to Egypt was the intellectual climate that he generated. Under his guidance the offices of *al-Jarida* soon became the meeting-place of the Egyptian intelligentsia; they became a forum for the exchange of ideas, and a school for perfecting a modern style of writing in Arabic. Apart from endowing nationalism with an articulate ideology, Lutfi infused politics with a pragmatic spirit which was to become the characteristic of a whole school of practical politicians; and lastly Lutfi introduced a method of thought which broke with tradition and replaced it with reason; in this sense Abduh can be regarded as the precursor of the group. *Al-Jarida* was therefore a link that brought together the liberal thinkers of Egypt. Almost every thinker, writer and politician of note who came from that generation either served his apprenticeship with Lutfi, or collaborated with him. Lutfi was an intellectual speaking in terms of Western liberal thought, and in arguments based on absolute trust in the power of reason to bring about Egypt's independence. He believed in reason on the part of the Egyptians to carry out the necessary social reforms, and reason on the part of the British government to evacuate Egypt. Because of his rational approach, Lutfi was out of touch with the masses; he had not the ability to rouse emotions, nor did he wish to do so. His trust in the ultimate power of reason was not the attribute of a political leader. He always felt a distaste for intrigue; the life he wished to lead was that of the detached scholar meditating on philosophical concepts. In time, he set politics aside and did become the detached scholar, who translated Aristotle into Arabic, and the rector of the national university—a position he held from 1923 until 1941, with only a few interruptions when he became a cabinet minister. By his life and doctrines he earned the affection of several generations of students; their name for him was *ustadh al-jil*—teacher of the generation.

Epilogue

Cromer's departure from Egypt, followed by the death of Mustafa Kamil a few months later, ushered in a different phase of British rule and of nationalist agitation. Although Cromer had turned Egypt into a British dependency in all but name, yet materially and in the best colonial tradition, he had given the Egyptians much. The first ten years of his rule, those of the Veiled Protectorate, were the most congenial. These were years of reform, the effects of which had been palpable to the average Egyptian who, after years of chaos, of financial ruin and frustration, welcomed stability of any sort. During that period Cromer established a reformed administration that was orderly and fairly efficient; he introduced a certain measure of justice in both the government administration and the courts of law; and, lastly, he brought about financial equilibrium, the *sine qua non* of any attempts at reform. The years of the second decade, those of open manipulation of power, witnessed a slow-down in reforms, and an increase in the inevitable paraphernalia of colonization, which was sooner or later to stir the population into manifesting its nationalism. For these reasons the Egyptians respected Cromer for his reforms, but they also feared and disliked him for having usurped power and thwarted their leanings towards self-government.

The relationship between colonizer and colony, between mentor and pupil, even between father and son, is inevitably one of antagonism, for the young, whether nation or individual, grow; they seek to try out their wings and to commit their own mistakes. To be constantly held in tutelage is not only exasperating, but is an invitation to break out into violence of some kind as a form of self-assertion. Today this is common knowledge, but then it was not even a principle of education. The same mistakes on the part of colonizing powers were thus to be repeated over and over again, not only in Egypt but in all other colonized countries. Nationalists made certain demands which were refused by the colonizing authorities and their puppet governments, only to be granted at a much later period when conditions had changed, and when the nationalists—no longer willing to accept the old terms —had made new demands. This was to be the pattern of Anglo-Egyptian relations for a long while to come: it took two revolutions, at a distance of thirty years from one another, to destroy that pattern in 1952.

In spite of his shortcomings Cromer was a worthy opponent. Through twenty-four years of uninterrupted rule he was able to sustain the myth of a man who was all-powerful, even invincible, who dominated Egyptians to the extent that his personal influence coalesced with the very might of the British Empire and became indistinguishable from it. His successors could not evoke the same feelings in Egypt. From the very beginning of his career in Egypt Cromer had occupied a top position in financial and government circles. Gorst and Kitchener, on the other hand, had served an apprenticeship in the lower ranks of the administration before they climbed into the top echelons; they were familiar figures to the Egyptians, and had none of the aura that surrounded the Pro-Consul. Cromer had made policy in Egypt: his successors received it ready-made from England, and applied it with some modifications of their own. The nationalists therefore could not regard them in the same light as they had done Cromer, and attacks against them were not as personal as those directed against *him*. Though they may have been equal in virulence, they were of lesser magnitude.

And yet, in spite of the disappearance of the Cromer myth, and in spite of the Liberal government's avowed intention to modify British rule in Egypt and replace the iron fist by more relaxed methods of administration, the nationalists were unable to wrest any marked concessions, and advanced little along the path of self-government. They waited for ten more years before they broke out into open revolt, and one might well ask why they waited so long before they took action. The answer, if answer there be to such a question, can be found only in a complex of fortuitous circumstances and personalities, both British and Egyptian; for though some revolutions may be plotted in advance, most of them are triggered off by accident—and the Egyptian revolution was no exception.

When Cromer resigned from office, Eldon Gorst was sent to Egypt to carry out a new, more liberal policy, which would grant some concessions towards self-government, without actually conceding self-rule. In theory this might have implied that the Assembly and the Council would be allowed a greater share in the governing process, and that a new kind of native minister, more active than Cromer's men of straw, would be appointed. In principle the new policy sounded as though it might appeal at least to the moderate nationalists. But it did nothing of the kind, because it offered the nationalists something they might have accepted twenty years earlier, but which they would not accept by 1908. The nationalists knew that it was precisely because of his friendship with the Khedive that Gorst had been appointed, and they quite rightly suspected that a policy of conciliation would ensue, one which meant that Gorst would defer to the Khedive on many minor points. Palace and Agency, in fact, would come together at the expense of self-rule.

Two mutually contradictory policies were thus once again to be adopted simultaneously, and quite naturally they were doomed to fail. For if a more liberal government meant in British eyes granting more power to the Khedive, it did not mean the same thing to the Egyptians who, from the time of Urabi, had been trying to limit the sovereign's autocracy. The Legislative Council and the General Assembly and all the nationalist parties were clamouring for a constitution to restrain both Palace and Agency; and since by 1908 even Turkey had restored her constitution, the previous excuses offered against granting Egypt one were no longer valid. The Egyptians wanted more teeth to their government and their representatives; instead, they were offered an arrangement straight out of *Alice in Wonderland*—municipal and provincial councils were to be gradually developed as a means of preparing the Egyptians for eventual self-government. The jam would always be dished out tomorrow, never today. One obvious solution, which was to encourage the development of truly representative institutions—Assembly and Council—was looked upon as incompatible with the policy then adopted of using a new kind of native minister. Consequently the Assembly and the Council, soured by the petty concessions, and by the choice of a new Prime Minister, hindered the running of the cabinet whenever they could.

Though a clever man, Gorst lacked sensitivity about public opinion in Egypt: he had even fettered it by reviving a law censoring the press at a time when he was claiming to introduce a more liberal policy. His candidate for the post of Prime Minister was not calculated to make his new policy any more palatable to the disgruntled nationalists. A capable and clever Copt, Butros Pasha Ghali was tainted by the service he had given as one of the judges of the ill-fated Dinshwai trial; he was also the minister responsible for having signed the Anglo-Egyptian Condominium Agreement in the Sudan. He was a good choice in British eyes; but either of these antecedents was sufficient to stigmatize him in the eyes of the man in the street, let alone the two combined. If Gorst's purpose was to woo the nationalists, his choice of Ghali as Prime Minister was bound to be its undoing. To make matters worse, in 1909 the Suez Canal Company presented a project for the extension of the Canal Concession for another forty years, until 2009, in return for one million pounds a year payable to the Egyptian government. Butros Ghali, together with the British Financial Adviser and many responsible Egyptians like Saad Zaghlul, were in favour of the proposal, which would have given Egypt some income from the Canal in return for all the money it had invested in the venture—an investment which had brought it nothing better than bankruptcy and a foreign occupation— especially since the Canal Concession was not due to end until 1969. Ghali presented the project to the National Assembly which turned it down; but for his share in the project, Ghali was assassinated by a young nationalist. The reasons al-Wardani gave for killing the Prime Minister were that he had served on the Dinshwai trial, signed the Condominium Agreement, and now wanted to extend the Suez Canal Concession. Ironically enough Ghali had never wanted to go to the Assembly with the project. When Ahmad Lutfi al-Sayyid had asked him in the name of *al-Umma* party to present the project to the people's representatives, Ghali had answered: 'Lutfi, why don't you come down from your cloud and join us mortals?' But Gorst in an attempt to try out some element of the new policy, had pressed Ghali to bring the project to the Assembly. In all fairness one must add that Gorst himself did not entirely approve of the policy he was asked to carry out, and eventually he had to admit defeat. But unlike Cromer, he could not impose his views on the Foreign Office. Overcome by illness, he resigned his post.

Ghali's assassination and Gorst's resignation brought the so-called liberal experiment to an end. The experiment had not been sufficiently liberal to be successful, and had not lasted long enough to bear any fruits. By then the British government was beset by a series of crises amongst the European Powers which threatened to explode into war, and had no time to devote to Egyptian complaints; hence Kitchener, who suceeded Gorst, was allowed to repress the Khedive and rule as an autocrat from 1911–14. Kitchener tried to walk in Cromer's footsteps, but he had neither the Pro-Consul's stature nor his ability. His dislike for the Khedive surpassed Cromer's, but he showed (as we shall see later) slightly more sympathy for the Egyptian nationalists.

Nationalist agitation had been muzzled by the press-censorship law, which Gorst had revived in 1909, and nationalist voices were now mainly to be heard in the newly-organized Legislative Council of 1913—one of the few sops Kitchener threw to the nationalists, which, while it did not appease them, served as a forum for the opposition. In the Council the voices of Saad Zaghlul, another of Kitchener's dislikes, and Abd al-Aziz Fahmi represented opposition to the government, and formed the nucleus that was to expand into the *Wafd*, the Delegation, and the nationalist revolution of 1919.

But what of the nationalist parties? The death of Mustafa Kamil in 1908 had left a gap which could not be filled. His successor, Muhammad Farid, though a dedicated patriot, lacked both the personality and the necessary political acumen to follow in his leader's footsteps. He allowed himself to fall into the hands of a Tunisian extremist, Shaykh Shawish, whose virulent articles were among the causes of the revival of the press law in 1909, and of the government's prosecution of *al-Liwa*. Eventually Farid had to flee from Egypt to escape imprisonment on a charge of inciting to violence. He spent the rest of his life in exile, forever striving for the nationalist cause, and died a bitter man.

The members of *al-Umma* party also lacked a leader. They had a president, and a spokesman, either of whom was only *primus inter pares*. Furthermore they were not revolutionaries, properly speaking; they were practical men who wanted order and security as well as self-government, and being moderates and pragmatists they were willing to compromise with the opposition. But besides lacking a leader, the party—perhaps because of its moderation—lacked the popular touch. It was composed of the middle classes, men with vested interests, and was led by people who chose to appeal to reason rather than to emotion. Hence it carried on a dialogue with fellow-intellectuals rather than representing a popular national movement. Consequently none of the national groups of the time had the characteristics of real political parties, that is, party discipline and party loyalty. And yet none of these reasons was a sufficient cause for the failure of the nationalists to take action. Could it be that they lacked boldness? One must remember that bloody uprisings were never a feature of Egyptian life, save in times of extreme duress like famine. Periodical massacres of officials were alien to the Egyptian soul, more given to compromise and submission in the tradition of a downtrodden people who had been misruled for centuries. Where a Slav or a Greek would have staked his life on a desperate gesture of liberation, the Egyptian nationalists were content to talk and squabble and wait. And yet that is not the whole picture, for one must also remember that in the meekest of people there is also a streak of violence, just below the surface, ready to break out if the victim is goaded too far. The nationalists chose not to goad the people yet. They preferred wresting concessions of self-rule by peaceful means rather than by violence, partly because they had been brought up in a liberal humanitarian tradition, partly because of the memory of the Urabi revolution and its consequences; but most of all because the situation was not desperate enough to warrant violence. In spite of its shortcomings, British rule in Egypt was benevolent. Perhaps had the British ruled Egypt in a more brutal manner, had there been more than one Dinshwai incident, the revolution might have come earlier. Violence and repression always arouse similar emotions in the opposition. The massacres of the Greeks and the Bulgars incited them to retaliate, but British justice in Egypt was at least better than the justice meted out by the Khedive. British methods of dividing the opposition in order to rule the more effectively, plus their brand of benevolent autocracy, encouraged the nationalists in the belief that autonomy lay just round the corner. The carrot was dangled with great effect.

Herein lay the basic reason for nationalist inaction. It was not fear of British might which restrained the nationalists, or lack of agreement amongst themselves that stopped them just short of revolution; for when they finally did break out in acts of violence they did so at a time when the British forces in Egypt were much greater in number than they had ever been, when martial law existed, and when Britain had just emerged victorious from a world holocaust. It was hope, not fear, that kept them quiescent.

There was aslo an added hitch to nationalist activity. Britain had no legal hold over Egypt, but Turkey enjoyed just this. Egypt was a vassal of Turkey, and though British troops might eventually evacuate Egypt, none the less it would still remain a vassal state. The Turkish bond, though a light and loose one, was at the same time guaranteed by international treaties, and could only be broken with the connivance of one or several Powers—that is, with British help. Hence we find one section of nationalist agitation concentrated on back-stage negotiations over issues which were perhaps as important as evacuation, but which were less spectacular, and which, for obvious reasons, could not be as much publicized. That is one reason why the period of 1908–14 is regarded by some writers as one of doldrums as far as nationalist activities went, when it was in fact an active period, but one which had different objectives from the movements coming before and after it.

Both Egypt and England had an interest in breaking the Turkish-Egyptian connection. At one time Mustafa Kamil had seen only the danger of British annexation of Egypt, were Turkish suzerainty to disappear; but at a later period the nationalists, specially those of *al-Umma* party, realized that there was nothing to gain by having both England and Turkey as overlords, and that to break the hold of one was an important prelude to breaking the hold of the other. But they had to step carefully, for Turkey as the seat of the Caliphate was dear to many Egyptians. The chance for back-stage action came in 1911 when war broke out between Italy and Turkey over the occupation of Tripoli. An Egyptian vessel was impounded by the Italians for flying the Turkish flag, and this seemed to Lutfi al-Sayyid to present a golden opportunity for breaking loose from Turkey. Through Ronald Storrs, the Oriental Secretary, he sounded out Kitchener on the possibility of declaring Egypt independent of Turkey, in order to protect her interests from Italian aggression. Kitchener did not turn down the idea, but he said that the British government did not wish to add to Turkish troubles just at this juncture. On the other hand, when the Egyptian Prime Minister, Muhammad Said Pasha, heard of Lutfi's proposal he called it high treason. The Khedive, by contrast, was delighted with the idea and suggested that a delegation composed of Lutfi, Saad Zaghlul and Adli Yaghan, the Minister of Foreign Affairs, should proceed to London and lay the plan before the British authorities. While pourparlers were going on between them, Prince Umar Tussun started a campaign in Egypt to help the Turkish forces in Libya, and called for donations and volunteers. Public feeling was roused to a high pitch by the appeal, and was sustained by most of the newspapers with the exception of *al-Jarida*, which, in an editorial entitled 'A policy of utility not one of emotions', advised moderation rather than blind sentiment. But public reaction to the appeal brought home to Lutfi and his friends that a bid for independence just at that time would be regarded as tantamount to a stab in Turkey's back in her hour of need. The plan would obviously fall flat, so it was shelved for the time being.

A second opportunity seemed to present itself in 1914 at the outbreak of the First World War, when martial law was declared in Egypt even though neither Turkey nor Egypt had entered the war. Lutfi suggested to Rushdi Pasha, then premier, that now was the time to bargain with the British for independence, and that he should inform the British officials that, if England were going to drag Egypt into a war, perhaps even against the suzerain, Turkey, then the British would have to pay a price—recognition of Egypt as an independent state. But Rushdi hesitated and said that the time was not yet ripe for such a step. Graham, the Adviser at the Interior, claimed that Turkey would not enter the war, so that Egypt would not find herself in an anomalous situation on that account; but Ronald Storrs was more sympathetic. By then Kitchener had become Minister for War in Britain, and since he had not shown opposition in the past to the suggestion of Egypt's independence, Storrs suggested to Lutfi that he work out a plan of action and present it to Kitchener. Together Storrs, Lutfi, Adli Yaghan, and Naguib Ghali, the Under-Secretary for Foreign Affairs, drew up the draft of a treaty between Egypt and England, in which Britain recognized Egypt's independence, and in turn Egypt recognized British interests in Egypt and the Suez Canal. But the plan came to nought, and Lutfi became so discouraged that he 'broke his pen', resigned from *al-Jarida*, and determined to give up politics. But not for long.

In 1915 Egypt was declared a British Protectorate, and Abbas Hilmi—who was in Turkey when the war broke out, and who had not been permitted to return to Egypt—was deposed. Egypt was now independent from Turkey, but was more than ever under British control.

Throughout the war years Egyptian resentment against Britain and the occupation was exacerbated by the exigencies of a war-time situation. For though Britain had promised Egypt that it would not be drawn into the war, inevitably the effects of the war were felt in the country. Requisitions of foodstuffs, livestock, and man-power by near-corvée methods affected the fallah, while the inflation consequent on quartering a large army in Egypt caused hardship to the whole population, and roused more discontent than had the previous three decades of occupation. For the first time all the Egyptians, irrespective of class or of interests, felt the pinch of occupation by virtue of a war for survival in which

Britain, not Egypt, was engaged. This was the necessary un-pleasantness needed to draw the Egyptians together, for they had to suffer hardship of some kind before it became worth their while to take drastic action.

During the war the nationalist leaders spent time in speculating on Egypt's fate after the war. What would happen to Egypt if Germany and her ally Turkey won the war, as many Egyptians hoped? The victories of the allies and Wilson's Fourteen Points brought conjecture to an end and pointed out to the nationalists the path they should take. For the Powers had proclaimed a principle which the Egyptian nationalists could only construe as willingness to grant them independence. In his memoirs Haykal wrote that on the day when Wilson's Points were made public in January 1918 he met a friend in the street who greeted him with the words: 'We now have the right of self-determination. The British will evacuate Egypt.'[1] Perhaps the friend was over-opti-mistic, but the nationalists were quick to make the most of a fresh opportunity. These men, many of whom were former mem-bers of *al-Umma* party or of *Hizb al-Watani*, had for the time being sunk their differences in an endeavour to find some way of loosen-ing Britain's hold on Egypt. Choosing three men from amongst them to act as their representatives, the nationalists sent a Delega-tion, in Arabic a *Wafd*, which eventually became the name of the Nationalist Party, to negotiate with the British authorities. The Delegation headed by Saad Zaghlul met Wingate, the High Commissioner, and asked to be allowed to present its case to the Paris Peace Conference. Wingate was sympathetic. Throughout the years 1917–18 he had kept the British government informed of the rising discontent in Egypt, and he now suggested that the Egyptian Delegation should be allowed a hearing. But Wingate did not have the ear of the British government, and his advice was disregarded. Rebuking him for listening to the nationalists, the British government adamantly refused to give the *Wafd* permission to leave the country.

By then an understanding between the Egyptian members of the government, the Egyptian sovereign, Fuad and the members of the *Wafd* had been reached. They all agreed to pool their efforts towards the common goal, which was to wrest some form of independence from England, each party probably thinking that it could dispense with its erstwhile partners at some later period. When the premier, Rushdi Pasha, offered to head a delegation, and his request was also turned down, matters became more serious. The nationalists stepped up their agitation, hoping to force England into doing something drastic; and, sure enough, on March 8 Zaghlul and a few companions were arrested and deported to Malta. The incident triggered off the revolution which, within three days, swept across the whole of Egypt and succeeded in rousing all the land—not only because it had been efficiently organized ahead of time, with an organization that went to the grass-roots, but also because it was given assistance by the Egyptian administration, which sent messages to the provincial Governors not to hinder the *Wafd* in its agitation. The revolution succeeded, and Zaghlul and his friends were allowed to sail to Paris (where no one had time to listen to them), and then to England—where Lloyd George showed them the seat reserved for Egypt when it became a member of the British Commonwealth. Such obtuseness increased the opposition of the *Wafd*, until the British government was finally made to realize through Allenby (who had replaced Wingate as High Commissioner, and who had Lloyd George's ear) that some concessions would have to be granted to the nationalists. But the magnitude of these concessions remained a constant source of friction between Egypt, intent on full independence, and Britain, reluctant to relinquish its grasp on the country.

If the 1919 revolution succeeded, the period of liberal nationalism which followed it failed. The aftermath of the revolution was one of autocracy and intransigence on the part of Zaghlul; of intrigue and corruption on the part of the sovereign, and his successor, Faruq; of highhandedness on the part of Britain. The brief honeymoon that had united all the parties into a nationalist front ended in the usual acrimony. In 1922 the British government, once again prompted by Allenby, abolished the Protectorate and declared Egypt independent, but hedged this independence with so many restrictions as to render it void. The *Wafd* refused to recognize the declaration even though the Egyptian sovereign did so, and successive governments fell through repeated attempts at negotiating some agreement with the British government which would be acceptable to all parties, and which would grant Egypt full sovereignty. In 1936, under the pressure of events in Ethiopia, a treaty between both countries was finally signed. By that treaty Egypt became an independent nation, she entered the League of Nations, and the system of Capitulations was brought to an end. Yet England still retained a firm hold on Egypt, for the treaty now gave her a legal right to protect the Suez Canal, and to station British forces on Egyptian territory. And since the treaty was a military alliance of a permanent nature, it really meant the permanent occupation of Egypt, as one segment of politicians pointed out. However, the treaty was a stop-gap. Every successive Egyptian government tried to negotiate a change in its terms, and failed, until it was unilaterally abrogated in 1951 by a *Wafdist* government.

It is not my intention to go into an account of the complexities of Egyptian political life in the intervening period, but Britain's lasting presence in Egypt gave the Egyptians a political pattern which was to continue until the revolution disturbed it in 1952. This pattern consisted of a trefoil—the British Embassy, the Palace, the *Wafd*—with all the other political parties playing minor but important roles. Inevitably one of the two Egyptian contenders for power was forever seeking to become an ally of the British Embassy so as to seize the reins of government, for Egyptian governments rose and fell when supported by the Embassy. This, then, became a convenient scapegoat on which Egyptian governments could blame all their administrative shortcomings; but it was also a guilty party, that actively interfered in the political life of the country, and contributed to its lack of stability. Lord Lloyd more than once called out the gunboats to settle his disagreements with the Egyptian governments, in a style that was reminiscent of Cromer; and Lord Killearn called out the tanks in the notorious incident of 1942.

It is perhaps a tragic, but not unusual, situation to find that in spite of the existence of a plethora of brilliant and capable men both in and out of government, the liberal experiment failed, for if Egyptian politics had a pattern, they lacked a system, and were too dependent on personalities. There were too many parties, all of them groupings round a leader rather than genuine parties with different platforms. The King was granted too much power through the constitution; and England was too much there, especially since the memory of Cromer seemed to inspire ambassadors with a desire to emulate his strong-arm tactics. In three decades not a single cabinet fell by reason of a vote of no confidence, and yet the average life of a government was only eighteen months. The *Wafd*, the majority party, came to power only five times, because the elections were usually rigged; and when it did come to power it ruined its standing by its blatant corruption, which obliterated the effect of any good it might have done. Good intentions were plentiful, but they foundered on the rocks of corruption, intransigence and intrigue. Nevertheless the government could have continued to function in such a fashion for a long while, had not King Faruq in 1948 made the drastic mistake of involving his country in a war for which it was not prepared, and supplied his men with defective arms in order to make a large financial profit. Up to then the army had remained aloof from political life, and had watched the various cabinets play at musical-chairs as a quiescent spectator; but the war in Palestine affected it too deeply, and was the necessary catalyst that moved the young officers to action. Once again young colonels, repeating the words that Urabi had told the Khedive, but with much more effect, seized the reins of government and deposed the King. This time the Powers did not interfere. The wheel had turned full circle.

The similarities between the three Egyptian revolutions are obvious. All three were planned by a handful of men but were immediately adopted by the mass of the population. All three wanted an Egypt for the Egyptians, and the end of foreign tutelage. Urabi failed completely, Zaghlul failed partially; only in 1952 was success achieved. For the first time in over two thousand years Egypt came to be governed by Egyptians.

American University,
Cairo 1968

Sources and Select Bibliography

Sources and Select Bibliography

A. UNPUBLISHED SOURCES

1. Harry Boyle Papers, 1884–1908, St Antony's College, Oxford.
2. Cromer Papers, 1882–1908, Public Records Office, FO/633.
3. Foreign Office Drafts and Despatches, Public Records Office.
4. Granville Papers, 1882–5, Public Records Office, PRO/30.
5. Correspondence between Mustafa Kamil and Abd al-Rahim Bey Ahmad, 1895–6, Egyptian State Archives.
6. Milner Papers, 1890–5, New College, Oxford.
7. Salisbury Papers, 1895–1902, Christ Church, Oxford.
8. Wingate Papers, 1884–1908, School of Oriental Studies, Durham.
9. Papers Concerning the Urabi Revolution, 1881–2, Egyptian State Archives.

B. GOVERNMENT PUBLICATIONS

1. Accounts and Papers, 1880–1910.
2. Parliamentary Debates, House of Commons, IV Series, 1882–1908.

C. WORKS IN ARABIC

1. Abduh, Muhammad and al-Afghani, Jamal al-Din. *Al-Urwa al-Wuthqa*. Beirut: 1933.
2. Amin, Ahmad. *Hayati*. Cairo: 1950.
3. —— *Zuama al-Islah*. Cairo: 1948.
4. Amin, Qasim. *Tahrir al-mara*. Cairo: 1890.
5. —— *Al-Mara al-Jadida*. Cairo: 1901.
6. Haykal, Muhammad Husayn. *Mudhakkirat fi al-siyasa al-Misriyya*. Cairo: 1951–3.
7. —— *Tarajim Misriyya wa Gharbiyya*. Cairo: n.d.
8. Kamil, Ali Fahmi. *Mustafa Kamil fi arbaa wa thalathin rabian*. Cairo: 1908–11, 9 parts.
9. Lutfi al-Sayyid, Ahmad. *Safahat matwiyya*. Cairo: 1946.
10. —— *Al-Muntakhabat*. Cairo: 1937–45, 2 vols.

11. Lutfi al-Sayyid, Ahmad. *Qissat Hayati*. Cairo: 1962.
12. Naqqash, Salim. *Misr l-il Misriyyin*. 1884.
13. Al-Rafii, Abd al-Rahman. *Misr wal Sudan*. Cairo: 1948.
14. —— *Mustafa Kamil*. Cairo: 1950.
15. —— *Al-thawra al-Urabiyya wal-ihtilal al-Injilizi*. Cairo: 1949.
16. Rida, Rashid. *Tarikh al-ustadh al-Imam al-Shaykh Muhammad Abduh*.
    Cairo: i, 1st ed. 1931; ii, 2nd ed. 1925–6; iii, 2nd ed. 1947–8.
17. Shafiq, Ahmad. *Mudhakkirati fi nisf qarn*. Cairo: 1934, 3 vols.
18. Tarazi, Philippe de. *Tarikh al-sahafa al-Arabiyya*. Beirut: 1913–44,
    4 vols.
19. Zaydan, Jurji. *Mashahir al-sharq*. Cairo: 1911, 2 vols.

D. WORKS IN OTHER LANGUAGES

1. Viscount D'Abernon (Edgar Vincent), *Portraits and Appreciations*.
   London: 1931.
2. Adam, Juliette. *L'Angleterre en Egypte*. Paris: 1922.
3. Adams, C. C. *Islam and Modernism in Egypt*. London: 1933.
4. Adams, Francis. *The New Egypt*. London: 1893.
5. Ahmad, Jamal. *The Intellectual Origins of Egyptian Nationalism*.
   London: 1960.
6. Arthur, George. *Life of Lord Kitchener*. London: 1920.
7. Blunt, W. S. *Gordon at Khartum*. London: 1911.
8. —— *My Diaries*. London: 1919.
9. Bowman, Humphrey. *Middle East Window*. London: 1942.
10. Boyle, Clara. *A Servant of the Empire*. London: 1938.
11. Broadley, A. M. *How We Defended Arabi And His Friends* London:
    1884.
12. Cecil, Gwendolyn. *The Life of Robert Marquis of Salisbury*. London:
    1921–32.
13. Chirol, Valentine. *Fifty Years In A Changing World*. London: 1927.
14. Lord Crewe. *Lord Rosebery*. London: 1931.
15. Lord Cromer. *Abbas II*. London: 1915.
16. —— *Modern Egypt*. London: 1908.
17. —— *Political and Literary Essays*. London: 1914.
18. Dugdale, E. T. S. *German Diplomatic Documents: 1871–1914*. London: 1928.
19. Fitzmaurice, Edmond. *The Life of the Second Earl Granville*. London:
    1905.
20. Freycinet, Charles de. *La Question d'Egypte*. Paris: 1904.
21. Gardiner, A. C. *The Life of Sir William Harcourt*. London: 1923.

22. Gooch, G. and Temperley, H. *British Documents on the Origins of the War: 1898–1914.* London: 1927.
23. Grey of Fallodon. *Twenty Five Years.* London: 1925.
24. Gwynn, S. and Tuckwell, G. *The Life of the Rt. Hon. Sir Charles Dilke.* London: 1917.
25. Headlam-Morley, J. *Studies in Diplomatic History.* London: 1930.
26. Hinsley, F. H. 'Bismarck, Salisbury and the Agreement of 1887'. *Historical Journal.* I, 1958.
27. Hornik, M. P. 'The Mission of Sir Henry Drummond Wolff to Constantinople: 1885–1887'. *English Historical Review.* IV, October 1940.
28. Hourani, Albert. *Arabic Thought in the Liberal Age.* London: 1962.
29. —— 'The Decline of the West in the Middle East'. *International Affairs.* XXIX, 1953.
30. Hutchinson, H. G., ed. *The Private Diaries of Sir Algernon West.* London: 1922.
31. Issawi, Charles. *Egypt at Mid-Century.* London: 1954.
32. James, Robert Rhodes. *Rosebery.* London: 1963.
33. Kamil, Mustafa. *Egyptiens et Anglais.* Paris: 1906.
34. —— *Lettres Egyptiennes-Françaises.* Cairo: 1909.
35. Kedourie, Elie. *Nationalism.* London and New York: 1960.
36. Knaplund, P. *Gladstone's Foreign Policy.* New York: 1935.
37. Lee, S. *Lord Kitchener at Khartoum.* London: 1925.
38. Lord Lloyd. *Egypt Since Cromer.* London: 1933.
39. Lyall, Alfred. *The Life of the Marquis of Dufferin and Ava.* London: 1905.
40. Magnus, Philip. *Kitchener.* London: 1958.
41. Marder, A. J. *British Naval Policy: 1880–1905.* London: 1940.
42. Milner, Alfred. *England in Egypt.* London: 1893.
43. Lord Newton. *Lord Lyons.* London: 1913.
44. Robinson, R., Gallagher, J. and Denny, A. *Africa and the Victorians.* London and New York: 1961.
45. Rodd, Rennell. *Social and Diplomatic Memoirs.* London: 1922.
46. Steppat, Fritz. 'Nationalismus und Islam bei Mustafa Kamel'. *Die Welt des Islams.* IV, Nr. 4, 1956.
47. Storrs, Ronald. *Orientations.* London: 1937.
48. Taylor, A. J. P. *The Struggle for Mastery in Europe: 1848–1918.* London: 1957.
49. Temperley, H. and Penson, L. *Foundations of British Foreign Policy.* London: 1938.
50. Ward, A. W. and Gooch, G. *The Cambridge History of British Foreign Policy: 1783–1919.* London: 1923.

51. Willcocks, W. *Sixty Years in Egypt*. London: 1955.
52. Wingate, R. *Wingate of the Sudan*. London: 1955.
53. Woodruff, P. *The Men Who Ruled India*. London: 1954.
54. Marquis of Zetland. *Lord Cromer*. London: 1932.

Notes

I. PRELUDE TO THE OCCUPATION *pp. 1–37*

1. Headlam-Morley, *Studies in Diplomatic History*, London: 1930, p. 56.
2. Salisbury to Lyons, in Lord Newton, *Lord Lyons*, London: 1913, II, p. 355.
3. Salisbury to Northcote, in Gwendolen Cecil, *The Life of Robert Marquis of Salisbury*, London: 1921–32, II, pp. 331–2.
4. Salisbury to Lyons, July 17, 1879, Newton, *op. cit.*, II, p. 357.
5. Milner, *England in Egypt*, 1893, p. 63.
6. Salisbury to Lyons, April 10, 1879, Newton, *op. cit.*, II, p. 175.
7. *Correspondence respecting the Affairs of Egypt*, 1882 (Accounts and Papers, LXXXII), Cd. 3161.
8. Abd al-Rahman al-Rafii, *Al Thawra al-Urabiyya wal-Ihtilal al-In'iliziyy*, Cairo: 1949, p. 127.
9. Rashid Rida, *Tarikh al-Ustadh al-Imam al-Shaykh Muhammad Abduh*, Cairo: 1931, I, p. 224.
10. *Ibid.*, I, p. 208.
11. *Ibid.*, I, p. 217.
12. *Ibid.*, I, p. 230. Also Broadley, *How We Defended Arabi*, London: 1884, p. 230.
13. September 24, 1881, FO/78/3324.
14. Gladstone to Granville, PRO/30/29/125.
15. PRO/30/29/124.
16. *Correspondence respecting the Affairs of Egypt*, 1882 (Accounts and Papers, LXXXII), C. 3105.
17. Granville to Gladstone, January 12, 1881, PRO/30/29/125.
18. FO/78/3459.
19. FO/78/3435.
20. FO/78/3448.
21. FO/78/3452.
22. FO/78/3436.
23. FO/78/3436.
24. FO/78/3437.
25. Gwynn and Tuckwell, *The Life of the Rt. Hon. Sir Charles E. Dilke*, London: 1917, I, p. 460.
26. Malet to Cromer, October 22, 1907, FO/633/XII.
27. *Correspondence respecting the Affairs of Egypt*, 1882 (Accounts and Papers, LXXXII), C. 3251.
28. Salim Naqqash, *Misr l-il Misriyyin*, Cairo: 1884, vol. V, p. 5.
29. Rashid Rida, *op. cit.*, I, p. 248.
30. Rafii, *op. cit.*, p. 302.
31. Gwynn and Tuckwell, *op. cit.*, I, p. 555.
32. Fitzmaurice, *Life of the Second Earl Granville*, London: 1905, II, p. 265.

33. *Correspondence respecting the Affairs of Egypt*, 1882 (Accounts and Papers, LXXXIII), C. 3391.
34. Yildiz 1208, Documents concerning Urabi.
35. FO/78/3449.
36. Temperley and Penson, *Foundations of British Foreign Policy*, London: 1938, p. 420.
37. FO/78/3470.
38. Knaplund, *Gladstone's Foreign Policy*, New York: 1935, p. 183.
39. PRO 30/29/126.
40. Egyptian State Archives, *Documents concerning the Urabi Revolution*, No. 128, box 3.
41. Freycinet, *La Question d'Egypte*, Paris: 1904, p. 311.
42. *Ibid.*, p. 231.
43. *Parliamentary Debates*, IV series, CCLXXII, Cols. 1586ff.
44. P.R.O. 30/29/126.
45. Gwynn and Tuckwell, *op. cit.*, I, p. 463.
46. *Ibid.*, I, p. 547.
47. *Ibid.*, I, p. 547.
48. *Loc. cit.*
49. *Further Correspondence respecting the Affairs of Control*, 1882 (Accounts and Papers, LXXXIII), C. 3461.
50. Gwynn and Tuckwell, *op. cit.*, I, p. 550.
51. *Correspondence respecting the Egyptian exiles in Ceylon*, 1883 (Accounts and Papers, LXXXIV), C. 3630.
52. FO/78/3442.
53. *Further Correspondence respecting the Affairs of Egypt*, 1883 (Accounts and Papers, LXXXIII), C. 3528.
54. Lord Cromer, *Modern Egypt*, London: 1908, I, p. 334.
55. Egyptian State Archives, *Documents concerning the Urabi Revolution*, No. 23, September 17, 1882. Letter from the *Irada Saniyya* to Sultan Pasha to be communicated to General Wolseley.
56. *Correspondence respecting the reorganization of Egypt*, 1883 (Accounts and Papers, LXXXIII), C. 3462.
57. *Correspondence regarding indemnity claims arising out of the Alexandria riots and subsequent events*, 1883 (Accounts and Papers, LXXXIV), C. 3468.
58. April 28, 1883, FO/78/3567.
59. Lyall, *The Life of the Marquis of Dufferin and Ava*, London: 1905, II, p. 14.
60. See Rashid Rida, *op. cit.*, I, p. 223, for passage by Abduh entitled 'Sultan Pasha's betrayal of Egypt'.
61. Egyptian State Archives, *Documents concerning the Urabi Revolution*, No. 128, box 6.

II. INTERNATIONAL ENTANGLEMENTS: 1882–1896 *pp. 38–53*

1. For a detailed account of the Mahdiyya movement see P. M. Holt, *A Modern History of the Sudan*, 1961, and *The Mahdist State in the Sudan*, 1958; R. Hill, *Egypt in the Sudan*, 1959; A. B. Theobald, *The Mahdiyya*, 1961, and others.

Notes

2. *Further Correspondence respecting the Affairs of Egypt,* 1884 (Accounts and Papers, LXXXVIII), C. 3844.
3. *Loc. cit.*
4. Baring to Granville, April 3, 1885, *The Boyle Papers,* henceforth referred to as B.P.
5. Magnus, *Gladstone,* London: 1963, p. 321.
6. *Correspondence Respecting Anglo-French Financial Control,* 1882 (Accounts and Papers, LXXXIII), C. 3447.
7. Communication handed to Lyons by Duclerc, from Tissot, *Ibid.,* November 24.
8. *Loc. cit.*
9. B.P., Granville to Baring, April 18, 1884.
10. Baring to Northbrook, April 4, 1884, Lord Zetland, *Lord Cromer,* London: 1932, pp. 117–18.
11. Hinsley, 'Bismarck, Salisbury and the Agreement of 1887', *Historical Journal,* I, p. 79.
12. August 7, 1885, FO/78/3821.
13. Salisbury to Drummond Wolff, September 8, 1885, in *Salisbury Papers,* henceforth referred to as S.P.
14. September 11, 1885, FO/78/3821.
15. May 25, 1885, Dugdale, *German Diplomatic Documents: 1871–1914,* London: 1928, I, p. 142.
16. S.P., Drummond Wolff to Salisbury, October 22, 1885.
17. S.P., Salisbury to Baring, February 18, 1887.
18. S.P., Salisbury to Drummond Wolff, February 23, 1887.
19. S.P., Salisbury, quoting Herbette's message to Malet, to Drummond Wolff, February 4, 1887.
20. September 6, 1885, FO/78/3821.
21. S.P., Salisbury to Drummond Wolff, February 23, 1887.
22. S.P., Baring to Salisbury, April 1, 1887.
23. S.P., Baring to Salisbury, May 8, 1887.
24. FO/78/3823.
25. S.P., Salisbury to Baring, February 25, 1887.
26. B.P., Salisbury to Baring, May 6, 1887.
27. Freycinet, *op. cit.,* p. 366.
28. A. Meyendorff, *Correspondence Diplomatique de M. de Staal,* Paris: 1929, I, p. 351, June 4/16, 1887 quoted in M. P. Hornik, 'The Mission of Sir Henry Drummond Wolff to Constantinople: 1885–1887', *English Historical Review,* LV, October 1940, p. 619.
29. Gwendolen Cecil, *op. cit.,* IV, p. 34.
30. S.P., Baring to Salisbury, November 10, 1888.
31. B.P., Baring to Iddesleigh, October 24, 1886.
32. Cecil, *op. cit.,* IV, p. 139.
33. Dugdale, *op. cit.,* II, p. 63. April 29, VIII, 151.
34. November 21, 1890, FO/633/VII.
35. Marder, *British Naval Policy: 1880–1905,* London: 1940, p. 159.

36. Taylor, *The Struggle for the Mastery of Europe*, London: 1954, p. 369.
37. *Ibid.*, p. 359, quoting Hatzfeldt to Holstein, July 30/31, August 5, 1895, in *Die Grosse Politik*, Nos. 2371, 2372, 2381.
38. Marder, *op. cit.*, p. 378 ff.
39. *Ibid.*, p. 569.

III. THE MAN ON THE SPOT *pp. 54–67*

1. Cromer, *Modern Egypt*, I, p. 341.
2. *Ibid.*, I, p. 343.
3. *Ibid.*, II, p. 356.
4. *Ibid.*, II, p. 359.
5. *Ibid.*, II, p. 360.
6. *Further Correspondence respecting the Affairs of Egypt*, 1884 (Accounts and Papers, LXXXVIII), C. 3844.
7. *Loc. cit.*
8. *Le Bosphore Egyptien*, January 8, 1884. Also see A. Rafii, *Misr wal-Sudan*, Cairo: 1948, p. 111.
9. B.P., Baring to Rosebery, May 18, 1886, recounting the incident at a later date.
10. February 24, 1884, FO/633/IV.
11. Cromer, *op. cit.*, I, p. 343.
12. *Loc. cit.*
13. B.P., Baring to Iddesleigh, October 24, 1886.
14. Blunt, *Gordon at Khartoum*, London: 1911, p. 454.
15. *Ibid.*, p. 45.
16. *Ibid.*, p. 56.
17. *Loc. cit.*
18. S.P., Blunt to Salisbury, April 7, 1887. Also W. S. Blunt, *My Diaries*, London: 1919, I, p. 58.
19. S.P., Baring to Salisbury, May 8, 1887.
20. Cromer, 'The Government of Subject Races', *Political and Literary Essays*: 1908–13, London: 1913, p. 12. The article first appeared in the *Edinburgh Review*, January 1908.
21. Cromer, 'The Government of Subject Races', *op. cit.*, p. 45 ff. See Roger Owen, 'The Influence of Lord Cromer's Indian Experience on British Policy in Egypt 1883–1907', *St. Antony's Papers* No. 17, London: 1965, for a thorough study of that aspect.
22. *Ibid.*, p. 45.
23. *Ibid.*, p. 25.
24. *Modern Egypt*, *op. cit.*, II, p. 146.
25. *Ibid.*, II, p. 148.
26. *Ibid.*, II, pp. 230 & 233.
27. 'Government of Subject Races', *op. cit.*, p. 28.
28. *Ibid.*, p. 28.
29. Woodruff, *The Men who Ruled India: The Guardians*, London: 1954, p. 14.
30. Ahmed Shafiq, *Mudhakkirati fi nisf qarn*, Cairo: 1934, I, p. 60.

Notes

31. Viscount d'Abernon (Edgar Vincent). *Portraits and Appreciations*, London: 1931, p. 14.
32. Cecil, *op. cit.*, III, p. 206.
33. D'Abernon, *op. cit.*, p. 15.
34. S.P., June 5, 1889.
35. *Reports on the State of Egypt and the Progress of Administrative Reforms*, 1885 (Accounts and Papers, LXXXIX), C. 4421.
36. Cromer, *Modern Egypt, op. cit.*, II, p. 326.

IV. THE GOVERNORS OF EGYPT *pp. 68–86*

1. B.P., Baring to Rosebery, February 15, 1886.
2. S.P., Portal to Barrington, September 4, 1887.
3. *Further Correspondence respecting the Affairs of Egypt*, 1884 (Accounts and Papers, LXXXIX), C. 4100.
4. S.P., Portal to Villiers, July 9, 1887.
5. February 25, 1888, FO/78/4144.
6. *Loc. cit.*
7. *Loc. cit.*
8. S.P., Salisbury to Baring, February 17, 1888.
9. S.P., Baring to Salisbury, March 10, 1888.
10. *Report respecting the Affairs of Egypt*, 1895 (Accounts and Papers, CIX), C. 7644.
11. *Loc. cit.*
12. S.P., Baring to Salisbury, April 18, 1889.
13. July 30, 1891, entry in Milner's Diary, in *Milner Papers*, henceforth referred to as M.P.
14. S.P., Baring to Salisbury, April 18, 1889.
15. M.P., Baring to Milner, June 16, 1891.
16. M.P., Diary, Summer 1897.
17. M.P., Baring to Milner, June 16, 1891.
18. *Ibid.*, June 27, 1891.
19. S.P., Salisbury to Baring, January 23, 1891.
20. S.P., Portal to Barington, July 22, 1891.
21. S.P., Scott-Moncrieff to Baring, June 9, 1888.
22. March 29, 1891, FO/78/4384.
23. S.P., Baring to Kimberley, 1894.
24. *Further Correspondence respecting the Reorganization of Egypt*, 1883 (Accounts and Papers, LXXXIV), C. 3696.
25. *Report respecting the Affairs of Egypt*, 1904 (Accounts and Papers, CXI), Cd. 1951.
26. B.P., Baring to Iddesleigh, October 24, 1886.
27. Muhammad Husayn Haykal, *Tarajim Misriyya wa Gharbiyya*, Cairo: n.d., p. 33.
28. M.P., Eldon Gorst to Milner, November 23, 1893.
29. M.P., Palmer to Milner, May 9, 1891.
30. M.P., Milner to Goschen, October 3, 1889.

31. M.P., Dawkins to Milner, 9 January, 1896.
32. November 4, 1893, FO/633/VI.
33. Clara Boyle, *A Servant of the Empire: A memoir of Harry Boyle*, London: 1938, p. 113, in a passage Harry dictated to his wife.
34. M.P., Diary, Summer 1891, p. 141.
35. Lee, *Lord Kitchener at Khartoum*, London: 1914, p. 76.
36. M.P., Milner to Goschen, January 5, 1890.
37. *Ibid.*, June 22, 1890.
38. M.P., Dawkins to Milner, August 16, 1896.
39. Willcocks, *Sixty Years in Egypt*, London: 1934, p. 118.
40. *Ibid.*, p. 119.
41. *Ibid.*, p. 269.
42. *Ibid.*, p. 116.
43. *Ibid.*, p. 119.
44. FO/633/VI, November 4, 1893.

V. RUMBLINGS OF OPPOSITION *pp. 87–97*

1. Cromer, *Modern Egypt, op. cit.*, II, p. 343.
2. Ahmad Amin, *Zuama al-Islah*, Cairo: 1948, p. 310. For a fuller study of Abduh's teachings see C. C. Adams, *Islam and Modernism in Egypt*, London: 1933; also Osman Amin, Muhammad Abduh: *Essai sur ses idées philosophiques et religieuses*, Cairo, 1944; Malcolm Kerr, *Islamic Reform*, Los Angeles, 1966; as well as Rashid Rida, *op. cit.*
3. Rashid Rida, *op. cit.*, I, pp. 11–12, translated in M. Kerr, *op. cit.*, pp. 108–109.
4. *Al-Manar*, VIII, p. 892, translated by C. C. Adams, *op. cit.*, p. 130.
5. Albert Hourani, *Arabic Thought in the Liberal Age*: 1798–1939, London: 1962, p. 139.

VI. THE KHEDIVE AND THE LORD *pp. 98–136*

1. Zetland, *op. cit.*, p. 193.
2. Cromer to Salisbury, April 15, 1892, FO/633/VI.
3. Cromer to Salisbury, April 19, 1892, FO/78/4451.
4. Zetland, *op. cit.*, p. 196.
5. Adams, *The New Egypt: A Social Sketch*, London: 1893, p. 148.
6. A. Shafiq, *Mudhakkirati fi nisf qarn*, Cairo: 1934, II, p. 52.
7. Lord Crewe, *Lord Rosebery*, London: 1931, II, p. 400.
8. January 1, 1893, FO/141/299.
9. *Ibid.*
10. January 2, 1893, FO/141/299.
11. January 3, FO/141/299.
12. January 25, FO/141/297.
13. January 9, FO/141/297.
14. *Ibid.*
15. B.P., Cromer to Rosebery, January 13, 1893.
16. *Ibid.*

Notes

17. Cromer, *Abbas II*, London: 1915, p. 19. This remark was made on December 29.
18. 'Memoirs', *Al-Misri*, April 9, 1951.
19. M.P., Malortie to Milner, January 27, 1893.
20. January 15, 1893, FO/141/299.
21. January 15, 1893, FO/141/299.
22. Cromer, *Abbas II*, p. 22.
23. January 16, 1893, FO/141/296.
24. January 16, FO/141/296.
25. January 16, 1893, FO/141/299.
26. January 16, FO/141/296.
27. January 17, 1893, FO/78/4517 B.
28. January 17, FO/141/299.
29. February 11, 1893, FO/78/4513.
30. January 19, FO/78/4517 B.
31. January 19, FO/78/4517 B.
32. January 19, FO/141/299.
33. January 20, FO/78/4517.
34. *Private Diaries of Sir Algernon West*, ed. H. G. Hutchinson, London: 1922, p. 123.
35. Gardiner, *The Life of Sir William Harcourt*, London: 1923, II, p. 226.
36. James, *Rosebery*, London: 1963, p. 280.
37. January 21, FO/78/4517 B.
38. West, *op. cit.*, p. 124.
39. *Loc. cit.*
40. *Ibid.*, p. 127.
41. January 23, FO/141/299.
42. 'Nasihat Mukhlis fi Khidmat Watanih', *al-Ustadh*, January 24, 1893, p. 545.
43. Rosebery to Dufferin, January 17, in his account of the exchange between him and Waddington, FO/141/296.
44. January 18, FO/141/296.
45. January 28, FO/141/297.
46. *Ibid.*
47. M.P., Malortie to Milner, January 27.
48. January 5/17, 1893, FO/141/397.
49. January 30, 1893, FO/141/297.
50. *Further Correspondence respecting the Affairs of Egypt*, 1893 (Accounts and Papers, CXI), C. 6956.
51. B.P., Cromer to Rosebery, January 30, 1893.
52. B.P., Cromer to Kimberley, March 25, 1895.
53. M.P., Wingate to Milner, January 30, 1893.
54. March 2, 1893, FO/141/297.
55. M.P., Garstin to Milner, April 18, 1893.
56. M.P., Wingate to Milner, July 23, 1893.
57. M.P., Malortie to Milner, July 27, 1893.

Notes

58. *Rapport sur le Budget de l'Exercise 1894 présenté au gouvernement par le Conseil Legislatif,* December 1893.
59. B.P., Cromer to Rosebery, December 25, 1893.
60. Cromer to Barrington, Salisbury's private secretary, FO/78/4576.
61. January 28, 1894, FO/78/4574.
62. See George Arthur, *Life of Kitchener,* London: 1920, I, p. 180 for details.
63. Cromer, *Abbas II,* pp. 53 and 55.
64. *Ibid.,* p. 58 in footnote.
65. January 24, 1894, FO/141/305.
66. M.P., February 18, 1895.
67. M.P., Dawkins to Milner, February 18, 1895.
68. M.P., Milner to Dawkins, March 1, 1895.
69. February 21, 1895, FO/141/308, No. 26a.
70. D. G. Hogarth, 'Lord Cromer', *Dictionary of National Biography, 1912–1921,* ed. H. W. C. Davis and J. R. H. Weaver, London: 1927, p. 22.
71. D. G. Hogarth, 'Lord Cromer', *op. cit.,* p. 22.
72. Robinson, Gallagher and Denny, *op. cit.,* p. 356. Repeated by French Ambassador in London to Hanotaux, October 3, 1896, *Documents Diplomatiques Français,* XIII, No. 468.
73. B.P., Cromer to Kimberley, February 24, 1895.
74. B.P., Cromer to Rosebery, February 25, 1894.
75. S.P., Cromer to Barrington, April 2, 1897.
76. Cromer, *Abbas II,* p. 10.
77. *Ibid.,* p. 15.
78. *Ibid.,* p. 34.
79. M.P., Birdwood to Milner, March 5, 1894.
80. Cromer to Salisbury, February 6, 1897, FO/633/VI, p. 277.
81. S.P., Cromer to Salisbury, December 11, 1897.
82. S.P., Cromer to Salisbury, June 5, 1898.
83. Storrs, *Orientations,* London: 1937, p. 52.
84. Zetland, *op. cit.,* p. 215.
85. Cecil, *op. cit.,* IV, p. 326.
86. February 29, 1896, FO/78/4986.
87. March 10, 1896, FO/78/4988.
88. Magnus, *op. cit.,* p. 118.
89. Robinson, Gallagher and Denny, *op. cit.,* p. 358.
90. Freycinet, *Ibid.,* p. 413.
91. S.P., Salisbury to Cromer, November 16, 1896.
92. Memorandum found in the Salisbury Papers, July 16, 1899.
93. Wingate, *Wingate of the Sudan,* London: 1955, p. 130.
94. Ward and Gooch, eds., *The Cambridge History of British Foreign Policy 1783–1919,* London: 1923, III, p. 309, footnote 1.
95. B.P., Cromer to Gorst, April 8, 1904.
96. Gooch and Temperley, *British Documents on the Origins of War: 1898–1914,* London: 1927, II, Nos. 387 and 415.

Notes

VII. THE RISE OF THE SECOND NATIONALIST MOVEMENT *pp. 137–154*

1. Cromer, 'The Government of Subject Races', *op. cit.*, p. 51 ff.
2. Issawi, *Egypt at Mid-Century*, London: 1954, p. 34.
3. See E. R. J. Owen, 'Lord Cromer and the development of Egyptian Industry, 1883–1907'. *Middle Eastern Studies*, July 1966.
4. Elie Kedourie, *Nationalism*, London: 1960, p. 101.
5. Bowman, *Middle East Window*, London: 1942, p. 39.
6. *Report of the Special Mission to Egypt*, Parl. Pubs. 1921, vol. XLII (Accounts and Papers), Cmd. 1131.
7. H. Haykal, *Mudhakkirat fi al-Siyasa al-Misriyya*, Cairo: 1951, I, p. 21.
8. Rodd, *Social and Diplomatic Memoirs*, London: 1922, II, p. 29.
9. Memorandum in Harry Boyle Papers, *op. cit.* Also *Modern Egypt*, II, p. 146.
10. Memorandum in Harry Boyle Papers, *op. cit.*
11. Alonzo Money, *The Egyptian Question*, 1896.
12. Elgood to Wingate, December 30, 1905, *Wingate Papers*, henceforward referred to as W.P.
13. Shafiq, *op. cit.*, III, p. 7.
14. Shafiq, *op. cit.*, II, p. 411.
15. Blunt, *My Diaries*, London: 1919, II, p. 90.
16. Shafiq, *op. cit.*, II, p. 348.
17. Cromer, *Modern Egypt*, *op. cit.*, II, p. 128.
18. Rashid Rida, *Tarikh*, III, p. 24.
19. Shafiq, *op. cit.*, II, p. 413.
20. Rida, *Tarikh*, I, p. 573.
21. Jamal Ahmad, *The Intellectual Origins of Egyptian Nationalism*, London: 1960, p. 43.
22. A. Lutfi al-Sayyid, *Qissat Hayati*, Cairo: 1962, p. 151.
23. Ahmad, *op. cit.*, p. 46.
24. A. Fathi Zaghlul, *Sirr taqqadum al-Injiliz al-Saksuniyyin*, Cairo: 1894, p. 23 ff. Translation by J. Ahmad.
25. Ahmad, *op. cit.*, p. 51.
26. Albert Hourani, *op. cit.*, p. 169.
27. *Loc. cit.*
28. Hourani, *op. cit.*, p. 173.

VIII. THE ORATOR, THE PRO-CONSUL, AND THE INTELLECTUAL *pp. 155–195*

1. Ali Fahmi Kamil, *Mustafa Kamil fi 34 rabian*, Cairo: 1908–11, II, p. 144.
2. Jurji Zaydan, *Mashahir al-sharq*, Cairo: 1911, I, p. 317.
3. See *Mustafa Kamil Correspondence*, Egyptian State Archives.
4. Juliette Adam, *L'Angleterre en Egypte*, Paris: 1922, p. 145.
5. S.P., Salisbury to Baring, February 17, 1888.
6. *Mustafa Kamil Correspondence*, Egyptian State Archives.
7. *Report on the Affairs of Egypt*, 1904 (Accounts and Papers, CXI), Cd. 1951.
8. Philippe de Tarazi, *Tarikh al-sahafa al-Arabiyya*, Beirut: 1913, IV.
9. Fritz Stappat, 'Nationalismus und Islam bei Mustafa Kamel', *Die Welt des Islams*, IV, Nr. 4, 1956.

10. M. Kamil, *Lettres Egyptiennes–Françaises*, Cairo: 1909, p. 64.
11. *Ibid.*, p. 238.
12. Rashid Rida, *Tarikh*, I, p. 593.
13. Storrs, *op. cit.*, p. 85.
14. *Report respecting the Affairs of Egypt*, 1902 (Accounts and Papers, CXXX), Cd. 1012.
15. *Correspondence respecting the Turco-Egyptian Frontier in the Sinai Peninsula*, 1906 (Accounts and Papers, CXXXVII), Cd. 3006.
16. Albert Hourani, 'The Decline of the West in the Middle East', *International Affairs*, XXIX, 1953, p. 31.
17. Findlay to Grey, January 27, 1906, FO/407/165.
18. Owen to Wingate, January 3, 1906, *Wingate Papers*, Box 278.
19. *Ibid.*, February 18, Box 278.
20. W.P., Owen to Wingate, April 29, Box 278.
21. W.P., Wingate to Cromer, April 10.
22. *Correspondence Respecting the Turco-Egyptian Frontier in the Sinai Peninsula*, 1906, Cd. 3006.
23. *Correspondence respecting the Attack on British Officers at Dinshwai*, 1906 (Accounts and Papers, CXXXVII), Cd. 3086.
24. April 1, 1887, letter from Baring to Salisbury, FO/633/VI.
25. *Correspondence respecting the attack on British Officers*, 1906 (Accounts and Papers, CXXXVII), Cd. 3086.
26. Husayn Haykal, *Tarajim Misriyya wa Gharbiyya*, *op. cit.*, p. 148.
27. Ahmad Amin, *Hayati*, p. 91.
28. Translated in Jamal Ahmad, *op. cit.*, p. 63.
29. Quoted in Memoirs of al-Rafii in *al-Jumhuriyya*, December 13, 1962.
30. *Parliamentary Debates, Commons*, Vol. 160, Cols. 280, 310.
31. *Ibid.*, Vol. 160, Cols. 286, 289.
32. Lord Lloyd, *Egypt Since Cromer*, London: 1933, I, p. 47.
33. Grey of Fallodon, *Twenty Five Years: 1892–1916*, London: I, p. 137.
34. November 19, 1906, FO/633/XIII.
35. Juliette Adam, *op. cit.*, p. 124.
36. March 3, 1907, FO/633/XIII.
37. October 27, 1906, FO/633/XIII.
38. Blunt, *My Diaries*, II, p. 40.
39. C.P., FO/633/XVIII, July 13, 1909.
40. Rashid Rida, *Tarikh*, I, p. 593.
41. Shafiq, *op. cit.*, III, p. 129.
42. *Al-Misri*, May 11, 1951.
43. *Report on the Affairs of Egypt*, 1911 (Accounts and Papers, CIII), Cd. 5633.
44. C.P., FO/633/XIII, March 28, 1907.
45. Clara Boyle, *A Servant of the Empire*, London: 1938, p. 107. Letter dated April 21, 1907.
46. *Report on the Administration and Finances of Egypt*, 1907 (Accounts and Papers, C), Cd. 3451.

Notes

47. *Report on the Finances and Administration of Egypt,* 1907 (Accounts and Papers, C), Cd. 3394.
48. Adam, *op. cit.,* p. 188.
49. Storrs, *op. cit.,* p. 85.
50. See *al-Jarida:* April 13, 1907; July 6, 1908; July 9, 1908, etc.
51. Kamil's speech in Alexandria on October 22, 1907, in *al-Liwa,* October 23. *Al-Muayyad,* December 22, 1907.
52. *Al-Manar,* December 5, 1907.

EPILOGUE *pp. 196–208*

1. A. H. Haykal, *Mudhakkirati,* I, p. 77.

Index

Abbas II (1874–1944), Khedive of Egypt, 1892–1914; succeeds Tawfiq, 83, 86, 97, 98–9; education at Theresianum, 98, 129, 145; befriends Ali Yusif, 97; relationship with Cromer, 99, 127–9, 130; changes in personnel, 99; grievances against Britain, 100; bid for independence, 100–10; and Fahmi's dismissal, 106–7; cabinet changes, 107; popular support, 111, 114, 117; visits Constantinople, 118–119; and the army, 121–2; let down by his government, 123–4; possible deposition, 124–6, 128, 130, 146–7, 147 n.; leader of young nationalists, 129, 137, 145–7; character and abilities, 129–30: and France, 133–4, 135, 136; espouses liberal cause, 145–6; his veniality, 146–7, 147 n.; disowned by nationalists, 147–8, 163; opponent of Abduh, 149 and n., 150–1; and Kamil, 156, 162–3; pro-British moves, 163–4; and *al-Umma*, 178: Gorst's policy towards, 183; visits Turkey, 185; and *al-Hizb al-Watani*, 186; deposition, 204

Abd al-Hamid, Sultan of Turkey, 92

Abd al-Raziq, Hassan, founding member of *al-Umma* and *al-Jarida*, 168

Abduh, Shaykh Muhammad (1849–1905), 7, 21, 61, 69; and Urabi, 11, 12–13; nationalist manifesto, 13–14; social and religious reformer, 62, 88, 92–3, 116–17, 149, 151, 153; in exile, 87, 92, 150; popularity, 87–8; interview in England, 90–1; appointed Grand Mufti, 92, 150 and n.; death, 92; the *ulama* and, 93, 94, 149; his importance, 94; his interests, 94–5, 149; and Abbas II, 146, 147, 149–50; and new nationalism, 148; resignation, 149 and n.; and Cromer, 150–1; accusations against, 151; and Kamil, 168; and Lutfi, 185, 197; his biographer, 189

Adam, Juliette, supports Kamil, 157

Adams, Francis, interview with Abbas II, 102

Adowa, Italian defeat, 131

al-Afghani, Jamal al-Din (1839–87), reformer and revolutionary, 7, 8, 12, 87, 88, 176; death, 92; and Lutfi, 185–6

Ahmad, Abd al-Rahim Bey, Khedive's private secretary, 156

al-Ahram, 96, 100, 106, 159

Alexandria, bombardment of, 1, 24–6; naval demonstration, 18, 21; riots in, 20–2, 112–13; burning of, 30, 31, 42; British forces and, 40

Ali, Muhammad, founder of ruling dynasty, 10, 69; bid for power, 2; and Mamluks, 7; his army, 11

Allenby, Edmund Hynman, 1st Viscount (1861–1936), 175; replaces Wingate, 206

Amin, Ahmad (1887–1954), 145 n., 149 n.; and Dinshwai sentences, 172–3

Amin, Qasim (1865–1908), and emancipation of women, 152–3, 187, 193; and Dinshwai sentences, 173, 183

Aqaba, 166

al-Aqqad, Hasan Musa, slave-trader, 20; and burning of Alexandria, 31 and n.

Arabia, Wahhabi movement, 38, 151 and n.

Armenia, 49, 52, 69; 1894 massacres, 116

Army, the, and nationalism, 6, 8–9, 10–13, 15; refusal to leave Cairo, 11; party in power, 17; defeat at Tal al-Kabir, 26; and trial of Urabists, 31; projected increase, 44–5; loyalty of European officers, 81; Abbas II and, 103, 117, 121–4; deposes King Faruq, 208

Artin Pasha, Armenian minister, 69

Assembly of Notables, 7; and Nationalist Party, 12, 13, 15; collapse after defeat, 36; Baring and, 59, 62

Aswan Dam, 131

al-Azhar University, 9, 92, 149

Index

Baker, Valentine, British Chief of Police, 72

al-Bakri, Shaykh, 119

Baligh, Muhammad, Deputy *Procureur Général*, 61, 62

Baring, Evelyn, Earl Cromer (1841–1917), and Anglo-Egyptian relations, xi, 58, 66; Commissioner of the Caisse, 3 n., 54; on Urabi's failure, 32; interpretation of Dufferin Report, 36, 55–6; Consul General, 36, 54, 55; and Egypt's finances, 39, 45, 54, 64–5, 86, 127, 135, 138–9, 196; and the Sudan, 39, 40, 56, 57, 131, 134; attitude to evacuation, 48, 49, 55–6, 59, 65, 85, 115–16, 135; and European politics, 50, 135–6; character, 54–5, 62–4, 127, 142; policy in Egypt, 55–9, 63, 68, 74, 79, 85–6; choice of administrators, 60–2, 66, 68, 72, 79–80, 142–3; and National Party, 61; and 'subject races', 62–3, 65, 79–80, 165; and the Oriental, 63, 77, 143; his unbounded influence, 66–7, 74, 83, 197; and Tawfiq, 68; crisis with Nubar, 73–4; and Fahmi, 78; low opinion of Egyptians, 77–9, 157–8, 165, 182; made Lord Cromer, 82 n.; personal opinions of, 83–5; suggested reforms, 85; and Egyptian nationalism, 90, 164–5, 193; opinion of Islam, 90–1; and Abbas II, 99–100, 101, 105–6, 107–10, 114–16, 120, 122, 127, 128–130, 137, 165; and Tigrane as P.M., 103–6; objects to Fakhri's appointment, 107–10; requests more troops, 110–12; fear of violence and fanaticism, 112–13, 116, 126, 174; and slavery incident, 120–1; and the army, 122; use of British officials, 142–3; and new nationalist movement, 148, 160, 162, 164–6; opinion of native press, 159–60; and Kamil, 164–6; and Taba incident, 166–7; and *al-Jarida*, 168, 188; admiration for Zaghlul, 176, 181; and moderates, 177, 178–9, 181–3; resignation, 179, 180–1; farewell speech on Egypt's future, 182–3; Egypt's debt to, 196–7; *Government of Subject Races*, 62; *Modern Egypt*, 63, 67, 83 n., 85

al-Barudi, Sami Pasha (1839–1904), accomplishments, 9–10; nationalist manifesto, 13; P.M. 17; resignation, 19

Bismarck, Prince Otto von, 2, 3, 47, 48; rapprochement with France, 29, 43, 46; and Salisbury's mission to Turkey, 46–7

Bizerta, 51

Blignières, M. de, French Controller, 69

Blunt, Wilfred Scawen (1840–1922), and nationalism, 13, 30, 35, 60–1; knowledge of Egyptian politics, 61–2; and Gorst, 147

Bond, W., and Dinshwai trial, 171

Bosphore Egyptien, Le, on Riaz, 77; and Cromer, 87; and Abbas II, 98, 100, 106–7, 119

Bowman, Humphrey, Cairo teacher, 139–40

Boyle, Harry, Oriental Secretary, 95, 143, 177; on Gorst, 82

Bull, Captain, and Dinshwai affair, 170

Cairo, 21, 38, 40, 99; strategic importance, 52, 130

Caisse de la Dette Publique, 3, 4, 42, 85, 137; share of revenues, 44; barometer of international situation, 44–5; additional Commissioners, 45 and n.; Baring and, 54; financing of Sudan expedition, 132; proposed abolition, 135–6

Campbell-Bannerman, Sir Henry (1836–1908), 161; meeting with Kamil, 175–6, 180

Capitulations, 121, 207; abusive system, 5–6, 32, 137, 145, 161; Baring and, 56, 79, 135; and foreigners, 186

Cartwright, Mr, Acting-Consul, 24

Cavendish, Lord Frederick, assassination, 22

Chamberlain, Joseph (1836–1914), and Egypt, 22, 28–9

Christianity, religion of occupying Power, 90

Churchill, Lord Randolph (1849–95), 60

Circassian Plot, 19

Civil Service, increase in British officials, 139–40, 141; cause of Egyptian discontent, 140–3

228

Index

Index

Index

Index

Suez Canal, opening of, 1; French policy and, 1–2; Urabist threat to, 17–18; Britain and, 22–3, 26–7, 28; project for extension of Concessions, 199–200

Sulayman, Muhammad Mahmud Pasha, founding member of *al-Umma* and *al-Jarida*, 168

Sultan Pasha, Egyptian notable, 7; and nationalism, 8, 11, 12, 13; President of the Assembly, 19, 20, 36; and Urabi, 23; his defection, 26, 36; his rewards, 37 and n.

Syria, 2, 49, 143

Taba incident, 160, 166–7, 188

Tal al-Kabir, battle of, 1, 26

al-Tashri ('Legislation'), founding of, 185

Tashyuz (Thassos) island, mining concession, 147

Tawfiq, Khedive of Egypt, 1879–92, 4; autocratic government, 7–8, 9, 20; and nationalism, 10–12; supported by Joint Note, 14–15; and Organic Law, 16; handling of Circassian Plot, 19; and Alexandria riots, 21; and Urabi, 23–4, 26; appeals to the Powers, 24, 31; British intervention and, 29; his guilt, 31, 89, 91; and Wolseley, 32, 36–37; and the occupation, 48, 58, 68; relations with Baring, 58, 59, 60, 68–9, 74, 76; his incompetence, 65, 74; character, 68–9; and Nubar, 72; and Riaz, 76; his foreign Advisers, 79, 117; succeeded by his son, 83, 86; and *al-Muayyad*, 96–7; and his premiers, 108; encourages liberalism, 145

Taxation, 6, 120, 138

Tharwat, Abd al-Khaliq Pasha, P.M. of Egypt, 176, 185

Tigrane Pasha, Minister for Foreign Affairs, 72, 73, 78, 100; nominated P.M. by Abbas II, 103–5; Cromer and, 119

Times, The, 13, 98

Tunis, 14, 15

Turco-Circassians, ethnic connotation, 6–7, 59 n.; privileged position, 7, 8, 60

Turkey, xi; European policy and, 2, 35; and the Khedive, 10, 12, 98–9, 114,

119, 130; and Egyptian affairs, 18, 20, 23, 24, 42, 52, 114; refused representation on the Caisse, 45; British missions to, 46–7, 48; Conventions with Britain, 47, 49–50, 137; naval strength, 51; seat of the Caliphate, 90; Kamil and, 160, 162, 166–8, 202–3

Turks, and trial of Urabists, 31; Baring's use of, 60, 61; as P.M. of Egypt, 75, 77; Egyptian attitude to, 90

Tussun, Prince Umar, 203

Umar Sultan, and *al-Jarida*, 168

Urabi, Colonel Ahmad Pasha (1839–1911), defeat at Tal al-Kabir, 1, 26, 208; nationalist movement, 6, 8; rise as a political leader, 8–9, 11–13; character and career, 9, 32; attempted assassinations, 10, 19; his demands, 11; Under-Secretary for War, 18, 20; and Alexandria riots, 21, 22; support for, 23; dismissal, 26; Holy War against England, 26; British government and, 29–30; trial, 30–1; exiled for mutiny, 31; belief in Dufferin's Report, 34; Nazli and, 95

al-Urwa al-Wuthqa ('The Indissoluble Bond'), 87, 88–9, 92; banned in Egypt and India, 89–90

al-Ustadh, 113, 185

Victoria, Queen, 28, 41

Villiers, F. H., Secretary to Salisbury, 72

Vincent, Edgar (later Viscount D'Abernon), Financial Adviser, 45, 70, 71–2; on Baring, 64

Waddington, William H. (1826–94), French Ambassador, 113

Wafd, the (Delegation), and 1919 revolution, 200; refused permission to negotiate, 205; and bid for independence, 205–7; in power, 208

Wahhabis, the, 38, 151 and n.

al-Wakil, Ibrahim, 61

Walker, General, 109, 110

Waqfs, the, use of its funds, 146 and n., 150

al-Wardani, assassinates Butros Ghali, 173, 199

West, Sir Algernon, 112

235